SALVAGE

A PERSONAL ODYSSEY

Captain Ian Tew

SALVAGE

A PERSONAL ODYSSEY

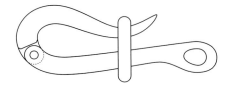

SEAFARER BOOKS

SHERIDAN HOUSE

© Ian Tew 2007

Published in the UK by
Seafarer Books · 102 Redwald Road · Rendlesham · Suffolk IP12 2TE · England
www.seafarerbooks.com
ISBN-13 978-0-9550243-9-9 paperback
ISBN-13 978-1-906266-00-4 hardback limited edition

British Library Cataloguing in Publication Data

Tew, Ian, 1943-
   Salvage : a personal odyssey
   1. Tew, Ian, 1943-
   2. Salvage
   3. Merchant marine - Officers - Biography
   I. Title
   387.5'5'092

ISBN-13: 9780955024399 (pbk) – ISBN-13: 9781906266004 (hbk)

Published in the USA by
Sheridan House Inc · 145 Palisade Street · Dobbs Ferry · NY 10522 · USA
www.sheridanhouse.com
ISBN-13 978-1-57409-256-1 paperback

A CIP record for this book is available from the Library of Congress

Photographs not otherwise credited are by the author
Maps and diagrams: Louis Mackay

Copy-editing: Hugh Brazier

Design and typesetting: Louis Mackay
Text set digitally in Proforma

Printed in China, on behalf of 1010 Printing UK Ltd,
via MBC Print Consultancy

Contents

PART 3 – *Salvanguard*

PART 4 – *Salviscount*

PART 5 – **Salvage master**

Maps

Foreword

'No cure, no pay' is the onerous responsibility taken on by a salvor when operating on the Lloyd's Open Form contract of salvage. It means that if – after putting himself, his crew, his tug and the assets of his company at considerable risk – he is finally defeated by the elements, a fire or a missile attack, he is not paid. No matter how much money, effort, sweat and tears have been expended, he receives nothing. It is not a business for the faint-hearted.

I first met Captain Ian Tew in 2001, when I published his book *Sailing in Grandfather's Wake*. He had just completed a four-year circumnavigation of the world, following a course across the Pacific that his grandfather had taken sixty years earlier. Two years later his mother completed an Atlantic crossing and at the age of 88 became the oldest yachtswoman to do so. Clearly, salt water has been coursing through the veins of the Tew family for generations. It was therefore no surprise to discover that Ian went to sea as a cadet at the age of 17, and spent thirteen years in the merchant navy before eventually accepting a job with the Singapore-based salvage firm Selco in 1974. The next ten years he spent as a salvor, operating anywhere from Cornwall to the South China Sea. This new book is an account of a series of epic salvage and towage operations, culminating in some particularly difficult and dangerous work in the Gulf during the Iran–Iraq war

I have been involved with salvage, tugs and towing for nearly 40 years and since 1995 have published *International Tug & Salvage* magazine, which is read all over the world by salvors and tug owners and operators, together with professionals associated with the industry such as naval architects, engineers, tug builders and marine lawyers. Ian Tew's book is written for all these people, and tug aficionados will relish this book – but, as a fascinating story well told, and for its insights into a world that to others may be little known, it deserves a far wider readership.

Ian's gripping narrative is a tribute to the seamanship, courage and resourcefulness of the captains and crews of salvage tugs – not least to his own share of these qualities. His story brilliantly conveys the flavour of the life lived in the business, with its periods of waiting on standby, alternating with bursts of intense action, and its dangers and uncertainties. In these pages you will find stories of adventure combined with a down-to-earth examination of the issues surrounding salvage and the life of a salvor – technical, commercial, and above all human. This book is a real eye-opener, a great tale of human endeavour in the face of countless difficulties and dangers, a veritable odyssey.

Alan Brunton-Reed
Managing Director,
The ABR Company Ltd. Publishers of *International Tugs & Salvage*
and organisers of the ITS Conventions and Tugnology Conferences

Acknowledgements

Two chapters in this book are revised versions of articles originally published in the *Nautical Magazine*, and I am most grateful to the publishers, Brown, Son and Ferguson Ltd, and to the editor, Leslie Ingram-Brown, for permission to republish 'A day off the coast of India' (from vol. 218, no. 2, August 1977) and '*Majmaa II* and *Pacificoeverett*' (from vol. 266 no. 1, July 2001, originally entitled 'Kadmat Island').

The painting of the *Dara* on fire (page 10) is the work of the marine artist Robert Lloyd, and I thank him for kindly allowing it to be reproduced here.

I am immensely grateful to Patricia Eve of Seafarer Books, who persuaded me to write this book: her skill at winkling out half-forgotten details of my life is amazing, and her enthusiasm is infectious. John Julian was the goad that started me off, and he kindly typed most of the manuscript in New Zealand (the internet is a wonderful thing). I would also like to thank Ray Clarke, who checked it for legal pitfalls, and the Seafarer team who put it all together: Hugh Brazier, who made sense of the incomprehensible, and Louis Mackay, for his patience and skill in designing the book, doing the maps and diagrams and organising the photographs.

Finally, to all those who salved ships with me, thank you for many unforgettable years.

Ian Tew

Dara burning. Painting by Robert Lloyd

Prologue – *Dara*

The *Dara* – there she was, burning, the smoke pouring out of her. I stood absolutely still, rigid with shock and surprise. It was so unexpected, a bolt from the past. I felt the strength leave my legs, and I sat down in one of the large bar chairs. I was attending the 150-year reunion of the British India Steam Navigation Company in May 2006, and I had just walked into the colonial-style Mount Lavinia Hotel outside Colombo.

My mind was racing. The photograph on the noticeboard in the lobby of the hotel took me straight back to April 1961. I could hear the bells ringing, the incessant fire alarm bells, so loud. I could see the shocked face of the third officer in the dim light of the emergency lighting telling me to go with the other cadet to our fire station with the breathing apparatus. I could feel the ship rolling heavily; it felt as though she was stopped in the water. I could smell the smoke and see little wisps of it curling round the alleyway outside our cabin in the poor light. And the screaming, oh the screaming. I could hear them screaming. I put my hands over my ears, but it was no use. The screaming was inside my head, and has haunted me all my life. The screaming and shouting and the figures running on B deck, running in panic, away from the glow and roar of the fire and the swirling smoke. Then silence, the silence of the sea, just the wind on my face and the occasional breaking wave washing over me.

She was my second ship, and I was the seventeen-year-old Junior Cadet. I had flown out from London in December 1960 to join the *Dara* in Bombay.

India was a shock. Nothing I had been taught or heard prepared me – not so much for the heat, I was young and fit – but for the mass of brown humanity, the hot and sweating bodies, the beggars, the noise, the hustle, the bustle and the smell. I had to make a conscious decision not to be frightened, not to be daunted and overwhelmed, if I was to stay in the East. I would have to get used to it.

The *Dara* was a single-screw passenger cargo ship permitted to carry 13 first class, 65 second class, 948 unberthed passengers and 132 officers and crew. She was built in 1948 by Barclay Curle, Glasgow, and her length was 382 feet, breadth 55 feet, depth 24½ feet, and gross tonnage 5,029. She was classed A1 at Lloyd's.

I was thrown in at the deep end within a few days of my arrival when we shifted ship out of the dock to Ballard Pier, with its great Gateway to India arch. The Junior Cadet's station was on the bridge manning the telephones, long before the days of walkie-talkies. The captain, pilot, third officer and myself were all dressed in immaculate whites, wearing caps, hot in the morning heat, the secunnies smart in their white tunics. I passed the captain's and pilot's orders to the chief officer forward and the second officer aft and relayed their messages back. Mistakes were not allowed, and I concentrated hard to report the messages word for word. It was a long manoeuvre with tugs, along the dock, into the lock, through the harbour and berthing alongside the pier, but it was exciting the first time.

Sailing day was always pandemonium, but organised pandemonium. The departure of the weekly British India mail ship to Basra was an event. The four D-class BI ships which maintained the service were the main way to travel around the Persian Gulf, to some places the only way, so they were an important link between India, Pakistan, Oman, the Gulf States, Saudi Arabia, Kuwait and Iraq. The ships were always full of passengers, mainly deck passengers. It was a busy day of hustle and bustle, with everything seeming to happen at the same time, and the shouts and babble of hundreds of people – men, women, children, servants, the cries of the porters carrying the luggage, huge bundles on their heads, and the street traders hawking their wares.

The cadets supervised the loading of the mail with the second officer. To lose a mail bag was unthinkable. There was a steady stream of humanity coming aboard via the gangways, and shouts and sometimes scuffles as men staked out their part of the deck for the voyage. Of course the more privileged or richer went second class and had cabins. Europeans were not allowed to travel on deck. First-class passengers came on board by a separate gangway, where the duty secunny kept watch. The tweendecks where the deck passengers lived seemed a form of bedlam to me on my first Gulf trip. The ship had a couple of holds forward, for passenger baggage and cargo, and the winches worked at full speed, swinging the cargo on board by the derricks, the stevedores sweating in the holds stowing it.

At long last everyone and everything was on board, the ship was fully bunkered and watered, and the trip to the money changer completed (for there was a nice little earner exchanging Indian rupees into Gulf rupees and up the Gulf the other way round). The pilot was on the bridge, I was showered and wearing my spotless whites for stations leaving, the tugs were made fast fore and aft, the gangways were put ashore, and with much shouting, wailing and waving from the passengers aboard and the families left ashore the ship moved off the pier. She was turned, the tugs were let go, and with a last blast on the ship's foghorn she steamed out to sea through the busy harbour, crisscrossed by country craft with their ragged sails, or if there was no wind the crews toiling at huge sweeps, all laden with cargo for trading up and down the coast, and when the monsoon was fair to East Africa, past anchored ships waiting for a berth, the buildings of Bombay to starboard – and so out to sea and up the coast to Karachi. With the northeast monsoon the weather was fine and the sea was calm.

The ship at sea was a world of her own. Apart from the noise of the diesel engines it was quiet. If my duties took me down to the tweendecks there was the continual babble from the hundreds of passengers in the vicinity and it was sometimes difficult to get through the decks because they had spread themselves and their belongings. The sea routine was very pleasant. We had to change into whites for all meals, and were expected to be in the saloon on time. When off duty I studied and worked the correspondence course we had to complete. The distances between the ports were quite short, especially in the Gulf, so we were in and out of port most days. The other cadet, Jos Grimwood, a strong handsome white Kenyan, was my senior, and he showed me the ropes and organised the work reporting to the chief officer. We got on well together – just as well, living in a small hot cramped cabin with a top and bottom bunk. I had the top bunk.

It was my fourth voyage, and we were on our way back to Bombay from Basra. The *Dara* was anchored off Dubai, the creek full of dhows, long before the days of Port Rashid, let alone Jebel Ali. The passengers were brought out on barges towed by tugs, although we had been ashore in the agent's launch, shopping along the creek for duty-free goods, the stalls all on the port side entering the creek.

I was on the bridge, looking down on the foredeck covered with its canvas awning, shelter for the deck passengers. A storm had blown up suddenly in the afternoon and it was now just before darkness set in, the normally clear sky covered by low cloud. The tugs were towing away the barges before they were damaged or they damaged the ship. I can still see in my mind's eye the *Zeus*, a Panamanian cargo ship dragging slowly towards us. Collision was inevitable, and her black hull crunched into the lifeboat on the port side forward and scraped down the white painted hull of the *Dara*. As soon as the *Zeus* was clear the anchor was weighed and Captain Elson took the *Dara* to sea, the ship pitching into the rough weather. When well clear of the coast he hove her to to ride out the storm for the night.

It was the bells which woke me at 0443 in the morning, the incessant ringing of the fire alarm bells. It was dark, and the bunk light did not work when I switched it on. I jumped down from my top bunk and went out into the alleyway, the noise of the bells louder. The ship was rolling heavily and it felt as though she was stopped. The shocked face of the third officer appeared in the dim light of the emergency lighting.

'Tell Grimwood to get the breathing apparatus and go with him to your fire station – the CO2 control panel on B deck,' he shouted, his voice difficult to hear over the noise of the ringing bells.

'Yes sir,' I shouted back, sticking my thumb up, my hand on the bulkhead to steady myself.

I returned to the cabin and shut the door, lessening the noise from the bells. I shook Jos's shoulder in the lower bunk.

'Wake up,' I said 'We have to get the breathing apparatus and go to our fire stations. There is smoke in the alleyway. There's a fire.'

Jos was instantly awake and out of his bunk. We quickly dressed in our working gear by the light of a torch, and I followed him out of the cabin. The noise of the bells was as loud as ever and the smoke in the alleyway was thicker. It was a relief to get out into the cool air on the boat deck, away from the ringing of the bells. I followed the light from Jos's torch, the sound of the wind blowing around the accommodation and funnel louder as we went aft, until it was overtaken by the sound of the screaming. The sea was rough.

We climbed down the companionway ladder onto the main deck and into the midst of the screaming, shouting, milling passengers. We had picked up the breathing apparatus on the way and pushed and shoved our way through the throng down onto B deck. We stopped in the glow, and could hear the roar of the fire, and I helped Jos put on the breathing apparatus.

The second engineer was instructing Jos how to set off the CO_2 fire-extinguishing gas into the engine room. The box was further up the deck on the side of the engine-room bulkhead. He gave a thumbs up and disappeared into the smoke, a ghostly red in the glow of the fire. Figures ran past, fleeing the flames, and there was a screaming man covered in blood. I wondered what had happened to him.

Some time later Jos returned, appearing out of the glow like some figure from hell, his face covered by the mask. He tore it off and gasped, 'I found the box but I couldn't find the key to open it.'

The fifth engineer had appeared and gave him a piece of metal to smash open the control panel. Jos put the mask back on and disappeared again into the thickening smoke. The continuous ringing of the bells stopped, to be replaced by the emergency signal, boat stations.

'Abandon ship,' I thought. (It was only eight minutes after what turned out to have been an explosion from a bomb: the speed of the fire was terrific.)

Jos reappeared, staggering, and I helped him off with the apparatus. 'Couldn't make it, too much smoke, too hot,' he cried.

'It's boat stations,' I shouted. We went up and back into the throng on the main deck, and to the motor lifeboat which was our boat station. It was chaos. People were shouting and screaming and running around, some already in the lifeboat and some trying to get in, although it was not properly turned out, let alone lowered.

'You go aft and I'll go forward and get it turned out,' shouted Jos. The second engineer had disappeared and we were alone amongst the passengers. The boat was incredibly heavy, and no one took any notice of us. I grabbed a man to help me turn the boat out, as did Jos, and we managed to get her hanging over the edge of the ship.

'You get in and take charge,' shouted Jos. 'I will lower.'

I climbed up and in and fought my way aft to the rudder. I found the tiller under a passenger and pushing him out of the way I shipped it.

'The plug,' shouted Jos.

I pushed and shoved my way through many legs to the bottom of the boat and found the metal plug. Even though it was dark in the bottom I could feel the hole and screwed it in. When I regained the tiller I shouted, 'Plug is in.'

Jos lowered away and stopped at the embarkation level. More and more passengers got into the already overcrowded boat, with people shouting and screaming and waving their arms around.

'Lower away,' I heard a voice shouting, and the boat disappeared below the level of the deck. People were still jumping in as she went down the side of the ship, the rolling making the boat hit the hull of the burning *Dara* with sickening jolts, and making the already panicked people more frightened. My efforts to calm the passengers were a complete waste of time.

The lowering slowed and then went down with a rush. The lifeboat hit the water with a splash and the lifting hooks swung clear both forward and aft. We were lucky. But then unfortunately a nearly empty boat appeared in the glow of the fires raging in the accommodation. The passengers saw it and made a rush to the side of my lifeboat, heeling her over. And then I was in the water. My boat had capsized.

I began to swim. I was not wearing a lifejacket. It had not occurred to me to pick it up when I left the cabin, for never in my wildest dreams had I imagined I would be swimming for my life in the Persian Gulf. After the bedlam and noise in the lifeboat it was suddenly quite quiet. What had happened to all the passengers in my boat? I could still hear shouting and screaming but it was becoming faint as the *Dara* drifted away, surprisingly quickly. It was rough, and waves were breaking over my head. I tried to swim back to the ship but it was no use and I soon gave up, treading water to preserve my strength. I was a strong swimmer but I found my shoes and dungaree trousers a hindrance so shook them off. It was much easier without them. I kept facing the burning *Dara*, smoke pouring out of her, the wind and sea behind me, the occasional wave breaking over my head. It became darker as the *Dara* moved away. I was alone.

In the dim light of the early morning darkness, the sky now clear, the stars shining brightly, the wind still blowing but not so hard, I saw a shape close by. A shark, I thought. 'Don't panic,' I told myself. 'Do nothing, don't move. I am not bleeding, maybe it will go away.'

Occasionally I had to kick my legs – it was too rough to lie on my back – but I did it as slowly and as little as possible, just enough to keep my head above water. I felt very vulnerable with no trousers, not that it would have made any difference if the shark attacked. I watched with exaggerated concentration as he moved closer to me. I felt utterly helpless as I waited, wondering if it would hurt when he attacked. After what seemed eternity, but in reality could not have been many minutes, I realised the shape was wrong and the movement towards me was my heightened imagination. It was not moving. I cannot express the feeling of utter relief as I realised it was not a shark, and I was not about to be attacked.

I quickly swam the short distance towards the shape and caught hold of the oar I found, at the opposite end to the head I had seen, not the fin of a shark.

'Hello,' I said as I clutched the wooden oar, but there was no answer.

'Hello,' I said more loudly, and shook the oar. There was still no answer, and the corpse slid off and sank. I realised it was the back of his head I had seen. The face, which I never saw, was in the water.

I was alone in the darkness. There was nothing in sight except the glow from the now distant burning *Dara*, like a false dawn. I felt a lot safer with the oar, and it was no effort to keep my face above the water, the salt drying. Daylight could not be too long away. It was just a matter of settling down and waiting, alone with my thoughts, my eyes constantly searching.

Some time later a slight lessening of the darkness in the east heralded the dawn, and it was soon light. The slowly rising sun felt warm on my face, and eventually I saw another shape, which turned out to be a lifeboat in the distance. At first I set off still holding onto the safety of my oar, but progress was slow and I soon abandoned it. I swam strongly, the lifeboat, people and safety a huge tonic.

'Ahoy there,' I shouted to attract the attention of the people in the lifeboat, but no one seemed to have seen me and there were no oars out. Brown faces peered over the side as I approached and helping hands assisted me on board.

'Hello, Ian,' said the assistant purser. 'Thank God you are here. You are a deck cadet – you can take charge.' Some kind person handed me a pair of swimming shorts, noticing I was only wearing a shirt.

'We'd better get organised,' I told the purser. 'Tell everyone to keep a good lookout for anyone else in the water.'

I took over my first command. The lifeboat was rolling quite heavily, beam-on to the sea and swell. I thought of using the sea anchor, but then decided it would be better to get the oars out. Keep the people occupied and busy. There were some crew in the boat, and getting the oars out was soon achieved. The activity seemed to have cheered everyone up. They all looked to me, facing aft.

'Remind everyone to keep a sharp lookout for others in the water,' I emphasised to the purser. He relayed my instructions in Hindi.

I soon had the crew rowing gently to keep the bow up into the wind and sea. The rolling was much reduced and it was much more comfortable. It became much warmer as the morning wore on and the sun rose higher in the sky. A tanker was heading in our direction and when she saw us she altered course and stopped, making a lee. The crew on my urging rowed with a will and I steered towards the lowered gangway.

'Tell the crew forward to have the painter ready,' I told the purser. I came alongside the gangway, and the painter was handed over to one of the Japanese on the gangway and taken on deck.

'We are safe now,' I said to the purser. 'We can let the men go first. It will be easier to get the women off then.'

The boat was soon empty except for myself and someone lying face down in the bottom of the boat . I thought he was asleep.

'Time to go,' I said. 'You're safe now.' I shook his shoulder, but he felt funny and there was no sound or movement. I pulled him onto his side and saw his face. His eyes were empty. He was dead.

'What should I do,' I wondered. 'Leave him? No, I'm sure the family will want the body. Must get him on board.'

I saw the purser among the faces looking over the side.

'Tell the Captain we have a dead body. We must put him in the freezer,' I shouted up to him.

The corpse was put on the stretcher the Japanese crew brought into the lifeboat. I followed it up the gangway onto the deck of the tanker and watched him being carried into the accommodation.

I had never been on a tanker before and she seemed huge and strange to me, all pipework and open metal deck instead of wooden decks, hatchways and derricks. The Japanese were looking after the people and I went up to the bridge. The foredeck looked huge.

I thanked the captain of the *Yuyo Maru No. 5* for saving us and looking after the passengers and crew. We arranged to make a list of all the survivors, which the purser did, and it was transmitted to the agents in Bahrain by Morse code that evening as soon as it was completed. Unfortunately my name was left off – unfortunate for my poor parents, who thought I was a goner. It was two days before they were told I was alive, two days of lurid newspaper headlines depicting attacks by sharks and sea snakes, and accounts of the many dead, 238 in total. I was given a cabin in the crew accommodation and went to sleep.

FROM *LLOYD'S CASUALTY REPORTS*, 1961

Dara – **Bahrain, April 8** – British motor vessel *Dara* (Basrah for Bahrain). Following SOS received from steamer *Empire Guillemot*, via Cable and Wireless, Bahrain, at 0230 GMT (0630 local) – closed on burning ship. Request all vessels stand by to pick up survivors. Name of distressed ship *Dara*, call sign GDTT. At 0700 local time – 'Am closing to distress ship and sending lifeboat to pick up survivors.' At 0710 – 'We have already taken on board some survivors.' At 0740 – 'We have on board 85 survivors. *Dara* (Master) informs originally 550 persons on board, none got away in lifeboat.' Master of *Dara* reported from motor tanker *Thorsholm*. At 0810 local – '*Dara* abandoned on fire in position Lat 22 55 N, Long 55 13 E.'

Dara – **Bahrain, April 11** – Captain Desmond Law, Commander HM Frigate *Loch Ruthven*, said that motor vessel *Dara* sank yesterday as she was being towed for beaching. 'About three miles off shore, the list in the *Dara* increased and she rolled over to starboard and sank. She is now lying on her starboard side with her davits just sticking out of the water.'

I SALVAGE APPRENTICESHIP

Hull

Falmouth Southampton

Toulon

PACIFIC OCEAN

Port Said

Suez

Dubai

Muscat

Bombay

Lakshadweep

Djibouti

Kochi Trincomalee

Colombo

Galle

Hong Kong

Bombay Reef

Bangkok

Songkhla Trident Shoal

Port Klang

SINGAPORE Labuan

Mogadishu

Mombasa

Jakarta

ATLANTIC OCEAN

INDIAN OCEAN

Europa I.

Cape Town

Singapore

After the *Dara* I remained at sea with BI until I completed my indentures. When I obtained my second mate's certificate I joined Ellerman Lines as a junior officer, running between the UK and India. A couple of years later I flew to Hong Kong and joined the Indo-China Steam Navigation Company, running round the Far East, India, Bangladesh, Burma, Malaysia, Singapore, Thailand, Japan, China, Taiwan and Australia. I obtained my foreign-going master's certificate in 1968. In 1973 I joined a firm of admiralty solicitors in London with a view to becoming a lawyer. They acted for Selco Salvage in Singapore, and a year later an opportunity occurred to join them. The lure of the sea was too much. I was interviewed in a pub near Dungeness and flew out.

I arrived in Singapore, which was hot and humid, and put up at the Orchid Inn on the Bukit Timah Road. I turned up at the office, out at Jurong, about 45 minutes' drive from the hotel, wearing a tie and jacket. I soon realised my mistake. No one seemed very interested in me so I wandered round the shipyard, for apart from tugs and barges Selco owned a yard and slip. Tony Church, an ex-seafarer, took pity on me and lent me a car for a couple of weeks to drive around and learn Singapore. Being a marketing man, he always wore a tie but no jacket.

Captain Peter Lankester arrived with a new tug for Selco. She was an old Japanese tug driven by two engines coupled to a single shaft. Manoeuvring was done on one engine and, to stop the propeller, the engine had to be stopped, big-ship style. The *Daisy*, as she was called, but to be renamed *Salvaliant*, was to be completely refitted at the Selco shipyard. Peter, being a most experienced tug master, knew exactly what he wanted done, regardless of expense. The refit was to take months, and I lived in the hotel, going to the tug each day with Peter.

Peter Lankester was a big, heavy, burly, tough Dutchman, with a heart of gold. It was hot in Singapore, being almost on the equator, so lunch was normally at the swimming club, accompanied by a few beers to replace all the sweat lost during the morning. It was the same in the evening on the way back to the hotel. Peter lived in a flat on the other side of the city with his wife Unke and their two children, Peter and Caroline. At weekends, I was sometimes invited for barbecues.

Nobby Halls, a retired naval petty officer, was the engineer superintendent, and in fact he doubled as the marine superintendent as well. He was a down-to-earth, capable man who got things done and was enormously helpful and supportive to me. He and his wife Anne lived in a flat at Sembawang, the naval base, and when I got to know Nobby better I used to go and stay for a night, away from the tug.

Ernie Kahlenberg, an older man, was a live wire, the dynamo of Selco, but I did not get to know him until later. He used to arrive at the office in a big chauffeur-driven car, a diminutive little man sitting in the back, his white, rather sparse hair just visible through

Salvana

the back window. He was the chairman and managing director, and owned the company.

One evening I received a call from Selco's operations room. We were all on pagers when away from the office or the tugs. A van would pick me up and take me to the office. In the operations room, I was instructed to go with the *Salvana* and her Filipino master, Captain Hannibul, and tow in a ship from the Malacca Straits. The *Salvana* was the original big Selco tug, with some 2,500 hp, and Peter had been in command. This was my first salvage job, and I was very excited. The *Salvana* was in the shipyard and I had to clamber over a couple of ships to reach her. It was near low tide and so she required a small tug to tow her out. We did not want anything to damage the propeller. Once clear of the yard Captain Hannibul, having obtained permission from Port Control, steamed west at full speed, through the Western Anchorage and into the Malacca Straits. In Singapore, no one moved in the port without permission, unless they wanted a one-way trip to Changi jail. Any other salvage tug in Singapore would be monitoring the VHF and would know that a Selco tug had sailed. What they would not know was whether it was a salvage sailing or not. Competition between the salvage companies in Singapore was very fierce.

It was a fine night and the sea was calm in the Malacca Straits, the Indonesian island of Karimun Kesil nine miles to port, Malaysia close to starboard, the jungle dark against the night sky, the lights on the fish traps twinkling. There was the usual traffic in the Straits, the main gateway to Japan – laden tankers from the Persian Gulf, container ships from Europe and small fishing boats from both sides. The tug seemed very small compared to the ships I had been on, and her 12 knots seemed much faster, being so close to the water.

I did not like to admit to Captain Hannibul, a very experienced salvage tug master, that I'd never been in a tug before, let alone done any towing. I suspect he knew in any event, because there was a pretty good bush telegraph in Selco, especially amongst the Filipinos. I went onto the tow deck to watch the crew preparing the towing gear. The casualty, as a ship in distress is known in the salvage world, was anchored about 40 miles north of Singapore. It was about 0200 in the morning when we reached her. Operations had given me the position.

Captain Hannibul stood by the anchored ship while I went across in the rubber boat. A wooden pilot ladder was lowered and I climbed aboard with a Lloyd's Open Form in my pocket. I was taken to the bridge and met the master, a Korean. I offered him the form. He knew we were coming and agreed to sign. I filled it in and we both signed. I was immensely pleased. It was my first Lloyd's form, a 'no cure, no pay' contract that salvors work on. I called up the *Salvana* on the portable VHF, using Selco's private frequency.

'LOF signed. You can come alongside and connect up, Captain,' I spoke into the radio. 'Inform Ops.'

'Roger Cap,' came the reply. Captain Hannibul did not waste words.

The casualty was stemming the tide – that is, bow to the tide. In order to make the connection easily and quickly, it was necessary for Captain Hannibul to bring the *Salvana* alongside in the 69 position – that is, the stern of the tug to the bow of the casualty. He had to come alongside with the tide behind him, not an easy manoeuvre with a single-screw tug, and to stop the propeller turning the engine had to be stopped. Captain Hannibul did it very well, with the crew of the casualty taking the lines. The *Salvana* salvage crew soon had the towing gear connected up, it being quite easy with the tug alongside. The towing wire was secured in a Selco pelican hook, a heavy-duty slip-hook, which was made fast to the mooring bitts with a wire lashing. I instructed the master of the casualty to heave up his anchor, and remained forward with the two *Salvana* riding crew.

'Anchors aweigh,' I told Captain Hannibul on the radio. 'Take her away.'

'Let go the tug lines,' I instructed the riding crew. When the lines were pulled in, the *Salvana* manoeuvred clear of the casualty, turning to starboard and steaming ahead to commence the tow. When I saw the towing gear was all in order, I went onto the bridge and remained there with the master. The Selco riding crew greased the fairlead at regular intervals to protect the tow wire. The ship followed the tug very well. At the pilot station, Captain Hannibul anchored the *Salvana* while the immigration and customs formalities were completed, and with the pilot on board we picked up the anchor and proceeded the short distance to the Western Anchorage. I was in the forecastle of the casualty when the towing gear was slipped and the anchor let go. The pelican hook and wire lashing were taken back to the tug.

The master signed the termination letter, and as I returned to the *Salvana* in the rubber boat the sun seemed to be shining particularly brightly. Captain Hannibul took the *Salvana* back to the yard where, feeling very pleased with myself, I took the Lloyd's Open Form to Operations, only to be told that Chris Herbert, the acting manager, had agreed a contract tow – which meant a fixed price and no bonus for the crew. So much for my first LOF and salvage bonus! And I had kept such good notes.

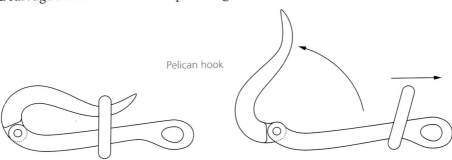

Pelican hook

Friedrich Engels

FROM *LLOYD'S WEEKLY CASUALTY REPORT*, 1974

Friedrich Engels (East German) – **Singapore, Sept 23** – Motor vessel *Friedrich Engels* (Rostock for Kobe) grounded on Nipa Shoal, off Singapore, in position lat 01 09 N, long 103 39 E. Vessel reportedly grounded at 22 knots at high tide and is hard aground with bulbous bow clear and dry ... owners have signed Lloyd's Open Form Salvage Agreement on 'no cure – no pay' basis. Salvors' equipment is presently on site. (Later) *Friedrich Engels*: Salvors advise vessel refloated at 15 33 today at high tide with use of ground tackles. – Salvage Association's Surveyors.

The *Salvaliant*, ex-*Daisy*, was moored alongside the yard, all sorts of shipyard gear on deck, pipes, bits of metal, all the usual chaos of a ship under refit. Peter received the word that there was a ship aground on Nipa Shoal and the *Salvaliant* was needed, refit or no refit.

'*God verdomme!*' he exclaimed. 'How do they expect us to get this heap of garbage away? Look at all the junk on deck.'

Within the hour, the *Salvaliant* was under way to Nipa Shoal. The shoal is just inside Indonesian waters, with the light maintained by the Indonesians, which meant it was out as often as it was lit. Nipa Shoal had been christened Selco Treasure Island because of the number of ships Selco had salved there. The crew and I worked like mad things to get the towing deck and gear ready. We were almost ready by the time we reached Nipa, about an hour's steaming from the yard. I had unfortunately badly twisted my ankle on one of the pipes on the towing deck, so strapped it up and wore a pair of boots. It was three months before I could take the bandage off but this did not stop me working: it was much too exciting! Peter told me to be more careful in future and handed me a cold beer. It was a hot and sunny day and I was drenched in sweat.

The *Friedrich Engels*, a modern East German cargo ship, was almost high and dry on the reef. She was in ballast and had gone aground at full speed. Peter anchored the *Salvaliant* close by and sent me across in the rubber boat to find out what was going on. I found Captain Hancox, Selco's salvage master, with the captain of the ship. Captain Hancox was a thin, dour individual who was forever writing, filling his notebook with neat, black print. He spoke in a monotone, Australian voice. Peter did not care for him, which was why I had been sent across. Captain Hancox told me that the Lloyd's Open Form had been signed and the *Salvaliant* should be connected as quickly as possible.

I was elated and was back on the *Salvaliant* as quickly as possible. Good portable radios were very expensive and heavy in those days and Selco only had a limited number. We were pretty sure our main rivals listened to our private frequency and so, until a salvage contract was signed, the radios were used as little as possible.

'*God verdomme!*' On the bridge of the tug, Peter opened a cold can of beer for himself and passed me one. It was hot and the sun was shining brightly. He proceeded to explain how he intended to connect. I was to sound round the stern of the casualty, which was still in the water. He would anchor the *Salvaliant* as close as possible and send away a messenger attached to a mooring line, attached to the towing gear. I would heave it on board the grounded ship using the capstan. The pelican, or quick-release hook, much bigger than the one on the *Salvana*, and its wire strop would be taken across to the casualty in the rubber boat. I would heave it up on deck, using the ship's capstan. I would make it fast round one set of bitts and back it up on another set for security. It was quite possible to pull out mooring bitts. When the eye of the towing gear was on deck, it would be connected to the pelican hook.

This was all done within an hour or so, and *Salvaliant* was connected. The crew worked really well under the bosun, Javier Patani, a big, heavy-set Filipino. The towing gear was paid out. It consisted of a 60-foot forerunner of eight-inch-circumference wire connected to a 50-foot double-nylon stretcher, the nylon being 12-inch circumference. This was connected to the main tow wire, which was 2,000 feet of six-inch-circumference wire on an electrically driven drum, enabling it to be heaved in or slacked out as required. The anchor on the *Salvaliant* was heaved up and Peter manoeuvred the tug astern of the casualty, no mean feat with a single-screw tug and no bow thruster, while the main tow wire was paid out. He then re-anchored to await Captain Hancox's instructions.

Salvaliant at speed

I was sent back on board the *Friedrich Engels* to see Captain Hancox. He was very informative, telling me the fuel and ballast situation and the results of the diving survey.

'Even after all the fuel, water and ballast have been taken off my calculations suggest the ground reaction will still be over 2,000 tons. We will have to cut her up,' he drawled, with a deadpan, serious face. It was some time before I realised he had made a joke.

'It will be high water in an hour and we will have a go with the *Salvaliant* to show willing, but it will be a complete waste of time. Keep the Salvage Association Surveyor happy,' he continued. 'Tell Peter to heave up his anchor and start towing. I'll keep in touch on the Selco network.'

I returned to the tug and gave him Captain Hancox's instructions.

'*God verdomme!*' exploded Peter, handing me a cold beer as he flipped one open for himself. 'What does he think he's doing: that thing won't come off in a hundred years!'

The anchor was heaved up and Peter showed and taught me his skill as a tug man, explaining everything he did. There was a slight cross-current, so he had to angle the tug with the tow line out on one side to keep the tug on course. He turned the tug each way to get the feel of her, because she was a lot bigger than the *Salvana* and, at the moment, was only on half power.

'I don't want to talk to him so you man the radio,' Peter instructed me.

I informed Captain Hancox of the situation and he told me to build up to full power.

The manoeuvring position on the monkey island had not been fitted with a telephone yet, so Peter shouted the engine movements he wanted to me from on top of the bridge, where he could see the tow wire. I rang down to the engine room and told the chief engineer to start up the second engine. When the engine was clutched onto the shaft, the surge of power could be seen as the tow wire almost came out of the water. Peter explained that the skill was to have enough tow wire out so it did not break when full power was applied, but not so much that it dragged along the bottom and damaged itself on the coral.

When the engines were on full power, I informed Captain Hancox on the radio.

'Throw her about a bit,' I relayed to Peter. He came down onto the bridge and shouted helm instructions from the bridge wing. The wheel was put hard a-starboard and the tug turned to starboard into the current, heeling as she moved sideways through the water. The tow wire came out of the water as the weight of the tug was added to the engine power. Then, when close to the shallow water, the wheel was put hard a-port, the tug turned, heeled, and started moving to port sideways through the water with the current. Peter turned back well before the shallows on this side so the current did not sweep the tug onto the reef as well. The sea was smooth but, even so, the tug heeled so much that water came onto the tow deck each time.

The tide had started to fall on my mark on the reef, and there was no sign of any movement. Captain Hancox's voice came over the radio. 'Cease towing and anchor for the night,' he instructed.

Peter heard the radio, put the engine telegraph to half speed, and I rang down to the engineers to go on one engine. Shortly afterwards, I let go the anchor and paid out enough chain so that the *Salvaliant* lay to the tide with the tow wire over the side and slack.

'We will keep anchor watches,' said Peter. 'If she starts to drag, it won't be long before we're on the reef ourselves. Tell the engineers to keep the engines on standby.'

I went over to the casualty and attended a conference between the master of the ship and the various shore people who had turned up, with or without the Indonesians' permission, including the Salvage Association surveyor. Captain Hancox explained that a bunker barge would be on site in the morning to take off the bunkers. The ballast and the fresh water would be pumped out and ground tackle would be laid.

Breakfast on Salvaliant's bridge, Peter Lankaster standing behind me

Early next morning, the bunker barge arrived, towed by a small Selco tug, and was put alongside the *Friedrich Engels* aft, where there was water. Ground tackle was laid by Dave Warner and the *Salvista*. The *Salvista* was a mooring and salvage vessel with horns on either side of the flat, rounded bow, designed to lay anchors. She was not in the first flush of youth, but had done sterling work for Selco over the years. The ballast and fresh water were pumped out of the *Friedrich Engels* and all was made ready for another attempt on the afternoon's tide. The ability to swing the *Salvaliant* about was limited by the ground tackle, and the attempt failed, with no sign of movement.

Salvage, as I was to learn, is an inexact science. By calculation, we did not have enough power with the *Salvaliant* and the ground tackle for the ship to refloat. However, on the next afternoon, just as the *Salvaliant* had built up full power, off she came unexpectedly. The ground tackle was hurriedly slipped and, when clear of the reef, the *Salvaliant* was slipped by the salvage crew on the casualty. The *Friedrich Engels* was anchored. A diving survey was made while the bosun collected our strop and pelican hook. Shortly afterwards, Captain Hancox dismissed us.

Peter took the tug to Western Anchorage to clear immigration and customs, and then back to the yard. It had been a fascinating experience, great fun, and we would get a bonus to boot. I was not unhappy with my decision to join Selco.

Sarah C Getty

FROM *LLOYD'S WEEKLY CASUALTY REPORTS*, 1974

***Sarah C Getty* (Liberian) – Singapore, Oct 2** – Steam tanker *Sarah C Getty* (Kharg Island for Sendai): Understood from agents that vessel reported to be stranded in Strait of Malacca approximately 15 miles from One Fathom Bank Lighthouse. United States Salvage Association, Yokohama, attending with owners' representative.

London, Oct 2 – Steam tanker *Sarah C Getty* went aground at 1200, Oct 1, in approximate position lat 02 39 36N, long 101 06 06E. Vessel completely surrounded by shallow water and fully loaded with crude oil.

Singapore, Oct 3 – Steam tanker *Sarah C Getty*: Now informed owners have signed Lloyd's Open Form 'no cure – no pay' ... – Salvage Association's Surveyors.

Wednesday 2 October 1974

I had gone ashore that morning, in the usual Singapore weather, hot and humid, to collect various stores. The Operations Room informed me that we were on salvage alert. Peter, the captain, was with me so we chased up those of our crew who were ashore in the yard and departed out to the *Salvaliant* in *Swallow*, a high-speed crew launch. *Salvaliant* was moored at the Selco mooring. As soon as we were on board we removed the shore workers and departed.

We were away at 1010, only 40 minutes after being informed of the alert. We steamed all day at full speed up the Malacca Straits, and that evening the weather started to blow up, with thunder, lightning and heavy rain.

We sighted the casualty just before midnight. She was aground on South Sands, about 15 miles from One Fathom Lighthouse, the lighthouse that stands at the entrance to the Straits proper. Somehow or other she had managed to get the wrong side of the banks and had steamed through numerous shoals, until finally running aground.

The sea had become quite rough by this time and, on the edge of the banks, a nasty sea was running and a moderate northwesterly swell. Peter and I discussed the situation. Although there was 5.5 m depth marked on the bank a little to the south of where the *Sarah C Getty* was aground, we did not think it a good idea to try and cross at night. Anyway, it was low water and the draught of the tug was five metres, and one is never sure of the depth of a sandbank: they often change.

Thursday 3 October 1974

We anchored just after midnight and called the *Getty* on the VHF. We spoke to the master, who said that he didn't want any help, but his owners' representative was arriving the next day and a decision would be made then about what to do. He told us he had run aground at the top of high water two days earlier, but there was no leakage from his tanks.

The sea by this time was even worse, and it was quite big running along the edge of the bank. We considered it imprudent to try to launch the Z-boat and motor over the bank to the *Getty*, which was about three miles away. We decided to go to bed and wait until the morning, and high water.

During the night the weather worsened, with continuous heavy rain, and at 0500 there was a violent thunderstorm, an inauspicious start to the day. It was high water just after 0600, and Peter decided to cross the bank at the five-metre patch, where there should now be 9.8 metres, so it gave us a little allowance if the depths had in fact changed.

I watched the echo sounder like a hawk as we steamed slowly over the bank. The depth increased and decreased as if the bottom was a series of sand dunes. It kept decreasing until we only had about six feet under the keel.

'Too late to turn round now,' commented Peter. And then, quite quickly, we were over the bank and in deep water. We heaved a sigh of relief.

We were about three miles to the south of the casualty, so we turned onto a northwesterly course and steamed up to the *Getty*. The sea was quite noticeably less inside the bank. The South Sands are a series of banks and we had only crossed the first. They stretched both north and south for miles, and at this time we were 20 or so miles from the shore. We

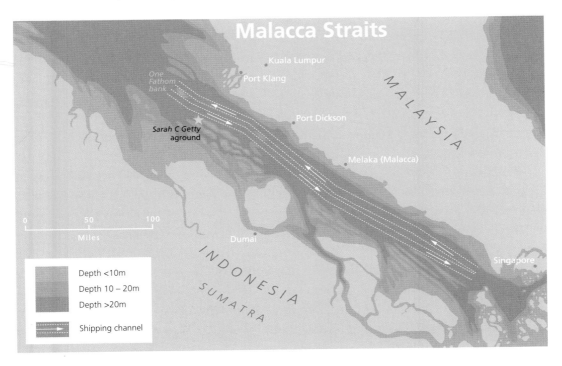

anchored off the casualty and called him up on the VHF, but he had received no word about the owners' representative and so would do nothing, nor would he let us on board.

After breakfast, we received word via radio-telephone from base that one of Selco's men was with the owners' representative and that they would arrive by helicopter just after 0900.

We immediately launched the Z-boat with a fierce sea running, without mishap, and I took it away to sound round the casualty and to act as rescue craft if the helicopter crashed. It was only a small one and could not hold more than four people, so there would be plenty of room in the Z-boat. I had the second officer and two ABs to do the sounding. I reckoned, when I was in the boat, to be the best person to handle her, and so I always drove – besides, I liked driving. She had a 50-hp Johnson and so could really move. It was much too rough to go at full speed to the *Getty*, and even at half speed she was jumping out of the water.

It was rather a strange sensation to be driving a Z-boat twenty miles from the nearest land, and *The Riddle of the Sands* crossed my mind, a connection enhanced by the poor visibility and driving rain that we were experiencing – although it was a bit warmer!

The tanker looked very large and forbidding from the Z-boat. She was lying in the same direction as the wind and waves and so neither side was a lee side. I motored round the whole ship, as close as possible, and continuously sounded as we went. I soon had a pretty good idea of the way she was aground. I then sounded round further off the ship to see where the deep water was and so find out which way she would have to come off.

At about 0920 I heard, and then saw, the helicopter arriving. It circled the *Getty* and landed on the foredeck. I waved to the Selco man who got out of the helicopter with the owners' representative.

'Better get on board,' Peter told me over the walkie-talkie.

They made their way aft and into the accommodation and I motored round the other side of the casualty. This was the side where there was a pilot ladder. The *Getty* was heading about east-south-east on the inside of a sandbank, so the bank lay on her port side, with the navigable part of the Malacca Straits on the outside of the bank, and the coast of Malaysia beyond, hidden in the haze. Luckily, there was a deep channel before the next bank inshore.

There was still quite a sea running, although it had gone down, so I decided to board the casualty from the pilot ladder, which I achieved without mishap. I told the Z-boat to stand off once I was on board.

There is always a certain strangeness boarding somebody else's vessel, especially miles from anywhere. I went up to the bridge and then down to the master's cabin, where I found the Selco man, Dave Warner with his red hair, and the owners' representative agreeing to sign Lloyd's Open Form.

They asked me for details of my soundings and I showed them a rough sketch I had made. It was pretty clear already that a lightening operation would be required. I was sent onto the bridge to tell Peter over the VHF to get hold of base and instruct them to order a lightening tanker. I gathered that there was a tanker already in mind: it only needed the word, and the charter would be made.

I had made out a tidal curve for the next few days, and it was clear that we would have to be pretty quick to get her off. She was now out of her draught about three feet and would require at least 7,500 tons of cargo to be discharged, and the longer we waited, the more cargo would have to be discharged before the tide started making again. She had 80,000-odd tons of light Arabian crude on board, bound for Japan, with over 3,000 tons of bunkers. Her floating draught was about 48.5 ft. I later discovered what he had done. Somewhere along the line, he was about nine miles out of his position, and had been for some time. This meant he had come inside the banks. He blamed his radar, which had given him distances that were twice the actual distance. I'm not sure how the radar managed to do this, but he succeeded in persuading the American owners' representative that this was the case.

Later on that morning, the Selco salvage master turned up on his salvage ship, the *Salviper*. We departed for our own tug after meeting for a beer and lunch. The salvage master was not very sociable, so we left him to it.

At the meeting, we had decided to attempt to tow her off at the next high tide, which was at 1836. We would make a towing connection during the afternoon. We had reminded the salvage master that the *Salvaliant* might look like a tug but she handled like a big ship. Her two engines were connected to a single shaft. You could only manoeuvre on one engine, in other words with half power. If you wanted the propeller to stop, you had to stop the engine and then, if

Salviper with Yokohama fenders on her towdeck

you wanted the propeller to move, you had to restart the engine, which was an air start. Everything took a long time in relation to what can be done with a modern supply boat or tug, where the engine is running all the time. As a result, one has to be extremely careful when manoeuvring in close proximity with this tug, and Peter was fairly forceful in informing the salvage master.

After lunch, the Z-boat was sent over with our diver to assist in the underwater survey of the casualty. The *Salviper* came alongside to transfer our slip hook and towing connection to the *Getty*. The *Salviper* was an ex-American fishing boat with an open deck aft, like a supply boat.

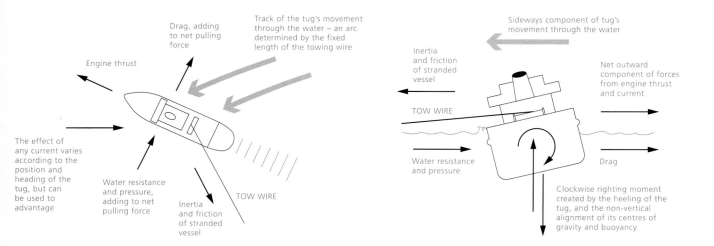

Drag, adding to net pulling force

Track of the tug's movement through the water – an arc determined by the fixed length of the towing wire

Engine thrust

The effect of any current varies according to the position and heading of the tug, but can be used to advantage

Water resistance and pressure, adding to net pulling force

Inertia and friction of stranded vessel

TOW WIRE

Sideways component of tug's movement through the water

Inertia and friction of stranded vessel

TOW WIRE

Net outward component of forces from engine thrust and current

Water resistance and pressure

Drag

Clockwise righting moment created by the heeling of the tug, and the non-vertical alignment of its centres of gravity and buoyancy

The forces acting on a tug sheering – pulling with the tow wire oblique to the tug's heading

The afternoon was spent getting the tow rigged and transferring men to and from the tug. Eventually, after manoeuvring very carefully around the stern, using one anchor, we managed to make a connection and were ready to tow by 1750. The gear, as might be expected, is very heavy. The towing wire is six-inch circumference and the nylon stretcher is twelve-inch circumference. A stretcher is used between the forerunner and the tow wire and acts as a shock absorber, which helps prevent breaking the wire. The shackles are 75 tons (breaking strain) and weigh nearly 2 hundredweight, and the slip hook is a hundred-tonner and weighs nearly 3 hundredweight. I think the gear is over-heavy, but at least you can rest assured that it will not break unless damaged.

Between 1800 and 1930 we towed without having the slightest effect on the casualty. Salvage towing is quite different from straight towing in that one tries to use the weight of the tug as well as its horsepower. This is achieved by sheering and, depending on the tidal direction and strength, one sheers off at an angle until the tow line, instead of being astern, is on the beam of the tug, causing her to heel over about 10 degrees. Thus, the whole weight of the tug is added to the horsepower or, at least, a lot of it. The problems occur in a tideway (which we were in), because if the tide is on your beam and strong, and you have a tow line too far on the beam, you cannot get back against the tide, which means you have to either cut or slip the tow, or run aground. Nothing quite as drastic happened, but we got rather a long way down tide and it took half an hour to get back, at full power with the helm hard over, which was all very interesting.

At 2000 we anchored for the night.

Friday 4 October 1974

High water was at 0646, so at 0600 we heaved up the anchor and commenced towing again, predictably with no result. However, it was good for morale aboard the tanker, and for the owners' representative! The *Getty* tried using her engine, as she had the day before, but there was absolutely no movement.

At 0735 we shortened in the tow wire. *Salvaliant* was fitted with a huge, 40-ton towing winch and all one had to do was press two buttons and move a lever, and in came the wire. At 0755, the forerunner was slipped from the *Getty* and we moved off to anchor and recover the rest of the towing gear, nylon stretcher and forerunner.

Just after noon, the *Salviper* came alongside and transferred four marker buoys. Once we had refloated the *Getty*, we would still have to get her clear of the Banks and back into the Straits. We decided that the easiest way would be to steer southeasterly for a distance of about 15 miles. We would take the tug and steam out and survey the route, dropping the buoys in the right places to mark the channel.

Once the buoys were on board and the anchor was aweigh, we proceeded to the proposed location for the first buoy. The echo sounder was, of course, continuously on. We decided to use the *Getty* as datum. We plotted the position of the casualty very carefully, using One Fathom Bank Lighthouse and the radar distance, which coincided with the shore distances from the radar. The casualty was so far away from the low-lying shores of both Sumatra and Malaysia that it was not possible to navigate, using bearings

STANDARD TOW

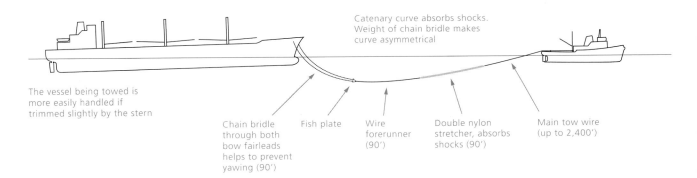

Catenary curve absorbs shocks.
Weight of chain bridle makes
curve asymmetrical

The vessel being towed is
more easily handled if
trimmed slightly by the stern

Chain bridle
through both
bow fairleads
helps to prevent
yawing (90')

Fish plate

Wire
forerunner
(90')

Double nylon
stretcher, absorbs
shocks (90')

Main tow wire
(up to 2,400')

SALVAGE TOW

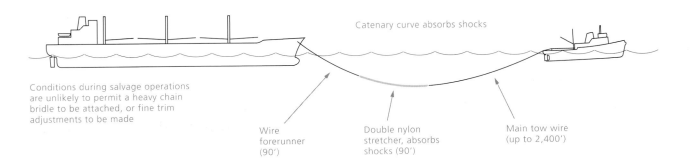

Catenary curve absorbs shocks

Conditions during salvage operations
are unlikely to permit a heavy chain
bridle to be attached, or fine trim
adjustments to be made

Wire
forerunner
(90')

Double nylon
stretcher, absorbs
shocks (90')

Main tow wire
(up to 2,400')

and distances from the shore, sufficiently accurately to negotiate a channel, which was in places only one mile wide. Therefore, by using the casualty as datum, we would be able to survey the channel. When the casualty was refloated and was steaming out, the *Salviper* would be left as datum in the casualty's old grounding position.

Just before lunch, we anchored in the position of the first buoy, five miles from the *Getty*. The crew prepared the buoys with an anchor weight and lines while we had a beer and lunch. The position of the shoal on which we were anchored was approximately correct, according to the chart. We dropped buoy number three and proceeded to the proposed second location after lunch.

Just after three o'clock, we anchored nine miles from the *Getty*. I took the Z-boat away to see how wide the channel was. I reported my soundings to Peter who, using the radar, plotted my positions and transferred them to the chart, so we had our own soundings chart. The northern edge of the South Sands, the inshore banks, was much further north than marked on the chart. The only indication of the sandbank was when it uncovered at low water, and it was one and a half miles out of position.

We dropped the second buoy and proceeded out a little to the south of the course we intended to use with the casualty, and found shoal water. We needed a minimum of 20-odd metres, or ten fathoms, to get the casualty out with any safety. We returned to buoy number two, went out again on a more northerly course and found plenty of water. We dropped buoy number one on the run and made a dummy run back to number two, which we found quite easy to see. The exit channel could only be navigated in clear, fine weather and in daylight.

We went out to the entrance of the channel and anchored, giving our position to the lightening tanker, which was arriving. We told him to anchor. When she arrived the next morning, I was to go on board and pilot her in through the channel we had marked.

Saturday 5 October 1974

The *Uranus* arrived while it was still dark. At 0800 we called him up on the radio and explained the plan to the captain, who thought it was a good idea. We said we would not be moving off until the cloud and rain, which were over the *Getty* (15 miles away), had cleared. I went over to the *Uranus*, a twin-screw motor tanker with a gross tonnage of 7,035, a length overall of 428 feet, a loaded draught of 23.5 feet, and a beam of 66 feet. She had been designed for river work, hence her wide beam and shallow draught. She had been built in France in 1957 with two 1,830 horsepower Nordberg engines, giving her a speed of nine or so knots.

I climbed up the pilot ladder and was shown to the bridge by a piratical-looking black man with hair down to his shoulders, dressed in a bright red shirt and grey shorts. I wondered what sort of ship I had let myself in for, but was pleasantly surprised to find the accommodation spotlessly clean and the master dressed in white shorts and a white shirt. He was a big, fat, ebullient Italian and welcomed me aboard as pilot. I was glad I had put on my whites.

The *Uranus* had two radars, which were both working. I asked the master if the echo sounder was OK and he informed me that it was. There was a quartermaster on the wheel, and the master told me he was ready to go. I explained to him that the *Salvaliant* would lead ahead and if she came to shallow water she would inform us. It would give us time to stop and anchor if they could not find deeper water quickly. Above all, we did not want to run aground. He sent two men forward and I informed Peter over the VHF that we were ready to go.

The master kept on calling me Pilot and said that the vessel was all mine, so I gave my first order on someone else's ship to heave up the anchor. It was childish, no doubt, but it gave me a thrill to be piloting a ship through a channel I had helped to buoy for the first time! It was completely different from normal, commercial shipping. I found it all very exciting and exhilarating.

At 0935 the anchor was aweigh and I ordered slow ahead on two engines. The piloting was, in the event, quite straightforward. We picked up the buoys at a distance of about three miles. I kept a running plot going and the personnel on the bridge could not do enough for me. I only had to hint that I wanted something, and it was done. It was rather amusing to have a 50-year-old master skipping around like a third mate at my behest. Luckily, nothing went wrong. I anchored the *Uranus* off the casualty, having turned her first on the engines, to stem the tide. The captain offered me a beer when we were anchored, which I gladly accepted.

The *Salviper*'s Z-boat came over to pick me up and take the captain and chief officer over to the *Getty* for a meeting to discuss the plan of action. The meeting was really very boring. I was not concerned with the discharge of the *Getty*. Peter and I removed ourselves fairly smartly and went back to *Salvaliant* for lunch.

During the afternoon, I took my crew over to the *Getty* to form the forward mooring party to make fast the *Uranus* when she came alongside. The previous day, the *Salviper* had put big fenders alongside on the starboard side of the *Getty*. The mooring proceeded without incident.

While mooring, I spoke with the captain and superintendent of the *Getty* and suggested that, when the *Getty* was afloat, the captain might like me to be on board to pilot her out through the channel, as I knew it. He thought it was an excellent idea, and so did the superintendent. So now I had landed myself the job of piloting an 85,000-ton tanker through a channel which in places was only a mile wide!

I took the crew back to the *Salvaliant* after some very welcome light refreshment aboard the *Uranus*. We rigged the big salvage pump as a fire pump, ready for when the *Getty* discharged into the *Uranus* overnight.

Sunday 6 October 1974

I was on the bridge with Peter at 0630 when we observed the casualty swinging to starboard towards us. We immediately picked up our anchor and moved out of the way. The *Getty* continued to swing, but stopped when she was across the tide. We re-anchored, and I took out the Z-boat to find the edge of the bank on the south side of the channel. It was raining and blowing quite fresh. I found the edge and reported to Peter by walkie-talkie and he then plotted the position on the chart. As we suspected, the bank was approximately one and a quarter miles further north than charted.

When I returned, the *Getty* was held across the tide by the ground tackle aft (this had been laid by the *Salviper*) and one anchor forward. I took the Z-boat round to the stern of the *Getty* and sounded the direction the stern would take if the ground tackle were let go. Within a couple of hundred feet, I found only 4.4 metres. Near to the stern, there was less than the draught. The casualty had re-grounded on another shoal. I went back to the *Salvaliant* and collected a marker buoy, which I laid on the shoal. This was a bit after the horse had bolted! I sounded round the stern of the *Getty* and found that she was aground aft as well.

I returned to the *Salvaliant*, and we were ordered to make a towing connection on the bow of the casualty. It was not very easy. Eventually, we had to run a messenger with the Z-boat so the *Getty* could heave our towing gear across.

In the middle of the morning we were made fast to the casualty and we paid out the wire. We then just steamed at slow speed while the *Uranus* was unmoored. At 1110 she was cleared and I told the captain he should steer southwest for one mile and anchor. We towed at full power, which was a waste of time because it was almost low tide.

We managed to get the bow of the casualty to move, but this was not surprising, as she was afloat forward. The rudder of the *Getty* then jammed over hard a-starboard. This was really serious because it meant that the *Getty* was ashore and resting on her rudder, in which case it would probably bend or be damaged. Apart from anything else, the expense of removing all the cargo and/or towing her to Japan would be enormous – and consequently the salved sum would be less and my salvage bonus would be less. We were not feeling too pleased with the salvage master, who we reckoned should have organised himself differently.

Just after noon, we anchored and had lunch. We had a sick man on board, and although we did not think he was going to die on us, he was not much good if he could not work, so we organised a helicopter to take him to Kuala Lumpur.

At about 1400, we started towing again, and towed all afternoon. The *Getty* refloated around 1700 and we towed her into the deep water we had surveyed. The casualty anchored just before 1800. We steamed round this for a quarter of a mile, then half a mile, just to make sure there were no shoals we had missed, and then we anchored for the night. Light refreshments were served before dinner, then to bed. We had said we could not possibly pilot the ship out in the dark – and indeed we couldn't – so it was arranged that we would go after the tide had turned the next morning.

Monday 7 October 1974

It had been decided to take the *Getty* to the Fairway Buoy off the Indonesian port of Dumai, about 70 miles down the coast, where her cargo would be reloaded. This was very much the *Salvaliant*'s part of the show, as we had done the survey and so we were in charge. At 0845, the Z-boat was launched and I went over to the *Uranus* and explained to the captain what we intended to do. He would be last in the convoy. Next, I went over to the *Getty*.

We did not intend to start until the ship had swung and was heading in the direction we wished to go. It was just too risky to try and turn her and run aground again. I spent the morning on the bridge of the *Getty*, imagining all the things that could go wrong and what I would do. I arranged with the captain that I would give all the orders, in other words pilot the ship, if he would translate them into Italian. I had already discovered that he was really the only one who spoke reasonable English. We tested his rudder and it seemed quite satisfactory.

At noon, the *Getty* had swung through about 100 degrees and I told Peter I was going to shorten the cable in. At 1210 the vessel continued swinging and at 1238 I told Peter that I thought I would have no difficulty getting round if I heaved up the anchor now. He had already picked up his anchor and taken station ahead of the *Getty*.

A little later, the anchor was aweigh and I ordered slow ahead, hard a-port. This was the first time I had handled a ship of this size on my own and I was not sure when to stop the swing, because it would be very easy to go too far. Anyway, I got it right, gave the helm orders, steadied up on the course, and told the quartermaster to steer it. I felt rather pleased with myself. I followed the *Salvaliant* and, of course, took my own bearings and positions. Once one got used to the size, she handled really very well.

Buoy number three was passed quite happily, but number two was out of position. We found it but, just afterwards, *Salvaliant* reported shoal water ahead. I immediately went to dead slow and altered course a little to starboard. I was certain we were to the north, and Peter confirmed this shortly afterwards. He went on ahead to try and find buoy number one, and to check whether there was enough water. He found deep water quite quickly and in fact, as we were to the north, I remained in deep water. Peter found buoy number one a long way out of position, being used as a mooring buoy by four Indonesian fishermen! By this time, we knew we were clear of the banks so I went to half ahead and altered course, out into the Malacca Straits. Just after 1500, I went to full ahead and the captain ordered light refreshments and sandwiches, which by this time were most welcome. It was an exceedingly hot day and I had been sweating buckets.

Though the captain stayed on the bridge with some of the officers, I was asked to navigate. *Salvaliant* went on ahead to anchor first and make a marker for me. I came up to the anchorage, taking way off in good time. It still took ten minutes at full astern to stop the ship, even though I had been going at dead slow and had stopped for half an hour before. Just as I was about to anchor, the salvage master came onto the radio to ask silly questions, so I pretended the radio was not working and left Peter to argue.

I anchored successfully and went below with the captain for a well-earned light ale and some cold beef. At 2230, just before the salvage master turned up, I went back to the *Salvaliant* in the Z-boat. And that was the end of that one.

We stood by while the cargo was reloaded and then went back to Singapore. I had already come to the firm conclusion that salvage work was much more amusing than sailing on cargo ships. Of course, I had only seen comparatively easy ones so far. I did not much fancy fighting a tanker fire.

FROM *LLOYD'S WEEKLY CASUALTY REPORTS*, 1974

Singapore, Oct 9 – Steam tanker *Sarah C Getty* – Following received from our surveyor on board *Sarah C Getty*: Vessel completed reloading cargo pm, Oct 8, and will resume voyage am today after salvage agreement terminated. Diver's inspection of underwater hull shows no damage other than scoring of paintwork over forward shell bottom and propeller blade tips scuffed due to working in sand; rudder and stern frame undamaged and sea-suction chests clear of sand/mud. – Salvage Association's Surveyors.

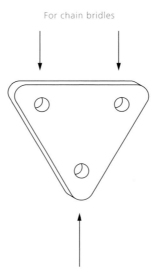

Fish Plate
(also called flounder plate
or towing triangle)

For chain bridles

For wire forerunner

Nienburg

FROM *LLOYD'S WEEKLY CASUALTY REPORT*, 1974

Nienburg **(East German) – Singapore, Nov 20** – Following received from Singapore Radio: SOS CQ (all stations), following received from Aeradio:

At 0025, Nov 20 – Following received from Australia, New Zealand and United Kingdom Forces at 0017, Nov 20, from Royal Navy Communications Centre, Hong Kong: Following SOS message intercepted on 500 kHz from motor vessel *Nienburg* DDXQ: Ship aground on Bombay Reef, Paracel Island, in position lat 16 03 30 N, long 112 33 00 E: request immediately help and assistance.

The refit was finally completed, and the first towing job was a barge to Songkhla in Thailand. Nobby Halls came with us to make sure the repairs and improvements worked. I made sure we had a good stock of soda water for him. After delivering the barge, we remained in Songkhla for a few days. The nightlife was not as varied as in Bangkok!

Back in Singapore, Nobby declared himself satisfied with the tug and we went on salvage station in Eastern Anchorage. It was not long until we were ordered to Loyang, on the northeast side of Singapore, where we picked up two crew boats for Brunei. The tow was in fine weather, and they were safely delivered.

Communication with Operations was by radio, and a regular schedule was maintained by the radio officer. The operations room was manned 24 hours a day. When the radio officer was not on duty, there was a speaker turned on in the wheelhouse with the medium-frequency radio tuned to the base frequency, in case an urgent message needed to be sent by base. The bridge was always manned. The VHF was always switched on to channel 16, the distress frequency. It became second nature always to have one ear listening in for distress messages. In the salvage world, minutes count. It is often the first tug to reach the casualty that gets the job.

While anchored off Brunei, we received instructions to proceed north and tow an oil rig. This turned out to be a most demanding job for us, being a single-screw tug with no bow thruster. We were often in considerable conflict with the tool pusher on the three-legged jack-up *Chris Seger*. Peter had to try and hold the tug across the current to comply with his instructions, while the anchors were picked up by a supply boat. The tool pusher would not agree to any of our suggestions and it was a tense and difficult time. Eventually, we got under way and with maximum power, or nearly so, we towed the rig at an average speed of two and a half knots. The rig was finally positioned and anchored, and the *Salvaliant* was dismissed. We took the insurance surveyor back to Brunei, plying him with our *Salvaliant* Special, which was a particularly lethal gin-based concoction.

———◆———

We were admiring the sunset, a gentle swell giving the tug slight movement to remind us we were at sea, as she ambled south at economical speed on one engine, relaxed in the glow of a difficult mission successfully completed. The speed of the tug through the water was enough to give a pleasant breeze on our faces as we sat on the bridge wing, in the late tropic afternoon.

The radio officer rushed out of the wheelhouse, disturbing the peace, and thrust a piece of paper into Peter's hand. The annoyed look on his face disappeared as he leapt out of his chair, which fell over on the deck, and he walked fast into the wheelhouse. I followed and heard him speak into the telephone: 'Two engines, maximum power.' He handed me the message.

'Drop the surveyor. Proceed maximum speed Bombay Reef,' it read. The message was signed Bond. Alan Bond was the Manager of Selco Salvage, a man of few words.

Shortly afterwards there was a further message from the Hong Kong Marine Department:

> Following received from motor vessel *Nienburg*: Present situation vessel aground with all bottom square lifted off draught about three metres forward apparently no damage to ship hull or bottom. Soundings cargo holds and tanks normal. Colours green hull yellow mast and funnel with blue red blue ribbon. Wx condition wind force five NE sea moderate forty-seven crew members no passengers. Two lifeboats and four liferafts on board. Main engine working. All attempts at refloating by own power without success and seems hopeless. No special place for helicopter landing. No special lift-off locations. Please advise urgently Hong Kong salvage tugs available. Will try refloating by means of heavy tugs.

I was electrified. My first chance of an open-ocean salvage. The surveyor was forgotten as I rushed into the chartroom to find the *South China Sea Admiralty Pilot*, the navigator's bible.

'Don't get excited, Ian,' Peter said. 'Expect there are lots of tugs around. We are days away and at the moment heading in the wrong direction.' His words were emphasised by the vibrating deck of the *Salvaliant* at full speed.

I was not put off, my mind racing ahead, as I pulled out the requisite book, boyish dreams of heroism and drama at sea coursing through my brain.

The sober, careful words of the *Pilot* soon brought me back to earth. I just noticed the vibrations ease and the engines stop as the elderly surveyor was dropped off into the boat waiting off Serai, Sarawak, and his friendly 'Best of luck,' as the boat pulled away. Peter turned the tug, and soon we were heading northeastwards, rushing through the dark night at full speed, the old tug pitching more heavily into the gentle swell.

Bombay Reef was the outermost reef on the eastern side of the Paracel Islands, which were in Chinese territorial waters about 410 miles south-south-west of Hong Kong, although the South Vietnamese claimed them as well. The main distinguishing features were four boulders and a wreck. The whole reef was under water at high tide. The forecast for the area was poor, wind northeast force five to six. If the ship was on the weather side of the reef there did not appear to be much hope for her.

Peter grunted when I told him.

'The Paracels are under commie control, whatever the South Vietnamese may think,' I continued. 'We'd better tell base to get permission to go into their waters. I don't fancy a communist prison.' But it turned out that Peking had no objection, so we continued on our way towards Bombay Reef.

There was a huge area of unsurveyed reefs between us and the casualty. We had to steam northeastwards through the Palawan Passage to clear this dangerous area, and then northwestwards out across the South China Sea, south of Macclesfield Bank. The weather was fine with a low swell, into which the *Salvaliant* dipped her bow as she thundered along at 15 knots. She pushed up a huge bow wave, leaving a foaming wake astern, her 200-foot length vibrating with the effort. We willed every ounce of speed in our endeavour to be first on the scene.

Further messages received during the night suggested the casualty was well out of her draught, and worse still she was on the windward side of the reef.

Once out in the China Sea, clear of the reefs, we felt the full effect of the northeast monsoon. It was blowing hard and a rough sea was running, and the *Salvaliant* rolled and pitched heavily. The towing deck was continuously awash and the occasional sea came on board forward. Some of the crew suffered from *mal de mer* but I knew they would perk up soon enough once the casualty was reached.

CHINA
Guangzhou
Hong Kong
Hanoi

The South China Sea
Bombay Reef

HAINAN I.

PARACEL ISLANDS

Nienburg on Bombay Reef

LAOS

CAMBODIA

VIETNAM

SOUTH

CHINA

SEA

Ho Chi Minh City (Saigon)

SPRATLY ISLANDS

0   200   400
Miles

Labuan
Bandar Seri Begawan
BRUNEI

MALAYSIA

Kuching

Singapore

My little-used sextant was back in use with a vengeance. I took sun and star sights when possible, the heavily rolling tug making it difficult, and the dollops of water reaching the bridge were an additional hazard. The closer we came to Bombay Reef the rougher it seemed to become.

Three and a half days after dropping off the surveyor we were approaching communist territorial waters. At 0506 on 24 November Bombay Reef bore west-north-west distance 22 miles by radar, and I confirmed that by star sights. We had found the right reef. Anyone with any possible excuse to be on the bridge was there, the tension palpable, watching for the first glimpse of the *Nienburg*. It had become overcast, and daylight seemed to be delayed in the gloom as the tug approached the reef. It was exciting and I was a little apprehensive at what was to come.

At 0700 the casualty was in sight. The bow was high in the air and stern well down, indicating how far out of her draught she was. The remains of a wreck were to the east of her, the boiler standing mute and alone, a stark reminder of what would happen to the *Nienburg* if we did not get her off.

It was a sombre and serious Peter, all joviality gone, who said, 'This is going to be difficult and dangerous. One mistake and we are on the reef ourselves. The reef is live coral; anyone thrown on it will be stripped of his flesh as quickly as if attacked by barracuda or piranha, a hideously painful death. Be warned, everyone, and warn the others below.'

The crew and officers on the bridge heard him and nodded their heads in agreement. I was the newcomer. I could see the remains of three other wrecks, a real ship's graveyard. The low cloud cover had closed in the horizon, making the whole scene dismal and uninviting. It started to drizzle, which made it seem cold as well.

The reef showed up well on the radar. Outside, the seas were breaking all along it and around the stern of the *Nienburg*. She was on a dead lee shore. The wind had picked up even more and it was now blowing a gale. It seemed an impossible situation to me.

'It's just like the *Lady Christine* salvage,' said Peter. 'The reef is steep to – look at the surf round the stern of the casualty – we cannot anchor.' The chart also suggested the same.

Peter spent half the morning manoeuvring the tug to see how she would lie. Unfortunately we could not go slow enough to just keep the bow up into the wind and sea. She fore-reached by about two knots, too fast to be able to make a connection.

There was a large mainland Chinese vessel to the west, silent and watching, like a black brooding beast waiting to pounce out of the drizzle. There was a large gun, uncovered, on the forecastle to add weight to their almost malevolent presence. Over the radio the captain of the *Nienburg* asked us to hoist a communist flag as a courtesy to them. Unfortunately none of us could remember what the flag looked like, so I had to elicit the information in guarded language. We were dead scared of upsetting the communists. Singapore did not have the best of relationships with China. The crew, all Filipino, with their usual ingenuity, soon had a flag made up and hoisted.

I called up the communist ship on the VHF and asked the captain for permission to make a connection. It was given. Peter took the tug in close to the reef astern of the casualty, the crew lining the rails watching. Our own crew were on the hatch and boatdeck, the tow deck being continuously awash. It was still drizzling and gloomy.

Peter turned the *Salvaliant* when off the stern. We were running parallel to the reef, and I really thought he had left it too late to get her round into the wind and sea. My heart was in my mouth, but of course I said nothing. If we touched the reef I reckoned we would be rolled over and that would be the end of us. Peter's face did not change, not a muscle moved. Then slowly, oh so slowly, she started to turn and we were clear. I slowly relaxed. I had not realised I had been holding my breath. I was not the only one. The helmsman called out the course as it changed.

Peter tried again and got to within one and a half cables of the stern of the casualty, when, for some reason, I went onto the bridge wing, the drizzle damp on my hair, and looked over the side. I could not believe my eyes.

'Bottom, the bottom,' I shouted, my voice high-pitched in excitement and shock. 'I can see it, I can see the bottom!'

Peter rushed over next to me, looked and exclaimed, 'Anchor, anchor, let go the anchor, Ian!'

The anchor was not even properly ready. The pilot book gave no indication of a ledge where it was possible to anchor – the reef was supposed to be steep to. There had been no indication on the echo sounder, although no doubt there was now.

I rushed up to the forecastle with Jesus (the second officer), the bosun, and some ABs. In no time the lashings were off and the anchor was let go, only a cable off the watching crew of the *Nienburg*. The anchor dragged wildly, the bow was falling off, and the tug was pitching and rolling, with only four shackles out. Remember that on the *Salvaliant* the propeller could only be stopped by stopping the engine, and it could only be started again using air, just like a big ship. Here we were, playing around on a dead lee shore in a gale with the engine stopped – literally dicing with death.

'Heave up the anchor,' shouted Peter from the bridge. 'We are too close and not enough chain out.'

I could hear the engine being started as the chain came rattling in. Luckily the windlass worked well and was fast. Peter headed out to sea, turned, and tried again. This time the anchor held with seven shackles out and the stern of the tug less than a cable off the *Nienburg*. If the propeller hit the reef it would also be the end.

I went aft with Jesus and the bosun, leaving two men on the forecastle to watch the anchor. The tow deck was continuously awash as the tug pitched heavily, and I found myself looking up at the faces of the East Germans on board the *Nienburg*. It was still drizzling, the low cloud making it seem dark and gloomy, although I was far too busy and hepped up to notice being wet. We tried floating down a lifebuoy but that did not work – it went nowhere near the casualty.

I went back to the bridge to report.

'Use the Schermuly rocket,' said Peter, standing by the engine-room telegraph. He was using the engine in short bursts to ease the weight on the chain. 'The sooner we connect the sooner I can get clear. I don't like it here at all, and I don't want to run out of air for the engine.' I could see he was very worried indeed.

I said nothing, not wishing to admit I had never used a rocket gun in my life before. It was a Japanese thing, but I had read the instructions. I went back aft to find Jesus laying out the rocket gear on top of the hatch. The towing gear was all ready to be paid out. I was very nervous – everything depended on getting a line across – but I tried to appear confident in front of the crew. The box and line were now ready, all neatly laid out. I picked up the gun, which had been loaded, and steadying myself against the roll, but mainly the pitch of the tug, aimed at the *Nienburg*. The bridge and accommodation were aft, which made a big target. I aimed, and squeezed the trigger.

There was a loud bang and all I could see at first was a red haze. When it cleared I saw the line heading towards the casualty. We all held our breaths, and then a cheer went up as it landed on the funnel. Eager hands grabbed it, and the messenger coiled on the hatch snaked out over the side, followed by a long polypropylene line.

I glanced up at the rock-like figure standing by the telegraph on the monkey island and Peter gave me the thumbs-up sign. The polypropylene line floated, and it was soon aboard the *Nienburg*. They put it on the capstan and it came out of the water as they heaved the towing gear across, the wire pendant

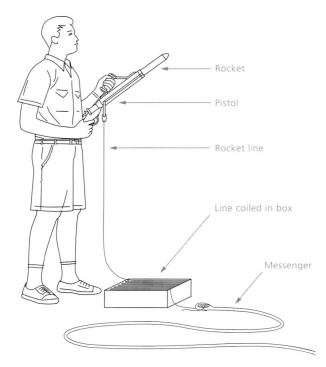

Rocket gun and line

Rocket

Pistol

Rocket line

Line coiled in box

Messenger

first, then the nylon stretcher and finally the main tow wire, the joining shackle slipping over the greased towing gunwale. The tow deck was constantly under water as the tug rolled and pitched, yawing to her chain. The tow wire was between the dolly pins, two movable bollards on the towing gunwale designed to keep the propeller clear.

There was another cheer as the crew on the casualty indicated they had secured the towing gear. We were connected. I went forward with the bosun and started heaving up the anchor, Jesus supervising the slacking out of the tow wire to Peter's directions. It was vital to keep it reasonably tight so it did not get round the propeller. Once the anchor was aweigh Peter steamed ahead. I went aft, to where the electrician was driving the electric towing winch, and when about 1,000 feet was out he secured it at Jesus' direction. The electrician was a stroppy-looking character, but a brilliant electrician. He had a wife and fourteen children.

'Ring down for two engines,' Peter said as I walked back onto the bridge.

Once power was increased, the dolly pins were lowered so the tow wire could run free and swing across the now empty tow deck, enabling the tug to be manoeuvred. The

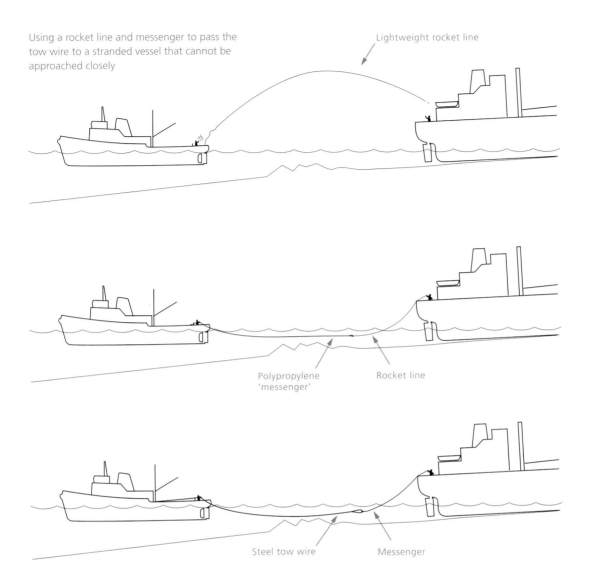

Using a rocket line and messenger to pass the tow wire to a stranded vessel that cannot be approached closely

Lightweight rocket line

Polypropylene 'messenger'

Rocket line

Steel tow wire

Messenger

Salvaliant was in a most precarious position on the windward side of the reef and now connected to the casualty. If we were unable to stem the current, which ran along the reef, or if anything went wrong, the tug would be aground on the coral in minutes, the waves breaking over her. Constant intense vigilance was required all the time.

Peter spoke to the captain of the *Nienburg* on the VHF, no doubt monitored by the watching communists, and told him we would have a refloating attempt. The engines were increased to full power. Peter flung the tug from port to starboard, shipping heavy seas on the tow deck as the tug heeled, being pulled sideways through the water, the additional weight of the tug pulling the tow wire out of the water. Too much wire out, and it would snag on the coral and break, too little and it would also break under the strain. It was a highly skilled manoeuvre to get it right. The captain used his main engine

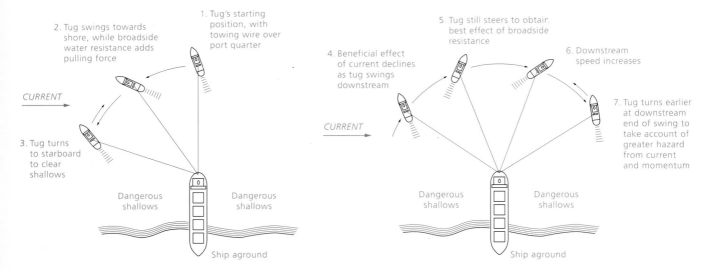

1. Tug's starting position, with towing wire over port quarter

2. Tug swings towards shore, while broadside water resistance adds pulling force

CURRENT

3. Tug turns to starboard to clear shallows

Dangerous shallows

Dangerous shallows

Ship aground

4. Beneficial effect of current declines as tug swings downstream

5. Tug still steers to obtain best effect of broadside resistance

6. Downstream speed increases

CURRENT

7. Tug turns earlier at downstream end of swing to take account of greater hazard from current and momentum

Dangerous shallows

Dangerous shallows

Ship aground

A tug working a stranded vessel free by alternating the direction of pull and using water resistance to boost the pulling force

but reported no movement. After an hour the refloating attempt was stopped and power reduced on the tug.

'1030 connected. Refloating attempt made. Failed,' was the laconic message Peter wrote and the radio officer sent by morse code via Singapore radio.

'*Albatross* on the way to assist,' came back the signal from the office.

'All help gratefully received,' remarked Peter. 'She's pretty heavily aground and we're going to be lucky to get her off. The *Albatross* is a Bugsier tug, all German crew. They will be good: just what we need.'

The Chinese ship was still silent, watching and waiting, her brooding shape indistinct in the drizzle and gloom.

In the afternoon a vessel was seen coming from the east.

'Wrong way from Singapore if it's the *Albatross*, observed Peter. We all watched as the mystery ship came closer, until one of the crew said, 'It's the *Virginia City*.'

'That's the last thing we want here,' grumbled Peter.

The tug belonged to the Filipino company China Pacific Salvage of Manila. I looked her up in the *Lloyd's Register* and saw she had been built in 1944, over thirty years ago. She was American-built and powered by diesel electric, but a big heavy tug.

Jesus spoke to the *Virginia City* in Tagalog on the VHF.

'Cap, they say they have a Lloyd's Open Form and want to connect,' he reported.

'Tell him he can do what he likes but keep clear of us,' replied Peter sharply.

There is intense rivalry between salvage companies and their people, and we certainly did not want a thirty-year-old tug getting in our way. After the refloating attempt, Peter had manoeuvred the tug up to the west of the *Nienburg* so the *Salvaliant* was up-current. This meant the *Virginia City* would have to connect down-current of us, so if anything went wrong they would be swept away from the *Salvaliant* rather than onto her.

The *Virginia City* was pitching and rolling in the sea and swell, shipping water on her towing deck, as was the *Salvaliant*, but our tug was pinned down by the tow wire, and we were quite comfortable. I felt sorry for the master of the Filipino tug: try as he would, he could not make a connection. The tug was bigger than the *Salvaliant*, but very slow to manoeuvre and the towing point, American-style, was much too far aft. Eventually he asked Peter over the radio if he could connect to our bow. I thought Peter was going to explode.

'*God verdomme!*' he exclaimed. 'Does he want to pull us onto the reef? He will pull us round – our towing gear is not strong enough for two tugs.' Peter was breathing heavily as he opened a can of beer, handing one to me.

'Let me think. Turn that bloody radio off,' he growled. He threw the empty beer can into the sea.

'OK Ian, rig the pelican hook on our port bow and make sure you can get it to slip in an emergency,' he continued. 'We'll make him fast to the pelican hook and, once connected, I want a man with a hammer standing by 24 hours a day. That is a big old heap of scrap and I don't want to lose my tug because of him. Jesus, tell him to come and connect to our port bow and, if he touches us, I will shoot him.' This was not an idle threat. There was a rifle and a pistol and ammunition in his cabin.

Jesus giggled nervously, and spoke into the microphone. The *Virginia City* steamed over to us. The bosun, Javier Patani, a big, burly, tough, experienced salvor, had his men ready with heaving lines. As the *Virginia City* went slowly past, water pouring off her tow deck when she rolled, they threw them at the tug. One of them was quickly picked up by enthusiastic hands and made fast to the messenger. The *Salvaliant* crew heaved it on board and put it round the windlass drum. The eye of the forerunner wire of the towing gear was soon brought on board through the forward fairlead and connected to the pelican hook. The *Virginia City* streamed her gear, heading straight out, with her master no doubt vastly relieved.

'Jesus, tell the *Virginia City* to turn to port and keep up-current of us, and then we will make a refloating attempt,' ordered Peter.

It failed.

Night fell. It was dark with a heavily overcast sky, no stars, low clouds scudding past. The lights on the *Nienburg* glowed brightly astern, and ahead were the dimmer lights of the *Virginia City*. It was still rough but the tug was quite comfortable, steadied both fore and aft by the tow wires. An AB was at the bow with a sledge-hammer, standing by the pelican hook. We steamed all night, monitoring our position on the casualty to make sure we were not swept down-current. Peter sent me off to bed at midnight.

Sometime later I was awoken by a tremendous roar. It must be a life or death emergency, I thought, jumping out of bed, still fully clothed.

'He's pulling us onto the reef. Slip, slip, slip ...' Peter's voice high in its despair, a terrible sound.

I rushed out of my cabin and onto the foredeck. The AB with the hammer gave the pelican hook a tremendous blow. The hook opened and the wire slid off, disappearing out through the fairlead. The *Virginia City* shot ahead. I looked aft and saw the *Nienburg* up to port: we were down-current. I could hear the waves breaking on the coral with that distinctive deep thump.

'Jesus,' I thought, 'we're on the reef.' I waited for the first terrible jolt, the awful shock as she hit the coral. I rushed up onto the bridge, my heart palpitating with fear, and took a bearing, which confirmed my worst thoughts: we'd been dragged right down onto the reef. I went into the wheelhouse fairly crackling with tension, and found Peter behind the wheel, the helmsman to one side, with it hard to port. The engine-room telegraph was at full ahead and I could see both engines were running at full power. I heard the slow click of the gyro compass as the heading changed. It stopped. The *Salvaliant* was not coming up. The tension was quite unbearable, and then the first click and I saw it was the right way; it stopped again for an agonising few seconds and then started, click, click, click, stop, and then again more clicks. She was slowly clawing her way off the reef. The *Virginia City* steamed off into the night.

'Never again,' was all Peter said as he picked up his can of beer, and that's all I ever found out. Once the tug was back up-current and holding her position on one engine, Peter said, 'All yours, I'm to bed,' and he walked off the bridge.

I watched the dawn to the east of the *Nienburg*, the black shape of the watching Chinese ship becoming more visible, her lights fading in the gathering day. The boiler of the wreck became more distinct, a continuing mute reminder of what would happen to the *Nienburg* if we did not refloat her. We had been towing for almost 24 hours and I had got used to the motion of the tug. The wind was less and the sea seemed to have gone down a little. I studied the stern of the casualty through the big powerful binoculars on their stand on the bridge wing. Only the occasional sea was breaking around it, and running along the side of the ship. I watched for some time and began to think it might be possible to get across with a skilful boat driver. The *Salvaliant* was equipped with a new rubber boat and powerful outboard, much better than the lifeboat. The more I looked the more I became convinced I could do it.

After an early breakfast, eaten on the bridge while continuing to watch the casualty, I called Peter and told him what I had observed. He looked himself and said, 'If you want to have a go, then OK, but be careful – if you get it wrong you'll be a goner on the reef, the coral will cut you to pieces.' He looked extremely serious. 'I would hate to lose you,' he added.

I called for volunteers and the rubber boat was launched. Peter told the *Nienburg* to put a cargo net over the side, along with the pilot ladder. I drove the boat with two salvage crew and stood off the stern to watch the sea. The entire crew of the *Nienburg* were lining the rails. There appeared to be gaps when the seas did not break, and after a wave broke round the stern I went in at full speed. I rounded up head-to-sea off the pilot ladder amidships and came alongside. The two salvage crew held on to the cargo net while I picked up the painter. Just as I was climbing out of the boat onto the ladder a wave half-swamped the boat, soaking my bottom half. I continued on up the ladder and at the top a willing crew member took the painter from me. I shouted down to the men in the boat to follow. Once on deck they took the painter forward and moored the boat in the comparatively calm but surging water around the bow.

Elmo Ramos, a young ex-Navy diver, had brought a sounding line with him. I told him to take soundings round the ship while I went to see the master, an East German, dripping water.

He offered me tea and a towel, which I gladly accepted, and I found out about the ship in his comfortably furnished cabin. There was another man along with the chief officer, who turned out to be the political advisor.

The *Nienburg* was almost fully laden with manganese in bags, coir fibre in bales, cartons of fruit in tins, textiles, lead and zinc ingots, so she had no ballast. She was due to bunker in Singapore, so was low on fuel and fresh water. It was quite clear, there was no other way: we would have to jettison the cargo if we were to get her off.

I went onto the bridge and talked to Peter on the VHF. He agreed and said he would tell the office. While on the bridge, I saw a boat coming from the Chinese ship, and it successfully came alongside. The communists had so far been silent and had not interfered in any way, but Bombay Reef belonged to them, and I was apprehensive. The last time I had been in communist waters was in Shanghai, at the height of the Red Guard madness, armed young guards everywhere, and loudspeakers blaring propaganda 24 hours a day.

Elmo came up with a sounding plan and, with the draughts I'd obtained from the master, confirmed the ship was very heavily aground and a lot of cargo would have to be jettisoned.

When I went back to the captain's cabin I found three communist Chinese inside, one of whom was obviously an interpreter and one, I guessed, was a commissar. They were telling the master they intended to lay ground tackle. I was aghast and feared for the *Salvaliant*. However I said I had no objection provided they did not interfere with my tug. It could do no harm, but how they were going to do it with their great big ship I did not know – nor, dare I say it, much care.

I returned to the *Salvaliant* in the rubber boat after we bailed her out: having done it once it did not seem so bad, and the sea had gone down even more. On the bridge I discussed the situation with Peter and studied the cargo plan I had brought back. If we could get at the zinc in the lower holds, we could lighten her quite quickly. Peter received a message from the office agreeing to the jettison and, at the same time, the weather forecast.

'*God verdomme!* There's a typhoon coming this way. Maybe four days: that's all we need. We will have to get a move on with this jettison.' This gave an added urgency to the situation. It was very doubtful if the ship could weather a typhoon, and there was no way the *Salvaliant* would survive. If we were to save the tug and ourselves we would have to leave before it arrived.

Half-a-dozen salvage crew came with me in the boat back to the *Nienburg*, together with various pieces of equipment. The boat, driven by a diver, returned for more. I immediately went to the captain and showed him the message from Selco and the weather forecast. He had received the same forecast so knew about the typhoon, and needed no persuading to start the jettison.

The jettison commenced within the hour and the race against time began. The ship's crew assisted, and a boat from the *Virginia City* turned up with more men. I drove a crane and the ship came alive as the cargo was lifted out of the holds with the derricks and cranes, swung across the deck, and thrown over the side. The Chinese commenced work to lay the ground tackle. Work continued all night and day, the *Nienburg* supplying the salvage crews with food and water. The rubber boat was hoisted out of the water and stowed on deck out of the way. Everyone worked with a will, knowing that with a typhoon on the way our very lives depended on success.

I had built a good relationship with the captain and ate my meals with him. He was glad of an 'outsider' to talk with, and I soon had his family history and those of his children. He was very worried about the women on board. If we were unsuccessful and lives were lost he did not want them on his conscience for not sending them off when he had the chance. We therefore arranged to send them over to another East German ship which was sheltering in the lee of the reef, and it was done without incident. It meant we had no stewardess on board, but the captain was much happier.

On the fourth afternoon the *Albatross* turned up, and I for one was extremely glad to see her. The weather was already beginning to deteriorate and the swell was increasing. She was a beautiful tug, black, long, lean, low in the water. Peter moved the *Salvaliant* up-current and the *Albatross* moved in stern-first, her bow thruster making manoeuvring comparatively easy. When about a cable off a man fired the rocket gun and the rocket and line came, or so it seemed, straight for me standing on the bridge wing. I ducked but it missed and luckily became entangled in a derrick. A nimble Filipino climbed the derrick and recovered the line, which was taken aft. The messenger was heaved on board and put around the capstan, and the wire heaved across. Something happened on the *Albatross* and the wire stopped moving; the messenger line became bar taught. Something is going to give, I thought, as I saw the bow of the *Albatross* swing round and the tug become parallel to the reef, drifting towards it. Suddenly there was a loud bang and the messenger parted. I hoped no one was in the way. The *Albatross* swung round, her bow into the wind and sea, her stern no longer pinned, and moved out to sea. I felt sorry for the master.

The increasing swell added urgency to the jettison, after the refloating attempt failed. The Chinese ground tackle was holding the *Nienburg*, preventing her from swinging onto the heading we wanted. There were definite signs of movement, which was encouraging, but more cargo needed to be discharged.

The *Albatross* made fast to the bow of the *Salvaliant* after the attempt. This was an asset, for she was a highly manoeuvrable tug with a bow thruster and not likely to pull the *Salvaliant* onto the reef. Once connected, a crowd of tough, burly Germans arrived on board to help with the jettison. Their rubber boat was nearly swamped alongside the *Nienburg* and it was quickly brought aboard by crane. It would be the last boatwork, for it was becoming too rough, with waves breaking along both sides of the ship.

The next morning it was worse. It continued dull and dismal. Seas were breaking around the stern of the casualty and sweeping along both sides of the ship, high up the side of the hull. The reef on either side was a seething mass of white water as the waves smashed themselves on the coral. We were trapped on board, there was no escape. It added further impetus to the jettison.

I discussed with Peter over the radio what we should do, apart from continue the jettison as urgently as possible.

'It's possible she may come off as the swell increases more from the typhoon. We are certainly feeling the beginning of it now,' he said. 'If she won't come off by the time I have to leave, you will have to ballast her down, double-batten down the hatches and pray. You're trapped on board.'

'All understood,' I replied. 'We've jettisoned well over a thousand tons now and there are definite signs of movement as the seas hit the stern.' In fact a lot of spray was coming on board aft.

'That's a good sign. We will have a last attempt at 1600.'

He signed off, and I spoke with the Germans from the *Albatross* and the Filipinos from the *Virginia City*. I told them the plan and to work as hard as possible to get as much cargo over the side as possible. I spoke with the captain to find out if he knew if the Chinese had any plan to release their ground tackle. There was no plan so I asked him to have the ship's cutting gear made ready by the wire. We all worked hard all day and a lot of cargo was jettisoned – 1,800 tons in all.

At 1600 I was on the bridge, the jettisoning continuing. It was overcast, grey and dismal. The sea and swell had increased to such an extent that the occasional wave came on deck. The *Salvaliant* was towing, with the *Albatross* ahead of her, and they made a fine sight. The Chinese ground-tackle wire was down-current to the east of the tugs, holding the stern against the pull of the tugs. The tugs increased to full power and I could see the water boiling around their sterns from the propellers. I was most apprehensive and tense: this might be our last chance.

The tow wire was bar taught with twice the normal load on it. Peter was taking a tremendous risk as in unison the two tugs sheered to port and then to starboard, heeling as they moved sideways through the water, water cascading off their tow decks. I told the captain to ring full astern, and the engine started, the deck vibrating under my feet as power was built up. Spray was coming aboard aft, soaking the men standing there. On the third swing to port there was definite movement: the *Nienburg* swung a few degrees and stopped. The ground tackle was holding her.

'Ian,' I heard my name over the radio, 'cut the ground-tackle wire.'

I told the captain what I was doing as I ran off the bridge and down to the aft deck. The *Salvaliant* welder, wet from the spray, was standing by the wire with the ship's cutting gear in his hand, already lit.

'Cut it,' I ordered.

I stood behind him to add moral support. The wire was bar taught, humming with the strain of the two tugs towing. It took courage to cut that wire. In theory if you stand at the place of parting it cannot hit you. But theory and practice are not always the same, and I knew what a flying wire could do to human flesh. Some Chinese were gabbling away but I took no notice and shouted for everyone to clear the area.

Suddenly there was the sound like a gun going off and the seaward end disappeared, taking part of the rail with it. The other, short end, flew back, lifting the blocks off the deck and hitting a winch.

'Well done,' I said, patting the welder on the back. He grinned. I ran back to the bridge as the *Nienburg* started swinging rapidly to port, the stern towards the towing tugs. The swinging stopped and then there was a tremendous bang and we were almost thrown off our feet. I rushed out onto the bridge wing to take a bearing of the wreck. She was moving and then stopped. Again there was a terrific noise and jolt and then she started pounding and moving astern. The shuddering and pounding stopped.

'She's afloat,' I said into the radio. 'Stop the engine,' I ordered the captain. I was walking on air, elated. The jettison had stopped, the crane hooks and derricks swinging as the ship rolled broadside to the swell. The crews were all cheering.

'Secure everything,' I shouted down to the men on deck.

'Ian, I will let go the *Albatross* first,' said the voice of Peter over the radio, 'then you slip me and steam round to the south side of the reef.'

It was getting dark when I made my way aft again. The *Salvaliant* crew, still grinning, were already at the towing connection. Once I saw the *Albatross* clear of the *Salvaliant* I told them to take the lashings off the forerunner eye, and it was slipped.

'I will pilot you round to the other side of the reef,' I told the master on my return to the bridge. 'Slow ahead,' I ordered. 'Hard a-port,' I instructed the man at the wheel as I walked to the radar. It was now dark, but as on the *Salvaliant* the reef showed up well on the screen. The two tugs were recovering their towing gear, the bright deck lights illuminating their tow decks. The *Nienburg* was rolling heavily in the sea and swell, and loose gear was rolling around on deck. It was not long before I altered south, and then west, into the lee of the reef, and the heavy rolling stopped.

There were mutual congratulations all round. Even the Chinese smiled, although they were not very pleased at the loss of their ground tackle. The men closed the hatches and lowered the derricks and cranes; all were keen to get away as soon as possible. The carpenter reported there was no leakage in the holds and tanks: the ship was sound. The chief engineer reported the engine to be in good order.

It was about 2200 when I finally reached the *Salvaliant* with the termination letter. I sat on the bridge with a beer and was suddenly engulfed by tiredness, a bone-deep weariness. I had had little sleep for the last few days and none at all for the last two days. Much of the time had been spent in heavy physical labour, jettisoning cargo; the rest had been high drama. I felt utterly drained and exhausted, down from an incredible, natural high. My first open-sea salvage, miles from anywhere, in communist Chinese waters, made more intense and dangerous by an approaching typhoon. I was extremely lucky to have had

Peter as the salvage captain in charge, a rock-like figure, full of experience.

We watched the *Nienburg* get under way and followed her on two engines to keep up and get south as quickly as possible, the *Albatross* following, but she slowly pulled ahead. The next morning she was out of sight and we were well clear of the typhoon. Peter slowed down to economical speed.

FROM *LLOYD'S WEEKLY CASUALTY REPORTS*, 1974

Nienburg (**East German**) – **London, Nov 26** – Information received states that motor vessel *Neinburg* has been refloated.

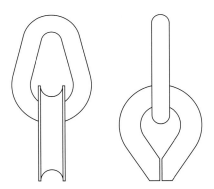

Thimble and link set
used in nylon stretchers

Damar

The beginning of 1975 was a busy time for me, and a vertical learning curve. Selco salved the fully laden *Showa Maru*, 238,000 deadweight tons, aground near Buffalo Rock in the Singapore Straits, at the time one of the largest ships in the world to be salved. I heard the distress and took the *Salvaliant* (Peter was ashore at the time) across the straits, and was first on board the casualty. Selco salvage master Captain Hancox made me his assistant for the 41-day operation. The *Salviking*, a mooring and salvage vessel built by Selco, was commissioned in April and I was given her command. It was all new work for me, maintaining the tanker mooring system at Port Dickson and other such work, with the occasional salvage thrown in.

I had left the *Salviking* in Balik Papan, Indonesia, after pulling a pipe from the shore at Sangatta, over a mile to the loading position, a set of buoys which we laid. I had then flown home, via Singapore to hand over my command to Hughie Murray, for my father's funeral.

Salviking in heavy weather on the way to Sangatta. Chief officer Arturo Briosi checks hatch fastenings

Now, at the end of November 1975, I was back on the *Salviking* for a nice little salvage job. A 100-ton tug had sunk just across the Singapore Strait from the Eastern Anchorage. She was at, or near, Pulau Sambu, Indonesia. It was about fifteen miles away from the Selco moorings in Jurong.

A Chinese fellow joined us from the Salvage Association and at first we did not see eye to eye; he expected everything to be done yesterday. I soon educated him, once I found out this was his first salvage. He had the second bunk in my cabin so it was important that relations were harmonious. I like to enjoy my work.

I took off after lunch on Thursday 27 November for Pulau Sambu. It was hot, as usual near the equator – 'mad dogs and Englishmen' and all that – but it was mitigated by my air-conditioned bridge.

During the *Showa Maru* salvage I had been there in a small boat, so had an idea of what it was like. The Singapore Straits were busy as ever, with heavy traffic in both directions, loaded tankers and bulk carriers bound for Japan, empty ones returning, together with loaded container ships for Europe, one of the main shipping routes of the world squeezing

Salviking

through a strait in places only a couple of miles wide. I was crossing the traffic, so being small I kept out of the way. The tides run strongly and the Indonesian side has lots of reefs. I had to keep a sharp lookout, aided by my officer of the watch, and watch my position. The *Salviking* was my command, so my fault if anything went wrong.

On the way over my radio officer, John, originally from Goa, India, called up Pertamina, the state-run oil company who owned the sunken tug. They told us she was at Batam, new port. I looked at my up-to-date chart but could not find it so told John to ask them where it was.

'Due south of Pulau Sambu,' was the reply. Due south on the chart showed nothing except a shallow bank on the west side and a channel leading south on the east. But they assured us there was a port there.

Nothing ventured nothing gained, I thought. I navigated through the channel, only two cables (400 yards) wide, with Pulau Sambu to port and houses on stilts in front of the heavily wooded island to starboard, dark green jungle on either side. Once past the little wooded island, Pulau Mariam, the *Salviking* was out into the Straits of Bulan, only a mile wide at this point, with its numerous islets all looking much the same. The tide was flooding strongly, running at almost four knots, increasing my speed over the land. There were strong eddies and whirlpools which threw the *Salviking* 20–30 degrees off course and the helmsman had difficulty holding her. I had to increase power to full speed on both engines to keep control and keep clear of the many reefs and numerous shallow patches. Even in my air-conditioned bridge I was sweating. It was really quite hairy.

I had just about run off the chart and was out of the Bulan Straits. I could see where the jetty was but had no idea how to get there. The whole area abounded with reefs. The tide had eased off now we were across the straits and I was just about to anchor, before running aground, when a local canoe turned up. The agent was aboard – shades of Lord Jim!

Two shore-based divers were on board the *Salviking* to supplement my own, and it turned out the agent was the brother-in-law of one of them. He showed me where the *Damar* was sunk, marked by a yellow conical buoy, and asked me to go to the jetty, clear customs and the usual formalities. I asked him if he knew the way. Luckily he did, and following his directions I moored myself alongside a barge at the landing.

It was dark once I had completed the clearing-in formalities (including 'honorariums' for customs and other officials), and too late to start work, so I decided to stay where I was for the night. It was pleasant on the monkey island in the cool night air listening to the jungle sounds, the smooth water reflecting the *Salviking*'s deck lights. It was exciting to be in charge once more and make all the decisions, but completely different from deep-sea salvage and the *Salvaliant*. An Englishman can be found in the most obscure places, I thought.

My 15-ton workboat was loaded on the foredeck, and she was launched early the next morning using the heavy lift derrick, the *Salviking* listing as she was swung over the side and took the water. The divers went off in her when it was light enough to make a preliminary diving survey. I moved the *Salviking* out and anchored close by the yellow conical buoy. Another salvage crew took the Z-boat away to sound round the casualty.

The divers reported to me that the *Damar* was lying in about 45 feet of water on her starboard side. The accommodation was touching the mud and the starboard deck was about three feet in the soft mud. They had marked each end of her with white marker buoys.

I weighed anchor and steamed up to the casualty, letting go the stern anchor. I manoeuvred the *Salviking*, with the help of the workboat, over the *Damar* and let go an anchor on each bow. Thus I had a three-point mooring and could position my salvage vessel wherever I wanted her in relation to the sunken tug.

The divers secured wire strops on the bow and stern and we lifted each end, using the wire from the main winch. The divers pulled lifting wires under the hull, ready for the lift. She turned upright when we lifted the bow, which made it all very easy. Once the slings were round the hull all we had to do was lift. My Filipino divers worked well with the Singaporean shore divers but it was slow work. At least the water was warm.

It took the whole of the day and the whole of the next day before we were ready. It was very hot working on the foredeck of the *Salviking*. The bright sunlight reflected off the steelwork and made it hot to the touch, as were the thick wires and heavy shackles, making the work arduous and tiring. There was no wind all day, making it doubly hot, but the calm sea made it easier for the divers. It was better to take a little time and do it properly than try and be quick and make a mess of it.

All was ready by about tea time, the day cooling. I had ballasted the salvage vessel so she was well down by the head. The lifting wires from the bow and stern of the sunken tug were led to the horns and back onto the main winch. The idea was to lift the tug as far as possible with the winch, then lift the tug's deck clear of the water by de-ballasting the *Salviking*. This would be the time of maximum weight and we would be working to the maximum pull of the winch and safe working load of the wires. It was important

Salviking on her way to a mooring job, with anchors hanging off her horns

to get it right, and I did not want anything to break. A broken wire could be a killer.

All went well, and the *Damar* slowly rose out of the water, first the mast, then the white mud-smeared wheelhouse and accommodation. The still water barely rippled until it poured off her deck. It was dark, and cooler after the heat of the day, by the time the deck was clear. We worked through the night, made short by all the activity. The sea was pumped out of her, the gushing water disturbing the still sea, the pumps shattering the silence. The tide took away the little wisps of oil, and the divers and engineers preserved the machinery.

The *Damar* had been assisting a vessel which was aground and the skipper got it wrong. He allowed her to be pulled over by having the tow rope on the beam of the tug. She turned over and sank. Luckily no one was killed. There was no damage to the hull, and we had been very careful with the lift not to 'cheese' her. At about midnight she was empty. We lowered her back into the water and brought her alongside. The salvage crew continued to clean her up ready to be handed over.

In the morning I was ready to leave. However, the authorities had a different idea and it took the whole day before permission was granted. It was most frustrating, and denuded my vessel of cigarettes. I took the *Damar* back to Singapore across the straits for a refit secured alongside the *Salviking*.

I was quite pleased everything had gone to plan. The salvage had been done well, quite quickly, and with no damage to the tug. Even better, it was done on a Lloyd's Open Form, so I and my crew would get a salvage bonus.

2 SALVALIANT

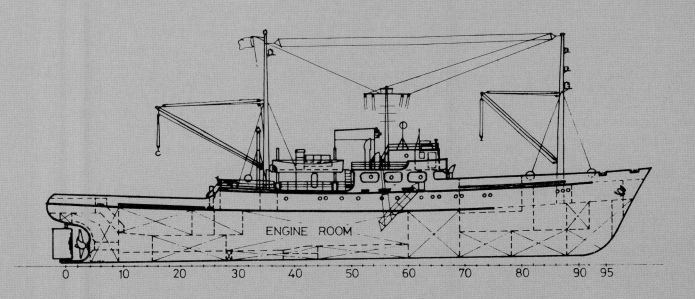

ENGINE ROOM

0   10   20   30   40   50   60   70   80   90   95

SALVALIANT

The *Salvaliant* was a single-screw motor salvage tug built in Japan
during 1961 of 993 GRT and 288 NRT. She had a length of 58.2 metres, a beam
of 11.5 metres and a loaded draught of 4.7 metres. She was powered by two
Burmeister & Wain six-cylinder diesel engines, which were coupled through a gearbox
to a single shaft. Her indicated horsepower was 4,600, which gave her a maximum
speed of 15 knots. Her navigational aids included radar, gyro compass, autopilot,
echo sounding device, radio direction finding, Loran, wireless telegraphy, radio
telephony, VHF, portable FM radios, and a weather facsimile chart receiver.
A secondary manoeuvring position had been built on the
monkey island for close-quarters work.

The *Salvaliant* was equipped with a 40-ton, single-drum electric towing
winch, which carried 640 metres of six-inch circumference towing wire.
Air-driven, remote-control dolly pins were fitted on the gunwale aft. There were
four powered reels in the after hold, which carried a spare towing wire 488 metres
long and ground-tackle wires. Also stowed in the after hold were chain bridles,
stretchers and pendants for every kind of tow. Stowed in the forward hold was a
quantity of salvage gear, which included a six-inch salvage pump, two air-driven
submersible pumps, two four-inch portable diesel pumps, a compressor, sheet metal,
angle iron, piping, wood, plywood, cement sand, epoxy, ground-tackle anchors,
wire pendants, buoys, assorted wires and other useful equipment. Among the
crew were two divers complete with diving equipment, including the
compressor for recharging the air bottles.

Her salvage firefighting equipment consisted of a dual-purpose Angus
foam/water cannon, which had a capacity of up to 19,800 litres per minute of
expanded foam and was mounted on the foremast. There were also two Kelly &
Lewis electric fire pumps serving the monitor and deck salvage fire main manifold,
305 metres of two-and-a-half-inch diameter Duraline fire hose with portable foam
branches along with jet/spray nozzles and extension pipes. A fixed welding
set was carried as well as portable oxyacetylene equipment.

The *Salvaliant* was therefore an extremely well-equipped salvage tug, able to
tackle a large range of jobs without recourse to outside assistance.

Oilfield work and a rough passage

Peter Lankester, captain of the *Salvaliant*, was going on leave. Much as I liked my command, I liked the *Salvaliant* better, a deep-sea ocean-going tug rather than a salvage and mooring vessel. On the *Salviking* there was not the excitement, the exhilaration – dare I say it, the heroics – of ocean salvage. It was hard, interesting work, but it was 'dead', not 'live' salvage. So I asked for the command of the *Salvaliant* when Peter went.

I was successful. On 12 December 1975 I took over the tug and set up residence in the captain's cabin, which occupied the whole of the fore part of the accommodation under the bridge, the sleeping cabin on the port side. I could look out on the foredeck from the portholes.

I was thirty-two years old, and in some ways I felt I had arrived. But I quickly had to relearn how to manoeuvre. The *Salviking* was comparatively easy, with twin screws, but

the *Salvaliant* was single-screw. She had two main engines but one propeller shaft, and only one engine could be used for manoeuvring. To obtain full power and speed the second engine had to be coupled in. Once in, the tug could not be stopped until one engine had been decoupled. Peter, a fine deep-sea salvage-tug captain, had been my mentor on the *Salvaliant* and had taught me much, in particular when salving the *Friedrich Engels* and the *Nienburg* – now I wanted to be better.

Before Christmas I was lucky and got some practice in. We twice went off on abortive trips up the usually calm Malacca Straits. Once for an Israeli ship which had a container on fire and once for a ship with an engine breakdown. Unfortunately for us, fortunately for them, they managed to deal with their problems themselves. But it gave me much confidence in myself and the

Salvaliant's new captain

crew. They like a captain who knows what he is doing and is a skilled ship handler. A lot of them were still from the time I had been chief officer.

Christmas eve, like the previous year, was spent with the Kahlenbergs – but I was a real captain this time, not just a chief officer! The table was beautifully set, the roast goose delicious, the candles gave out a soft light highlighting the decorations, the air conditioning cool, all utterly alien to the tropical heat outside. Old man K went off to bed early but I stayed chatting to Mrs before going back to my ship. Christmas day was spent at the Bonds, who held open house, and was a jolly occasion.

I took the *Salvaliant* out of Singapore on the morning of 30 December 1975, bound for Brunei. The weather had been bad in the South China Sea for weeks so there was quite a heavy swell running once past Horsburgh Light at the entrance to the Singapore Straits. Still, it was not like the winter North Atlantic, and at least it was warm. We rolled all the way. I took the southern route to look for a missing ship but did not find her.

We arrived off Kuala Belait on 2 January, a muted new-year celebration on the way. Days were spent at anchor, rolling heavily in the open roads, and very boring it was too. The welder welded rings at strategic points round the bridge and wings to hold my glass or mug steady. The tug was on charter to Shell for three weeks, which was not my idea of fun – no salvage, and I had to do as I was told! However, it was all experience.

Shell had a series of large oil and gas fields off the Brunei coast, with lots of installations which needed maintenance. At night the whole area was lit up from the burnt waste gas. We were taking the place of the regular supply boat, which was off for her annual refit. Some rigs were drilling for new wells, while production was from platforms built over the oil-producing ones. Servicing and expanding the complex system were a series of supply boats. They supplied the rigs and platforms with fuel, water and equipment. These vessels were also equipped for anchor handling. A couple of very large crane barges maintained the rigs and installations.

These barges were moored with anything up to sixteen anchors when on location. The anchors were run by the supply boats. The anchor was hung off the stern of the supply boat, which steamed out at full speed to a predetermined location and let go. The anchor was marked by an anchor buoy. To lift the anchor the supply boat picked up the buoy and heaved the anchor off the bottom. The barge or rig then heaved in the anchor wire until it was home and the supply boat let it go. Sometimes the supply boat heaved the anchor on deck and disconnected the anchor wire. But the *Salvaliant* was neither equipped not manoeuvrable enough for this sort of work. She could only tow, not handle anchors. She did not even have a bow thruster.

The first job was to tow an empty barge to Labuan for heavy lifts and back again, loaded, to Kuala Belait. A few minutes after getting rid of the barge I was told over the radio to tow the *Mardock*, a large crane barge, to Champion Shoal, a field about sixty miles to the north. It was dark, being night, so I called the barge up. They told me they had two anchors down and I should come and pick them up. I said they had the wrong boat and they had better find an anchor handler. Impasse – so I went to bed. Of course it cost thousands of pound a day to run these barges, not including our hefty charter rate. I don't think I was too popular, and I grew to hate the voice on the radio.

At about 0200, a particularly dead time of the night, the voice called up and said they had got hold of an anchor-handling boat and were now ready. It was raining, overcast, very dark and most unpleasant in the heavy swell. The chief officer heaved up the anchor and I navigated over to the barge in the poor visibility. The tug, as I have mentioned before, was difficult to handle. A supply boat is like a dinghy while the *Salvaliant* was like a long-keeled heavy displacement yacht. I did not have a workboat to help me. I had to be very careful not to hit the barge because I would have holed her and myself in the eight- to ten-foot swell which was running. Yet I had to get close enough to connect my towing gear.

After two hours, and more white hairs, the connection was made and off we went towing the barge. My crew were very good, thanks to Peter's training. At the other end of

Salvaliant's crew with a sailfish caught in the South China Sea

the passage I had to tow the barge into location while she anchored. I had no help until the very end and then the workboat pushed in the wrong direction and the *Salvaliant* got across the current. I could not hold her and the barge had to cut my towing gear to prevent a collision. Luckily no damage was done except to my tow wire and nerves. I did not like oilfield work!

Our next job was to tow a drill ship off location and put her on a new one. The tool pusher, or man in charge of the drill ship for the shift, was Tom someone. He had been on the *Salvaliant* when we shifted the jack-up rig *Chris Seger* in 1974, so he knew my difficulties. This one went OK and I towed her onto the new location with no damage and first time – just a few more white hairs. Again the towing connection was made at night and there was a twelve-foot swell running. To make matters more difficult my radar had broken down.

Back in the anchorage we rolled, waiting for the next call. Suddenly I came alive. There was an SOS distress message. I obtained permission from Shell to depart and left at full speed in a heavy rain storm. The radar could not be repaired so I was running blind. I posted extra lookouts. There was no radio direction-finding station so the only aid to navigation was my echo sounder. It was blowing force seven so there was a rough sea over the heavy swell. The tug was very lively and shipping water overall.

I had to round a point of land before heading southeast. If I cleared the point a good distance I would be running through an oilfield where there were unlit bits of oil junk to hit. It was still raining heavily. I decided to trust my echo sounder. As we closed the point the water shallowed and the sea and swell heaped up, becoming very rough indeed. The seas were crashing right over the after deck, making a seething mass of white, and heavy spray was flying right over the bridge and funnel.

As long as I did not let the tug get inside the 10-fathom line I knew we were safe. As the soundings decreased or increased, so I altered course. My stomach was tied in knots. The noise of the rain and spray hitting the bridge, the violent motion, the vibration as the engines ran at maximum speed, running blind in the dark, relying solely on the echo sounder, all made for a tense atmosphere in the wheelhouse, and no one spoke. I wondered if I was being foolish, but an SOS is an SOS and we were a salvage tug, an emergency ambulance of the sea.

Quite suddenly the rain stopped, it was quite light, and I could see where the tug was, safe. It was a release from the tension and I called for a cup of tea.

My radio officer was in touch with the casualty, who said his engine room was flooding. The engine had broken down and the ship was drifting. A few hours later he said all was OK, he was proceeding. I then heard him arranging with some crony to meet up in a night club in Kuching. I was not pleased.

On returning to Kuala Belait at economical speed, Shell said they had nothing for me and I could go. After obtaining clearance I set course for Singapore.

The whole of this area is a navigational nightmare. The shoals, reefs and unlit islands are numerous, not to mention oilfields. Navigational lights are few and far between and often do not work. If the radar is working then navigation is not too bad, but without it navigation at night is dangerous, and it is better to anchor and only proceed in daylight.

Selco salvage master Captain Hancox had salved a dredger in Indonesia and loaded it onto a barge which he was towing to Singapore. He sent a radio message to me saying he was in heavy weather and not making any progress against the westerly wind. His position was east of Billiton island off the south coast of Indonesian Borneo, way to the south. Would I go and help?

With no radar working I was not too happy. However, salvage is salvage and it is a risk business. I checked with the office and altered course for Api Passage and the south. It was still blowing force seven, rough, and visibility was almost nil in the heavy rain storms.

There was a light at Api Passage, and if it was working I would see it at night. If not and I was outside the course line there was an island to hit. If inside there were cliffs to be wrecked on. The only thing I had was soundings. If the soundings became less than 10 fathoms I would stop and head north. The echo sounder was in continuous operation

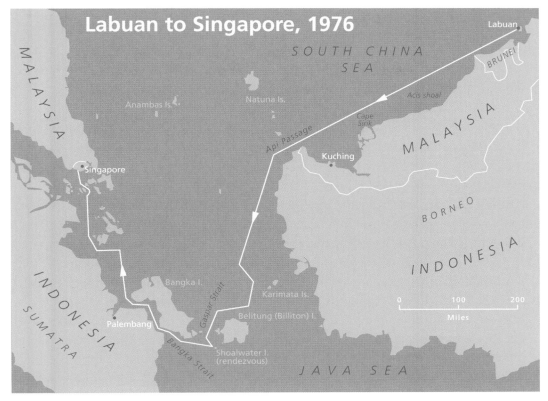

Labuan to Singapore, 1976

SOUTH CHINA SEA

MALAYSIA

BRUNEI

Labuan

Anambas Is.

Natuna Is.

Acis shoal

Cape Sirik

Api Passage

MALAYSIA

Kuching

Singapore

BORNEO

INDONESIA

INDONESIA

SUMATRA

Bangka I.

Gaspar Strait

Karimata Is.

0   100   200

Miles

Palembang

Belitung (Billiton) I.

Bangka Strait

Shoalwater I. (rendezvous)

JAVA SEA

with an officer permanently watching it. I had not been able to take any sort of position for twenty hours and the currents were variable to say the least.

At about midnight the tension was building up. There were anxious looks on my officers' faces. We had run our distance and seen nothing. However the soundings were OK so I decided to carry on for another hour. Half a knot out in my speed calculations would mean about an hour out in the timing.

The tension continued to build. I had lookouts on both bridge wings peering out through the darkness, their oilskins glistening with water, spray as well as rain. We all looked for the light, making an assumption – not necessarily correct – that it was working.

At the end of the extra hour my nerves were beginning to go. We had still seen nothing. The soundings started to decrease. I ordered half ahead on the engine room telegraph and told the officer of the watch to tell the engineers to go one engine, so I could manoeuvre. The tug slowed down and I had just ordered the course to be altered to the north to retrace our track when a voice shouted –

'There it is, off the starboard bow.'

There was a collective sigh of relief as I resumed course. The rain had stopped. Ahead were the cliffs bathed in moonlight, the sea breaking white at their feet. We were seven miles inside the course line. I resumed full speed.

There was a shallow patch about three miles off the point and I decided to go inside it to save time. We rounded the light close to, the rocks off the base of the cliffs clearly visible. I dismissed the extra lookouts and went back to normal watches, although I stayed on the bridge.

Once clear I made for the next light, on an island, and then headed off south. The wind, still blowing force six, was now behind, and the tug was rolling and pitching with heavy water coming aboard all over the aft deck.

I was heading for the light off Karimata island. The soundings would not be any help so it would only be a visual sighting, and the visibility had to be good. I allowed a reasonable speed and once the distance was run if we had not seen anything I would have to stop and wait for daylight.

During the day we had been able to obtain positions from the various islands. Surprisingly the current appeared to be negligible or even against us. The wind had been blowing from the north for weeks and the current should have been running the other way. This made estimating the position even more difficult because it was different from the information in the pilot book. Not all that many ships sailed in these waters, although the area had been used by sailing ships – what a nightmare!

As it turned out the night remained fine and we saw the light at twenty miles, so all was well. The next problem was to make the north end of Billiton island, which the pilot book advised against. Soundings are no help, for once in 20 fathoms the ship is amongst the rocks and shoals. I did not see the light on the northwest point.

It was hazy when day broke and the higher mountains were not visible. The coast was not easy to identify. At about 0700, when I was trying to identify a hill through the binoculars, I saw waves breaking on a rock. The tug was inside the course line and soundings had given no indication. The current had been running at about one and a half knots, yet previously there had been none.

A little later everything fell into place. I altered course to close the coast and pass through the Gaspar Strait between Billiton and Bangka islands. It turned into a fine sunlit day. Although the wind still blew hard from the northwest it was very pleasant in the straits. I stopped to offer assistance to a ship at anchor. She had engine failure but the captain declined my offer.

The rendezvous was behind Shoalwater Island, south-south-west of Billiton. A reef surrounds the island and I anchored about a quarter of a mile off it, about a mile offshore. We had arrived first at the anchorage. It was well sheltered by the island and reef. The *Salviper*, towing the barge loaded with the dredger, came alongside later that day.

The tow was passed over to the *Salvaliant* by the efficient *Salviper* crew led by chief officer Juanito Ventura, whom I got to know well. I departed for Singapore the next morning, passing through the Bangka and Durian straits. It was sheltered waters, perhaps, but strong tides and many country craft to contend with made it an interesting and different passage – and much better than oilfield work!

On arrival in Singapore I handed over the barge to Selco harbour tugs, and then we were on standby, which was very frustrating. The longer we waited for a salvage the more

Attending the freighter *Wan Fu*, on fire in Singapore's Eastern Anchorage

the tension built up. The famous Dutch company Smit's had a base and a tug on salvage standby as well, so we had hot competition.

It was a bit like a war: intense activity or nothing. The only incident in February was a mini ship fire next to where the *Salvaliant* was anchored in the Eastern Anchorage. A cargo ship was undergoing repairs. Just beyond her our main opposition tug was also anchored.

I saw the ship catch fire and called emergency stations. The anchor was aweigh and I manoeuvred the tug alongside the casualty before the Smit tug even noticed. Unfortunately for us the fire was out and we got nothing. But I was very pleased that at least we beat the competition.

Sophie B
One that got away

FROM *LLOYD'S WEEKLY CASUALTY REPORTS*, 1976

Sophie B (Greek) – **Singapore, Feb 20** – Motor vessel *Sophie B*: Tug *Mississippi* left Singapore pm, Feb 18, for engine trials and Feb 19 intercepted a call from a Russian vessel advising casualty on fire in way of engine-room and accommodation and requesting further assistance. *Mississippi* proceeded and owners at Piraeus signed Lloyd's Open Form contract. *Mississippi* was alongside vessel 1700, Feb 19, and combating fire with her firefighting equipment and advised that Russian vessel was also alongside fighting fire but she had exhausted her foam. Understand Russian master also has salvage contract with vessel. Also believe salvage tug *Salvaliant* is standing by in vicinity. – Salvage Association's Surveyors.

The previous evening, I had been instructed that the *Salvaliant* was to sail for the Persian Gulf the next day. We were anchored in the Eastern Anchorage, Singapore, amongst many other vessels. I immediately took steps to have the tug taken off salvage standby so that my crew could go ashore for any last-minute shopping. As usual this was a panic; the tug that was towing two stacked barges to the Gulf had broken down. The barges were in Port Klang, Malaysia, in the Malacca Straits. I also went ashore to arrange for last-minute provisions – and to give myself a good dinner as well. I returned on board at about midnight, having decided to sail at 1400 the next day, when my stores and bond would be on board. I went to bed.

The telephone above my head buzzed.

'Base wants you, sir,' said the AB who had been on watch. I turned on the light and looked at my watch: 0520. It must be salvage, I thought, as I ran up to the bridge.

Our private FM frequency was known by the opposition, so salvage messages were always given rather garbled, intended to outwit the competition. Nonetheless, they usually had the same information as soon as we did!

It took about half an hour to get the engines ready from a dead cold start. As I was talking to base, I heard an urgent voice over the other radio extension:

'Pan Pan Pan. Pan Pan Pan.'

I dropped the microphone to base and went into the radio room to listen to the distress message, telling the AB to get everybody up quickly and to stand by.

Following information received on 500 kilohertz from XVS – *Sophie B* / SXQV, receiver out of order, position last 2 32 N, 105 04 E, require help urgently, fire in engine room at 1930 GMT, stop. Ships in vicinity please render assistance as required.

I called base to ask them if it was the distress I had just heard and they replied '*Hong Wei No. 7*.' This was a fishing vessel we had picked up in this direction last year, and presumably meant yes.

I picked up the microphone for the ship's internal loudspeaker system.

'Emergency, emergency: stand by, stand by: ship on fire, ship on fire.'

The radio officer arrived and took over from me, and I told him to call Singapore Radio for any further information. I knew that the opposition, the Smit tug *Mississippi*, must have heard the same message. They had the same sort of shore base for listening to the distress frequencies. I could do nothing until I had the engines. What was more, we were facing the wrong way and would have to turn among the anchored vessels before I could head out to the east.

I walked out onto the wing of the bridge to get some fresh air, trying in vain to curb my impatience as the engineers got the engines ready. I was astonished to see the Z-boat pulling away from the tug's side. Upon investigating the matter I was informed that a 'friend' was being taken ashore. 'Friends' of any type were strictly against my instructions, purely for the reason that they delay a getaway. What was more, the boat had been taken away without my permission. I was not pleased. I told the chief officer what I thought about the situation and if they were not back by the time the engines were ready, I would go without them and they would be fired.

It is very difficult to keep up morale and enthusiasm sitting around in Singapore with no work. We had been on standby for over a month and had not had a salvage for four months – at least the *Salvaliant* had not. If one does not ease up a bit or turn a Nelson-like blind eye, then the crew gets bolshie and there is trouble, but if one eases up too much, the tug becomes a shambles.

At 0540 the engine was ready and I picked up the anchor. I was turning the tug, with other anchored vessels close by, some unlit, when I saw out of the corner of my eye the lights of the *Mississippi* moving. Then I saw her steaming lights. She had got under way as well. The Z-boat was still not back from the shore, so you may imagine the imprecations I was muttering to myself.

I had just completed my turn and rung down to the engine room for full ahead on one engine when I saw the Z-boat. It came alongside as I rang down for two engines and maximum possible speed. The sea was calm and we had become quite good at sending away boats and picking them up when under way. I was much more worried about the unlit ships that were around, which were very difficult to see. I was taking a tremendous risk in going on two engines before clearing the anchorage. Once on two engines, I could not stop until one engine was declutched, which might take five minutes. It's like driving a motor car in a town at 30 mph with no brakes and the accelerator jammed.

After what seemed a lifetime of altering course around the ships and hoping that any sampan would get out of the way – but which in fact was about fifteen minutes – I was clear. The *Salvaliant* was thundering along at 180 rpm, which gave her about 13 knots. Thirteen knots among anchored vessels. I thought of what would have happened if something had gone wrong – the steering, for instance – and I had hit one. Thirteen knots times 2,000 tons displacement. I gave up to think about more cheerful things.

I looked inshore, and there was the *Mississippi* about a cable ahead of me going hell for leather as well. Thirteen knots may not sound like much speed but for tugs it's not bad, and they kick up a huge wash.

In a sailing dinghy or yacht, as I knew from years of experience, there are many things that have a bearing on speed and distance made good, and the crew must be constantly alert to gain maximum advantage from every wind shift. But here I was wholly dependent on the engines as to whether I beat the *Mississippi* or not so, once on course, a feeling of total frustration overcame me. I gave instructions that the rudder was not to be moved more than a couple of degrees for altering course. A large rudder angle would reduce the speed. I could almost stop *Mole*, my old Firefly, in a gentle breeze with zealous use of the rudder, and what in principle applied then must apply now. I called the chief engineer to come on deck to see the *Mississippi*, as I thought it might inspire him.

The *Sophie B* was about ninety miles north of the entrance to the Singapore Straits, or, upon more careful inspection, to the northeast of the Straits.

If the course was due north, then it would pay me to take a short cut through the narrow North Channel, which is OK if the visibility is good as it is not marked by buoys. It is about 30 feet deep at its shallowest part, which is deep enough, but at full speed and even with 12 feet under the keel, this would slow the tug down fractionally. I looked up the tide, which should be south-going by the time we reached the channel, in other words against me. The tide in the North Channel runs more strongly than in the deep-water channel about nine miles further on, being funneled between the banks. To pass through North Channel, I would have to head due north, right into the tide, but if I went along Remunia Shoal, which was to seaward of North Channel, the tide would be on my beam. When I turned into the deep-water channel, I would still be able to keep the tide on my bow – in other words, I would not have to head straight into it. The *Sophie B* was just far enough to the east: it would be about half a mile shorter to go through North Channel, but I came to the conclusion that I would gain more by not heading into the tide.

This was worse than sailing a race. The two tugs had just about the same speed (this became apparent) so every inch helped. I took a look at the *Mississippi*, still inshore of me, and was elated to see that she was now abeam. He should have altered course out a little, otherwise he would have to steer through a maze of fishing nets and boats from Johor whereas I would be able to steam straight and so gain a little more. I'm afraid to say that no thought passed through my mind about the luckless people on the *Sophie B* except to pray that the wretched ship would not sink before I got there. The dominating thought, overriding all others, was to beat the *Mississippi*.

It was now about 0700 and I suddenly realised I was still only dressed in a towel. I went below for a shower and shave. I was back on the bridge when I received the following message:

XXXXXXXX Urgency Signal CQDE9VG (from Singapore Radio). Following message received: Motor Vessel *Sophie B* – SXQV in position 2 32 N, 105 04 E is on fire in engine room and in all aft accommodation. Require salvage boat. Radio station is out of order. *Rubinovy* / UUXK helping us. Please come immediately. Master.

The *Rubinovy* was a Russian trawler, and as the master of the casualty was sending messages through her, he could obviously receive them through her, so I told the radio officer to send the following message:

To Master *Sophie B* / SXQV via UUXK / *Rubinovy*: Salvage tug *Salvaliant* fully equipped for firefighting coming to your location. ETA 19 / 1400 local. Offer assistance on Lloyd's standard form. What is your latest position? Regards, Salvage Master.

I thought Salvage Master sounded a bit more impressive than just Master and, anyway, I am a Salvage Master. I knew the *Mississippi* would be sending a message, and we picked one up on Singapore Radio from Smit's in Rotterdam and then another from the *Mississippi* itself. It was just signed Master.

I ate my breakfast on the bridge as I altered course along Remunia Shoal. By now, just over two hours after I had left Singapore, the *Mississippi* was about half a mile astern. I felt sorry for the master as there was nothing he could do to make his engines go faster. I had gained on him as he had had to alter through the fishing nets and eventually was directly behind me. I thought that, if I were in his shoes, I would go through the North Channel as a last resort: it might just pay. It didn't. When, about three hours later, she was back behind me on the same course as myself, I was three and a half miles ahead. I had gained a further one and a half miles on top of the half-knot speed I seemed to have on him by going through the main channel.

I thought I had it in the bag as long as nothing broke down. All I had to do was cover the *Mississippi* in case the *Sophie B* was not in the position that had been broadcast and I would be there first.

My radio officer told me he had picked up part of a message indicating that the *Mississippi* was going to be given the job. The *Mississippi* had sent an ETA of 1500 local, so I sent the following:

To Master *Sophie B* / SXQV: *Salvaliant* will be at your position by 1400 local. Am fully equipped for firefighting with over 500 gallons of foam and pumps if required. Offer assistance on Lloyd's standard form. Please confirm my assistance required. Regards, Master.

I received the following reply:

Informal from SXQV to 9VIG: Thanks, but the fire is stopping. Captain informed me just now. You can come or not.

This was a really helpful and encouraging message to receive, when I was going to be there first. Obviously Smit's of Rotterdam had been on to the owners. I looked the *Sophie B* up in the latest supplement to *Lloyd's Register of Shipping* and her call sign in the latest *Ship Station* book, but could not find her, so did not know who their owners were, except that they were Greek. There was nothing more I could do from my side except to get there first and try to persuade the master to sign with me. Maybe the fire would flare up again and he would be only too thankful for my assistance, especially as the distress was not cancelled, and Singapore Radio were still broadcasting his request for a salvage boat to come quick. I therefore sent the following to base:

Urgent

1. Have been calling all morning but no one answering

2. Received message indicating opposition have job

3. We will be on location at least one hour earlier

4. Can you contact owners, please

5. Message from vessel standing by says fire under control

6. Offers of assistance made under LOF but so far no answer

Tew

At about noon, I received the following:

From SXQV to 9VIG: Do not come for assistance because HP3461 [*Mississippi*] and UUXK [the Russian] are enough for helping. Thanks and regards. Master.

You can imagine how I felt. Maybe the *Mississippi* would break down or blow up, or there would be some other disaster, I thought. I therefore continued, muttering imprecations at the office for not getting hold of the owners first. Maybe I could still persuade the master to sign once I was alongside. I continued, but the urgency and thrill of the race was missing.

I sighted the vessel after lunch, with smoke coming out of the after end. So she was still on fire, there was a faint glimmer of hope, and the *Mississippi* was all but out of sight behind us.

The *Sophie B* was a cargo ship with the engine aft and officers' accommodation amidships. She was a vessel of about 6,000 gross tons and was flying light, so the salved value would only be that of the vessel – and that would not be very high so there would only be a small reward, I thought. The Russian trawler was alongside to windward, which was the north side. I circled her once and then went alongside to leeward. As expected, the Greeks refused to take my lines, so I had to hold the *Salvaliant* alongside by using the engines.

'Would you like our assistance?' I asked one man, who was almost indistinguishable from all the other crew, but who was wearing a sweatshirt and could have been an officer.

He turned out to be the chief officer. 'All my equipment is ready,' I continued, pointing to the *Salvaliant*'s deck where the firefighting hoses were laid out along with jerry cans of foam, nozzles with foam attachments, a man standing by the big fire monitor on the mast, a portable diesel pump with fire attachments already running, as well as breathing apparatus and firefighting suits.

'No, the fire is out,' he replied, and then an older man, looking just as scruffy, turned up and introduced himself as the master.

'Thank you for coming,' he said, 'but we do not need your help. The fire is out and we are waiting for the *Mississippi*. Our owners have made a contract with the *Mississippi*.'

'But the *Mississippi* is not here and I am,' I replied. 'What is all that smoke pouring out of the engine room? If you sign with me, I will put your fire out and tow you wherever you want to go. Would you like to come on board?'

He was quite adamant that he would not sign, and by then the *Mississippi* was clearly visible.

The ship was in the usual Greek tramp state and the crew appeared to include every nationality under the sun. Some were amidships watching us, while others were hanging over the rail by the tug. There were some Russians taking breathing apparatus back aboard the trawler, but I could see hoses being played near the engine-room skylight, from which clouds of black smoke were billowing. It was quite clear that the fire was not out – but if he wouldn't sign, he wouldn't sign.

I called up the *Mississippi* on the VHF and asked him which side he wanted to come alongside. He wanted my position, and there was nothing I could do unless I got my pistol out, so I moved off and let him come alongside. I decided to stand by and watch.

The crew on the tug started preparing their firefighting equipment. The first hose was not on board the casualty until half an hour after the tug had gone alongside. It was another ten minutes before the second hose went aboard. I was surprised, to say the least.

I called the *Mississippi* again on the VHF and asked if he would like my assistance, and he asked me to stand by. I think I would have preferred to lose the casualty under the circumstances than to ask for the opposition to stand by.

I stood by for an hour and a half, slowly circling the *Sophie B*, watching the firefighting, which seemed ill-coordinated. I was feeling very disappointed and despondent: to have arrived first and then to lose the job was a bitter pill to swallow, especially after the long time we had been on standby. I consoled myself with the thought that the award would not be very big, there was a small salved value, the fire had been mostly put out by the Russians and there was other assistance available (namely us), but it did not help much.

Eventually, the smoke stopped and the *Mississippi* called me up to say the fire was out and thanked me for standing by. I departed and headed for the location of a Norwegian tanker I had passed on the way north, which had been displaying 'not under command' signals. I saw her earlier than expected and she was proceeding merrily on her way.

I returned to Singapore hoping the Persian Gulf job had been cancelled. It hadn't.

Barge salvage report, Iran

Sunday 21 March 1976

The *Salvaliant* was at anchor in the Khowr-e Musa waterway at Bandar Shahpur with Buoy Number 19 bearing 195 degrees, distance 8.3 cables with 90 fathoms of chain out in 22 fathoms of water. At 0600 the weather started to deteriorate, with an increase in wind from the southeast to force four and a slight sea in the waterway. At 0800, the wind had increased to force six with passing rain and I was thankful that I was not at the pilot station with the barges.

I considered that the *Salvaliant*, anchored where the pilot boat had indicated, was too close to the mud bank in the prevailing conditions. At 0805, I commenced shifting the *Salvaliant* and was re-anchored by 0835 with Buoy Number 19 bearing 211 degrees, distance 6.4 cables in 15 fathoms with 75 fathoms of chain out.

At about this time I heard the tug *Essard* calling the Khowr-e Musa pilot vessel on VHF channel 16. The *Essard* had brought a similar tow of barges, including three loaded one on top of the other. She had arrived a couple of days after the *Salvaliant* and had had an unfortunate accident while anchoring. The tow wire knocked a man over the side and his body was never recovered.

The *Essard* asked the pilot vessel for the use of the tug which transported the pilots from the pilot station to incoming and outgoing ships. One of her barge tows had broken adrift. The pilot vessel answered the *Essard*, informing him that the tug was above the bar, due to the rough sea, and so could not assist.

I immediately called up the *Essard* on VHF channel 16 and offered my services to recover the barges. I knew he must have disconnected his tow and secured them on light lines, which would be unsuitable in rough weather. The only way he could recover the lost barges would be to reconnect his tow, which was probably impossible in the prevailing weather conditions, or anchor the barges and then go after the drifting ones. I doubted whether he would have the men or equipment to recover the barges in rough weather.

Although I called for about half an hour offering my services, the *Essard* either could not or would not hear, for he did not reply.

The *Salvaliant* was waiting for port clearance. This could not be delivered until the following day, due to the Iranian New Year holiday. If the *Essard* accepted my services, I intended asking Shahpur Radio for permission to proceed to the pilot station. As I had

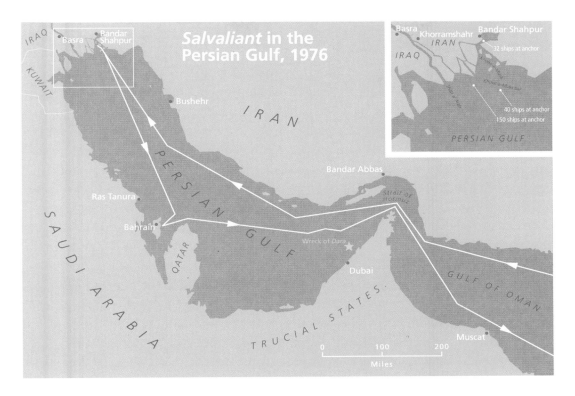

Salvaliant in the Persian Gulf, 1976

IRAQ
Basra
Bandar Shahpur
KUWAIT
Bushehr
I R A N
P E R S I A N   G U L F
Ras Tanura
Bahrain
SAUDI ARABIA
QATAR
Bandar Abbas
Strait of Hormuz
Wreck of Dara
Dubai
TRUCIAL STATES
GULF OF OMAN
Muscat

0   100   200
Miles

Basra
Khorramshahr
Bandar Shahpur
IRAN
IRAQ
32 ships at anchor
40 ships at anchor
150 ships at anchor
PERSIAN GULF

brought the *Salvaliant* upriver with the tows and without the services of a pilot, I felt I would have no trouble proceeding downriver without a pilot.

I knew that it was important to recover the barges quickly, due to the nature of the Khowr-e Musa waterway. It is a flat, featureless area, shallow and unsurveyed outside the main channel. If the barges drifted far, it might be impossible to recover them from the shallow area.

I tried calling the *Essard* on the SSB radio and the distress frequency, 2182 kHz, but she did not answer. As I did not have a contract, I did not feel justified in leaving Bandar Shahpur at this juncture.

By noon the weather had moderated somewhat, and as I had heard no more over the VHF, I assumed that the *Essard* must have managed to recover the barges. This was borne out by a report in the evening from a Filipino-officered ship at the pilot station that the barges had been recovered.

Although the tides were taking off, the current in the waterway ran very strongly and at 1920 the *Salvaliant*, despite having five times the depth-of-water length of cable out, started dragging. I therefore shifted anchorage and re-anchored to two anchors at 1950. Unfortunately, when the tide eased, I found I was too close to a large Greek bulk carrier, so shifted anchorage once again. At 2230 I re-anchored in position Buoy Number 21 bearing 168 degrees, distance 1.7 cables in 11.5 fathoms with 75 fathoms of chain out. The weather at midnight was cloudy and the wind southeast force three.

Monday 22 March 1976

The day dawned cloudy but calm. During the morning the cloud mainly cleared and a light east-south-easterly breeze sprang up. I made a radio link call via Khorramshahr Radio to the home of Mr Costello of Sealand to enquire about my port clearance, and was assured that Mr Ong would bring it on board between 1300 and 1400 hours local time.

At 1235 four pilots boarded for the passage out to the pilot vessel. Mr Ong, the senior representative, boarded at 1320 with the port clearance. He told me that the three-stacked barge from the *Essard* was adrift. I informed him that I had heard about it but that it had been reported that the barges had been recovered. It turned out that a two-stacked barge had broken adrift as well and it was this that had been recovered, not the other.

I immediately offered my services on Lloyd's Open Form, pointing out to Mr Ong that, as agent to the barge owners, he could sign it on their behalf. He said it was up to the master of the *Essard*. I pointed out that the master of the *Essard* might not sign unless instructed to do so by the agent and, anyway, the *Essard* was at the pilot station. If Mr Ong signed, I would get the master of the *Essard* to sign as well. I said that in the absence of any instructions from his owners, he must do the best he could to protect his owners' property and, in this case, it appeared that the barges had been adrift for 36 hours or so. I was offering the services of a fully equipped salvage tug, including divers, to locate and salve the barges if possible.

Mr Ong still refused to sign, so I offered him the use of the radio telephone to contact Mr Costello and obtain his instructions. Unfortunately, the radio officer was unable to get through so, as the pilots were becoming restive at the further delay, I said I would sail.

Mr Ong asked me to look for the barges on the way out. I replied that as he had declined to sign a Lloyd's Open Form, if I found the barges, I would attempt to salve them as derelicts. If I was successful, I would tow them out to the pilot station, informing Sealand of my actions. If a Lloyd's Open Form was signed or security acceptable to Selco was put up, then I would deliver the barges to Bandar Shahpur. He agreed that this was acceptable, and meanwhile he would seek instructions from the owners of the barges.

Mr Ong left the *Salvaliant* at 1355 and I commenced to heave up the starboard anchor. The anchor was aweigh at 1400 and *Salvaliant* proceeded downriver to master's orders and pilots' advice. Once clear of the shipping at Buoy Number 20, maximum safe revolutions on two engines were ordered.

The tide was still flooding. High water at Bandar Shahpur, the refined-products loading terminal of the National Iranian Oil Company, was predicted for 1611, height 5.3 metres, while high water at the bar was predicted for 1440, height 3.6 metres. The *Salvaliant* made good just over ten knots in the first hour at full speed, so the last of the flood was running at something like three knots. The barges had been reported to be about five miles north of the pilot station, which would have placed them in the unsurveyed shallows to the east of the bar.

At 1600, when about midway between Buoys Number 12 and Number 9, I sighted through the powerful binoculars what looked like a three-stacked barge. I immediately took a bearing, ordered that speed be reduced to one engine, identified the object on the radar, thus obtaining a distance, and plotted the position on the chart. The object, which later proved to be the barge LT 1, with barges LT 11 and LT 12 stowed on top, was about five miles away in the unsurveyed shallows of Khowr-e Vosta. They were about 13 miles from their last reported position.

I asked the pilot if it was safe to pass northwards of Qassar bin Siswan rock, which is marked by Number 9 Buoy, as I wanted to go and investigate. I apologised for what would probably be some hours' delay, but as there was only about two and a half hours' daylight left (sunset was predicted for 1827), I must investigate and secure the barges. They agreed to the delay but were not very happy about going over to the east side of the river. It looked reasonably safe on the chart and so I said I would pilot the tug, absolving them of all responsibility. I suggested they might like to partake of the light refreshments available in the owner's cabin.

The tide was now ebbing, so I decided to anchor up-tide of the entrance to the Khowr-e Vosta. As soon as I was informed that the tug was on one engine, I altered course and passed to the north of Qassar bin Siswan. The weather at this time was fine with light airs. It was high tide, so none of the mud banks or waterway banks was visible. There was water as far as the eye could see. The only visible objects apart from the barges were Buoys 9, 10 and 12.

The echo sounder was running continuously, and when a depth of nine metres was reached, I let go the anchor. The tug was brought up at 1633 with one shackle of cable in nine metres of water in position Buoy Number 9 bearing 228 degrees, distance eight cables. I warned Jesus Armasilla, my chief officer, to be careful of the unexamined, dangerous rocks visible at low water, marked on the chart as lying across the Khowr-e Vosta, and to sound continuously with a hand lead line when he proceeded towards the barges in the Z-boat. At 1635, Jesus and his sounding party were away in the Z-boat and they reached the barges at 1705. I gave the following message to the radio officer for urgent dispatch to Selco:

From *Salvaliant*, DTG 221315Z, to *Salvenger*, urgent attention Mr Bond:

1. Three barges, similar to *Salvaliant*'s tow, broken adrift from tug *Essard*, agent Sealand

2. I am anchored in river and Z-boat over to now abandoned barges

3. Barges three miles from nearest *Salvaliant* can approach

4. Have four pilots on board

5. Agent has not signed LOF

6. If I deliver pilots to pilot vessel, shall return and try for salvage

7. If disagree, cable soonest

Tew

Jesus reported over the radio that the barges were still afloat but there was shallow water close by. I instructed him to anchor the barges and I would come over with the lifeboat to tow the barges into deeper water.

The ebb was now running strongly and it seemed that the most important thing was to keep the barges afloat. If they grounded near high water, we would have great difficulty refloating them as the tides had taken off and become neaps. It was out of the question to take the *Salvaliant* closer to the Khowr-e Vosta without surveying and buoying the channel, so the barges would have to be warped to the tug.

I had informed the pilots that there would be a further delay, as I was going to tow the barges with the lifeboat. The steward was looking after them with refreshments, and they agreed, one of them going onto the bridge to inform the pilot vessel over the VHF what was happening.

At 1710, the lifeboat was taken away by the second officer, and I accompanied him and his party. Torches, lifejackets and an anchor had been added to the lifeboat's equipment, together with extra diesel fuel. The chief officer had reported shallow water on the direct course to the barges so a southerly course was first steered and then easterly towards the now anchored barges.

The barges were reached at 1745 and a towing line immediately made fast. The extra men in the lifeboat climbed on board the LT 1 and assisted in raising the anchor. This turned out to be a common anchor and, once it was raised, towing commenced at 1750 towards the main channel. At about 1820, I was informed by the radio officer that he had received a message from Selco. I asked him to read it out and I understood that I was to safely anchor the barges and proceed. I therefore instructed him to send the following message:

From Master *Salvaliant* DTG 221458Z, to *Salvenger*, urgent attention Mr Bond:

1. Yours understood

2. Will anchor barges and proceed soonest Bahrain

3. Suggest salvage claim can still be made as we towed barges clear of shallow water and anchored

Tew

I returned to the *Salvaliant* on the Z-boat, arriving on board at 1843. I gave instructions to heave up the starboard anchor and checked that I had correctly understood the message. I had. At 1850, the starboard anchor was aweigh and the *Salvaliant* started to drift downstream on a fast-running ebb. My plan was to have the tug heading straight

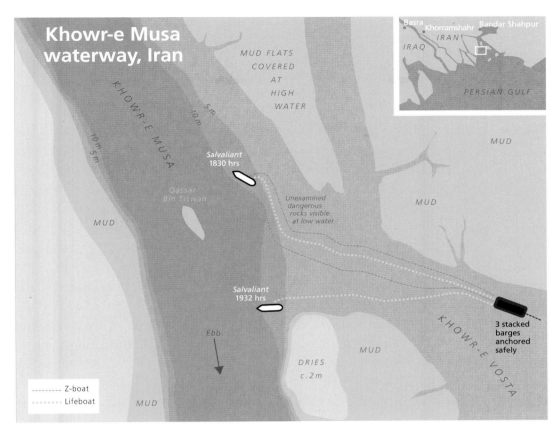

Khowr-e Musa waterway, Iran

KHOWR-E MUSA

MUD FLATS COVERED AT HIGH WATER

Basra Khorramshahr Bandar Shahpur
IRAQ IRAN
PERSIAN GULF

MUD

5 m
10 m

10 m
5 m

Salvaliant 1830 hrs

Qassar Bin Siswan

MUD

Unexamined dangerous rocks visible at low water

MUD

MUD

Salvaliant 1932 hrs

Ebb

DRIES c. 2 m

MUD

KHOWR-E VOSTA

3 stacked barges anchored safely

-------- Z-boat
·········· Lifeboat

MUD

into the waterway across the stream on a heading of about 270 degrees, and if the depth shown on the continuously running echo sounder indicated less than eight metres, I would go ahead on the engine into deeper water. In this way, I could safely close the distance with the lifeboat, which, once in the main stream, would have difficulty heading against the ebb.

I instructed the second officer to check that there was sufficient water to anchor the barges, bearing in mind that the tide still had about three metres to fall. When he had safely anchored the barges, he was to return to the *Salvaliant* immediately.

At 1855, the barges were reported as anchored and I plotted their position, which was 30 11.15 N, 49 01.15 E, meaning that the barges had been towed about a mile from the shallow water. I informed the master of the *Essard* over the VHF that I had safely anchored his barges and that he could collect them.

At 1915, Number 9 Buoy bore 290 degrees, distance one mile, and at 1932 it bore 318 degrees, distance 1.4 miles, when the lifeboat arrived alongside. The lifeboat was clear of the water by 1935, and I proceeded down the waterway. I had the following message sent to Sealand via Khorramshahr Radio:

Number One *Salvaliant* – 9VIG – CK49 221640 GMT. Sealand Khorramshahr

1. Have anchored your three stacked barges on LT 1

2. As towed into deeper water and anchored safely, I claim salvage

3. Risk of barges becoming lost if I had not anchored

4. As Selco's agent, please telex the contents of this message to them

Regards: Tew

There is no doubt that a valuable service was performed. Speed in securing the barges was the important thing, hence the necessity of taking *Salvaliant* as close as possible. There was considerable risk of *Salvaliant* grounding on an uncharted or shifted shoal, which in a swift-running ebb stream could have proved disastrous. There was the ever-present risk of the Z-boat hitting a rock or underwater object, which would have smashed the engine and/or ripped open a side tank, thereby immobilising her. The water was muddy and visibility was nil. If the lifeboat had grounded on a falling tide, at best she would have remained there until the next high water, or capsized in the current.

The barges had drifted twenty miles during the time they had been adrift, and it was fortunate for their owners that we were able to get to them when we did. If we had not towed them clear of the shallow water, they could have grounded nearer high water and become neaped. If they had not grounded, they could have drifted far into the unsurveyed mudflats and become totally inaccessible. They could have holed themselves on a rock and, with such a high deck cargo and with one or more tanks breached, LT 1 might have capsized. If this had occurred, it is doubtful whether the barges could have been salved as it would have been impossible to bring a salvage vessel into the shallows.

I went at full speed to Bahrain. I had been told there was an urgent job for us in Colombo, but fuel was cheaper in the Gulf. On arrival, I found there was some hitch and I was not able to bunker straight away. To add insult to injury, we were not allowed ashore.

And then, two days out of Colombo, I slowed down in anticipation of helping a ship on fire, but evidently she dealt with it herself or someone else got the job.

Barges

Barges LT 11 and LT 12 were 110 feet long by 40 feet wide by 8 feet depth with a gross tonnage of 309.48. They were twins of the ones *Salvaliant* had towed from Port Klang, and the same gear was secured on the top barge, namely, rubber-tyre fenders, stanchions, anchor, and navigation-light stands. They were in a brand new condition. LT 1 was a second-hand barge, but was in good condition. She was about 125 feet long by 40 feet wide by 10 feet depth, and her draught was one metre. There was a small, plywood box-like shelter at the forward end of LT 1. All three barges were registered in Panama.

Volosko
A difficult tow

FROM *LLOYD'S WEEKLY CASUALTY REPORTS*, 1976

***Volosko* (Yugoslav) – Colombo, Mar 12** – Motor vessel *Volosko*: Agents report vessel aground off Pottuvil, east coast Sri Lanka, with motor vessel *Kumrovec* standing by for assistance. Sri Lanka Navy alerted to stand by. – Lloyd's Agents per Salvage Association.

London, Mar 18 – *Volosko* refloated and now in tow of sister ship.

Colombo, Mar 18 – *Volosko* arrived Mar 17.

Colombo, Mar 23 – Motor vessel *Volosko*: Owners seeking offers of tug for tow to Singapore. – Lloyd's Agents per Salvage Association.

Colombo, Mar 29 – Motor vessel *Volosko*: Arrangements in hand to tow vessel to Singapore for repairs. Salvage tug *Salvaliant* due Colombo Apr 1. – Lloyd's Agents per Salvage Association.

When I ask for full speed again, one of the engines breaks down. This does not augur well for the towing of a fully laden ship from Colombo to Singapore. We carry on with one engine and I enter the harbour without a pilot. The pilot comes on board inside the breakwater.

As usual, the pilot does not want to handle this tug, so I put her alongside the Yugoslav vessel *Volosko* myself. She has had an engine breakdown, and I am to tow her to Singapore. I feel a bit of a fool having to tell the captain we cannot leave because I have to repair my own engine! In the event, the engine repairs take a lot longer than expected. The air conditioning on the tug breaks down, so I take myself ashore and stay in the Oberoi Hotel.

It is evening, and I am sitting in the green-grassed beer garden of the hotel, watching the sun set. There is a low swell running in from the Indian Ocean, which we have just crossed from the Persian Gulf. It is breaking quite loudly on the beach below, hidden by a low wall. A white-clad, barefoot waiter replenishes my glass with a smile. What a contrast to Bandar Shahpur, or even my own poor, broken-down tug in the harbour.

The sun is just beginning to enlarge as it closes the clear horizon. The bottom of the fair-weather cumulus clouds are already tinged with pink. As it sinks, the sun becomes a formless mass of molten steel, almost too bright to look at. The sea changes colour as the light fades. A long line of cloud to the northeast, near the horizon, is purple. Now, quickly, the bright colours of the tropic sunset form, purples and all shades of red. The sun has sunk, the final bright spot gone with the suddenness of switching off an electric light. No green flash tonight.

Some lenticular clouds above the sun, now below the horizon, shine with a silvery brightness. The sea has lost its daytime green. The colours in the sky deepen – crimson, purple, violet, orange, red, all shades of green and yellow – until the still light blue in the zenith.

It is quickly becoming dark, the fierce heat of the day already beginning to cool. The higher clouds are now grey; the silvery clouds now a furnace-red. The sea has lost its allure as it continues to darken. The colours fading, the ruby-reds have lost their richness, the fiery reds have lost their fire, but as much of the sky as I can see is brushed with a faint coat of pink.

The silence of the fast-approaching night, broken only by the breaking waves, is shattered by the slamming of a car door and the starting of an engine. The car, now gone, has disturbed the peace and other sounds intrude: the murmur of the servants' voices, the sound of female laughter, the clink of a bottle on glass. The magic has gone, more people filter into the garden, their voices loud. Electric lights have been turned on, and the strange silence of the sunset is gone.

As I leave I can hear thunder overhead, a long, rolling, deep-throated sound stretching into the distance, prelude to a monsoon, when the streets run with water and the sea is lashed by strong winds. It is time to be away with my tow.

———◆———

Finally the engine was repaired and the tow connected. The *Salvaliant* was alongside the *Volosko*, bow to bow, with the forerunner lashed on the side. My idea was to move ahead and tow the *Volosko* out through the breakwater. I would have to make a turn approaching the entrance but felt happy it would not be a problem. I discussed the departure with the chief pilot, old Razzle Dazzle. He had been fourth officer on the *Dara* before she was blown up when I was a cadet. He said he would put the two port tugs one on each side of the tow to help steer her.

When all was ready, I manoeuvred the *Salvaliant* ahead of the *Volosko* while they let go from the buoys. With my air-start engines, and given that I could only manoeuvre on one, thus half-power, you can see that a certain amount of skill was required – even though I say so myself! I found by now that, in general, I could get her to do anything I wanted. A lot of it is a matter of feel. I just knew what she would and would not do, and acted accordingly.

I was ahead of the *Volosko* and she began to move. I quickly increased to full ahead on my one engine, and the towing gear came right out of the water. It was short while manoeuvring in the harbour. I managed to build up enough speed to make the turn but not so much that the fully laden *Volosko* would yaw out of control.

Salvaliant, towing in heavy weather with the towed vessel out on the beam – note the wire over the side. In this case, the ship is the old liner, Fairsky, on her way to Hong Kong. Destined to be converted into a casino, she was damaged by fire and finally scrapped in 1979.

Once in the entrance, with the breakwaters either side, the *Salvaliant* felt the swell and the two harbour tugs let go. The tow followed meekly until clear and then took on a life of her own. She yawed. I had the second engine connected and built up to full speed. The tow yawed even more.

The voyage proved very difficult, as the *Volosko* yawed or sheered all over the place. Her weight was twelve times mine and she wanted to take control. Part of her rudder was missing and therefore inoperable so she could not be steered. She would yaw out to one side, the tow wire creeping round on the towing gunwale until she was abeam. It looked as though she was trying to overtake me. The tow wire, all 1,700 feet of it, was dragging through the water. *Salvaliant's* helm was over on the opposite side to hold her on course. The speed through the water reduced, the tow wire hummed and sang and occasionally rattled on the gunwale.

Then quite suddenly, for no apparent reason, the *Volosko* would alter course and head towards me as though she wanted to collide with the tug. Weight came off the tow wire, it sagged, and the tug picked up speed. The helmsman would have to be alert to keep the *Salvaliant* on course. As the speed picked up, the tow wire remained tight. The *Volosko* altered course even more and would swing past the stern, sometimes fast, sometimes slow, and then would go out onto the opposite beam. Sometimes she would stay there for hours, sometimes minutes, before altering course again. Sometimes she would stay astern and follow meekly, and then we would make good speed.

There was absolutely nothing I could do to stop the yawing, except slow down. But we were not making very good progress even at full speed, so I just had to put up with it and make sure the bosun greased the towing gunwale and wires every few hours. I would slow down and adjust the length of the tow wire so it would not chafe the same spot. Greasing was a skilled job. The man doing it had to keep his head down because the wire was free-running, due to the yawing. If he got hit by the tow wire it would take his head off – and I did not want that to happen.

At night I could sometimes see just a green side light, sometimes a red one, and sometimes both together, which told me what she was doing. She did not show her steaming lights, of course.

All the time, at the back of my mind, was what would happen if the *Salvaliant* had a power blackout or engine failure. The *Volosko* would start towing the *Salvaliant* and, if she was abeam and I lost control, the *Salvaliant* could be pulled over and capsized. As a result I found, I think for the first time ever, that I could not switch off properly and so could not sleep, and I spent most of each day and night on the bridge.

There was quite a swell in the Indian Ocean and both tug and tow rolled. The weather was typically pre-monsoon, with rain squalls.

Once past the northern tip of Sumatra, the swell went but the traffic increased. In the rain squalls, there was always the worry that some ship would not realise that the *Volosko* was under tow and would pass over my tow line. The radio officer sent a navigational warning every few hours.

I asked Selco to send a tug to help me through the narrowest part of the Malacca Straits. The heavily yawing *Volosko* was difficult to handle and I wanted more control in the heavy traffic with loaded tankers overtaking and empty ones bound for the Gulf, not to mention cargo, container and passenger ships, along with many fishing boats. She brought up the mail, which was very welcome.

During the last night, we had the most tremendous thunder and lightning storm. It made me thankful that I had taken a different route from usual to keep out of the traffic as much as possible. Having got so far and worked so hard, it would have been a pity for something to go wrong at the last moment. My nerves were a little stretched. At one time, I had six loaded supertankers thundering down behind me and an equal number of ships coming the other way.

Early in the morning I received a message telling me of another ship in trouble. I arranged with Selco to leave the *Volosko* at the Immigration Anchorage, and I would proceed as fast as possible. I towed the *Volosko* into the anchorage, where she anchored. This had been a tow port to port, as opposed to a salvage pickup at sea, so I was towing her on chain bridles.

My crew and I, of course, were in a fever to leave for the ship in trouble. The bosun took his team across to the *Volosko* and slipped the chains and emergency tow wire. These were recovered and I set off at full speed. Not having cleared in, I did not need to clear out.

We were successful, even if the salvage was short. This time I cleared in, and I was steaming to the mooring when I heard of a collision only twenty miles away. I turned the tug round and steamed out at full speed. On arrival I found neither ship was badly damaged, so we were not required. I returned to the Selco moorings and retired to a hotel.

Not for long. As soon as some repairs were completed, we were off again. Time was of the essence to beat the forthcoming southwest monsoon in the Indian Ocean. I steamed at full economical speed, about 12 knots, up the Malacca Straits and rolled heavily all the way to Dondra Head, on the southeast end of Sri Lanka. This was back along the way we had towed the *Volosko*, but now, running free, the *Salvaliant* was much livelier.

FROM *LLOYD'S WEEKLY CASUALTY REPORTS,* 1976

Volosko **(Yugoslav) – Singapore, Apr 19** – Motor vessel *Volosko* arrived Singapore Road Apr 19.

Standard stud tow link chain

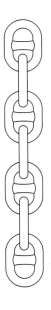

A day off the coast of India

It was a fine, clear night, dark with no moon, and little cloud above the horizon. We rounded Sri Lanka the previous night and were now approaching the northern side of the Gulf of Mannar. I stood on the monkey island to give me more height, the tropic night warm in my face, searching in the north for Cape Comorin Light. Just before 0400, I sighted the loom, faint in the distance to the north-north-west, group flash two every 20 seconds, the light far below the horizon. It was in the right place, so I returned to my bunk.

It was daylight when I returned to the bridge, and we were off the Indian coast, the faint smell of incense on the light morning breeze, which rippled the long, low southwesterly swell. The coast was hidden behind a thin mist, except for the occasional glimpse of the undulating sand hills behind Cape Comorin.

By about 0800, Cape Comorin, the southernmost point of the Indian subcontinent, was quite clearly visible. The lighthouse, a square masonry tower with black and white bands, stood on the low sandy cape, and nearby the bungalow 'formerly occupied by the British resident'.

I had kept well out to clear Crocodile Rock, which, with only six feet of water over it, was a danger to be avoided – and in fine weather the sea did not break. Muttam Point Light, another black and white banded lighthouse, was abeam just after breakfast. Crocodile Rock was inshore to starboard, invisible with the calm sea, so I altered course into the land, which lies in a generally northwest–southeast direction. When about one mile off the coast, I altered again, parallel to the shoreline, to observe the scenery.

Numerous sails were putting out to sea on the last of the offshore breeze, and all, without exception, were brown. The canoes at first looked like log dugouts, but upon closer inspection appeared to be bamboos lashed together, the bow and stern blunt. A small mast held the long, bendy bamboo yard to which the sail was attached, the rig a very crude form of lugsail. Most of the boats had one man on board, dressed only in a loincloth; a few of the larger ones had three crew. Once the grounds were reached, the fishermen lowered the sail and mast and started fishing, drifting on the south-going current. A few of them had nets but mostly the fishing was by hand line with a single hook. The grounds had not been ruined by trawling and modern fishing methods, so there was still an abundance of fish off this coast, despite thousands of years' continuous fishing.

The coastline was one continuous sandbank onto which the swell broke, the water surging almost to the top. It must be spectacular during the southwest monsoon. Behind the bank were rows of coconut trees, occasionally broken by a field, the land burnt brown and tinder-dry by the winter sun.

On the beach were large groups of people. At first I could not see what they were doing, then I realised they were fishing by a method described in the Bible! It was fascinating. Here was a place where parts of the population were dependent for their food, especially protein, on methods that were old in the time of Christ.

The net was shot off the beach with a boat propelled by oars. Attached to the two ends were ropes, which were apart on the beach. Twenty or thirty men on each rope pulled, while more men in the water thrashed the surface to drive fish into the net. The backbreaking task of heaving the net in by hand continued until it was dragged above the high-water mark. All concerned gathered around to empty the net, while circling the men were hopping crows and scavenging dogs. This was no isolated group; every few hundred yards, all the way along the coast, were groups of fishermen with their nets.

I had never seen so many churches in such a short distance before. Every little village or hamlet of mud huts with reed roofs had its own church, a large imposing brick building, each with its spire. All were well maintained and one, painted white, looked large and impressive enough to be a cathedral.

On the chart there was quite a large opening in the sandbank at Puvar, a small town with a couple of churches. I had the greatest difficulty in spotting it, a mere gap in the sand with the entrance quite silted up. No doubt during the rains the entrance would have cleared. A church was also marked, meaning it must be an unusually formidable edifice amongst the many we had already passed, but it was almost totally obscured by palm trees. Above, and a little to the northwards, however, a new and modern-looking building had been put up, the only sign that this was the twentieth century.

Pre-lunch aperitif time saw us off Vilinjam, where the lighthouse had red bands. There was a breakwater built out southwards from the point, forming a small harbour, although only suitable for small craft.

On Kovalam Point, a bluff with reddish-coloured rock or sandstone, was an important-looking building with a bright red roof. There was a well-kept garden with purple flowers setting off the green grass, a haven compared to the parched earth seen earlier. Originally it must have been one of the maharajah's palaces but some white-painted, chalet-type buildings had since been put up close by, suggesting it might be a hotel.

By lunch we were off Trivandrum (8 29 N, 76 57 E), capital of the state of Kerala. The main city lay about a mile inland, but a road led down to and along the shore to seaward of the small airport. A large white building with a slate-grey roof stood almost in a direct line with the runway, on which was parked a solitary, propeller-driven aeroplane. I saw two bicycles, one old, black Morris Oxford and a lorry which would not have disgraced Montagu's Motor Museum. Men, walking with their dhotis hitched up, stopped to watch us pass while women carrying loads on their heads found us an excuse for a rest.

A breeze from the north had sprung up and the sea was dotted with brown sails as the fishing fleet made for the shore with its catch. White horses shattered the deep blue of the sea, making the water appear clean and invigorating, in sharp contrast to the burnt-out brownness of the land around the city.

I was interested to see how the boats were beached and carefully watched. On approaching their particular collection of mud huts, the canoe was luffed up into the wind and the sail and mast lowered. The crew would then paddle, waiting for the right wave to surf in. As soon as the boat landed on the beach, they jumped out quickly and heaved to clear the next wave. It looked very simple!

By 1400, siesta time, the sea was almost empty of craft and the beaches denuded of people. I had to keep slightly further off the coast as the coastal bank extended further offshore, and so I followed the local custom. At 1800 we were off Quilon, a small port only open during the northeast monsoon, and Tangasseri Point Lighthouse, clearly visible with its black and white bands.

As the sun slowly set, gradually becoming larger and redder as it closed the horizon, I took my departure from the Malabar Coast. I watched the sun sink slowly out of sight, the sky a fiery red, and then looked at the darkened, receding coastline with Tangasseri Light and Kovilthottam Light further northwards, bright flashes amongst the yellow kerosene lights sprinkling the shoreline.

Majmaa II and *Pacificoeverett*
A leper colony in the Laccadives

FROM *LLOYD'S WEEKLY CASUALTY REPORTS*, 1976

Pacificoeverett **(Liberian) – London, June 3** – Motor vessel *Pacificoeverett* reported aground 1 mile NE of Kadmat Island, Laccadive Islands.

Bombay, June 3 – *Pacificoeverett*: Local agents confirm vessel aground since approximately 1400 May 31. Vessel still aground at 1045 today. Understood salvage tug *Salvaliant*, which reported in vicinity with tow, requested to assist. Understood crew safe.

On the way to the Fateh oilfield off Dubai, I passed the wreck buoy marking the remains of the *Dara*, which brought back memories. I slowed down and dropped a plastic flower in memory of the dead and wondered what had happened to the living. I briefly thought about myself – survivor to salvor – but not for long. Arriving at the oilfield, we were contracted to tow the *Majmaa II*, an old floating storage tanker, to Singapore for a refit. The *Salvanquish*, with Peter Lankester in command, was already there to tow the *Majmaa I*.

They were tankers, or rather just over half a tanker. The engine room and accommodation had been cut off. This meant that the stern was completely square and would cause tremendous drag, rather like trying to drag a quay wall through the water.

I put the *Salvaliant* alongside, keeping clear of the chains which secured the tanker. She was flying light and towered over my tug, making her seem very small. The derrick was just long enough to lift the towing gear, chain bridles again, on board.

During the operation, I heard the most terrible scream. My God, I thought, someone has been killed. I looked around, but could see nothing on the tug. I climbed up the ladder and boarded the *Majmaa*. Lying on deck, close by, was the figure of one of my divers, but I could not see any blood. He was surrounded by other crew members.

'Just knocked out, he's coming round,' said one.

He had been knocked off the rail and had fallen, luckily, onto the *Majmaa*. Obviously he had thought he was falling to his death on the tug.

It was very hot, being summer. The monsoon was breaking in the Arabian Sea – we were too late. It was therefore ultra-important that everything was prepared to withstand heavy weather.

The first row I had was with the surveyor, who wanted to ballast the *Majmaa*. I told him I did not want to tow a lot of water around, and the lighter she was the faster I would go. He did not agree. Eventually I gave in, but put my electric submersible pumps and generator on board. As soon as I left, I pumped most of the ballast out and proved my point!

The field manager was in charge of the departure operation. He was a fit, good-looking Englishman. Oil workers are a different breed, heavily influenced by the Americans. I invited him on board for dinner, my cabin table being laid with a tablecloth, cut-glass wine glasses, and plastic flowers. Don't forget we are in the middle of an oilfield in the Persian Gulf. It was still hot in the evening when the manager turned up to sample my roast duck and drink my best wine.

'Do you mind putting on a shirt?' I asked as his bare torso entered my cabin.

He looked so startled. I don't think anyone had ever questioned his attire before, certainly not on his own oilfield. He left without a word, and I thought that was that. But five minutes later he returned wearing a bright shirt and a jolly time was had after all, classical music playing on my tape recorder. It was surreal.

The next day we left. The securing chains holding the *Majmaa II* were slipped and I towed her out of the oilfields without incident. It was 13 May, a bad omen, but I did not have the nerve to delay a day. The Z-boat took the pumping crew over to the tow and the next two days were spent pumping her out.

She followed meekly, like a lamb, her bow pointing at my stern, the tow wire straight astern, almost never moving. What a difference from the *Volosko*. The weather was fine and the speed slowly increased as ballast was reduced. I went over in the Z-boat. At the stern of the *Majmaa*, it was like being in a river eddy, with a whole mass of water being dragged along. No doubt this drag contributed greatly to the good course she followed.

The omen was indeed bad. Three days after leaving, one engine broke down. We were through the Straits of Hormuz, but still in calm waters. On one engine, speed was more than halved. The monsoon had broken and the weather in the Arabian Sea was bad. However, a temporary repair was made by the engineers and we carried on, albeit at reduced speed.

I persuaded Jesus, now chief officer, to make some sails. The wind was mainly on the beam and sometimes abaft it. With a strong wind beginning to blow, it made sense to try and utilise it.

'But what if anyone sees us?' he complained. 'The crew will die of embarrassment. Whoever heard of a sailing tug?'

However, I prevailed and, as usual, the Filipino crew proved most inventive. Eventually, we had five sails hoisted with a combined area of about 1,000 square feet. At its most advantageous direction, it increased our speed by about a knot. I was more than pleased. The sails had to be rigged in such a way that they could be quickly lowered in a squall. I did not want to break anything.

Slow progress was made towards the lee shore of the Indian coast. The sun was permanently obscured by heavy monsoon clouds. It was like living in a permanent tent.

As a result, of course, we could not obtain any sights and so the position of the tug was estimated only. The direct course goes through the Laccadive Islands, but there are lots of reefs and shoal waters. It was a difficult and tense time.

The sea was very rough, with continuous, breaking white horses which came on board the towing deck, the thud clearly audible on the bridge. The *Salvaliant* was quite comfortable, held steady by the tow and, of course, the sails. The *Majmaa* followed benignly, although it was too rough to make the daily visits we were supposed to. It rained a lot, the heavy raindrops like pellets on the windows. The air was damp with heavy humidity. Everything was damp on board and it was surprisingly cold.

The dismal, overcast rough weather, the damp atmosphere on board, the lack of sunlight, the continuous gloom, together with the engine problem, all conspired to sink my normally buoyant feelings to a low ebb. The crew, normally cheerful and smiling,

Heavy-weather towing on the way to Kadmat island: *Salvaliant* being dragged sideways through the water by the tow

Salvaliant, pooped by heavy seas

became dull and sullen. There was a nervous, anticipatory feeling pervading the tug, as if to say, 'What more could go wrong?'

Ten days later, approaching the islands, without having had a sight, the engine broke down again. It was very rough and the weather was bad. It was blowing a full gale, raining and overcast. In the worst of the rain squalls we could not even see our tow, normally looming so large astern. I felt enclosed in the wheelhouse, my own small world in time and space with the wind, rain and waves. That was all that mattered. It was as though we were the only things left on the planet. I stayed continuously on the bridge, catnapping in the captain's chair. I was increasingly concerned about our position approaching the islands.

The weather became worse, with a cyclone approaching, and the sails had to be lowered. There was nothing I could do to keep her out of the way unless I slipped the tow, and I was not prepared to do that.

It was overcast, the low cloud enveloping us in our own small world. The rain squalls reduced visibility to almost nil, obliterating the breaking seas – we just heard the thud as they hit the tug, the spray mingling with the rain hitting the wheelhouse. The noise was considerable. Underneath my feet, I could feel the slight vibration of the engine, the beating heart of the tug.

The chief engineer was not well: he seemed to have given up and retired to his bunk. He was not a young man, but was very experienced. I went to the engine room to consult with the second engineer and to see if we could do anything to get the starboard engine working. There was a crack in the engine casting and it was getting worse when the engine was used. We had to find some method to strap up the engine so that it could be started.

We retired to the chief engineer's cabin and discussed the situation. A plan of action was made, and the chief engineer perked up a bit and went below. Twelve hours later, the starboard engine was started and could be used, although not at full power. I felt a lot better with two engines running.

The weather became even worse with the approaching cyclone, but with the damaged starboard engine not having full power, I could not make much progress. We were to all intents and purposes hove-to. At times, I suspect, we were going backwards, although I had enough power to keep the *Salvaliant* into the sea and swell. I could not continue on course until the weather moderated.

On the last day of May, the cyclone passed within 150 miles. It continued to be very rough, but I felt the worst was over. I had asked Selco to send the *Salvanquish* to assist me, once she had delivered her tow.

Just as we were beginning to feel that things were getting better, the starboard engine packed up again. I was back to one engine. The weather was still very bad, but we were making about half a knot, which was better than going backwards.

'Proceed to Kadmat Island at best speed and salve the *Pacificoeverett*,' said the message that the radio officer handed me.

I laughed. I was trying to keep clear of the islands and was unsure of my position, with the coast of India under my lee. What a difference from our passage up. The Admiralty Sailing Directions for the west coast of India were not encouraging. The Laccadive Islands are low and not easily seen, even with their coconut trees, and that is in fine weather. They should be avoided and, to make matters worse, there was no anchorage at Kadmat Island, only at Andrott Island, which was sixty miles to the east-south-east.

I set course from my estimated position and headed for Kadmat Island. The radar was working, but the heavy rain squalls often obliterated any echoes and there was considerable clutter from the rough seas. The weather was beginning to moderate to more normal southwest monsoon conditions. But it remained overcast, with low, scudding clouds, and I still felt enveloped in a tent.

Early in the morning of 2 June, an echo was seen on the radar. Kadmat Island, I thought. But no, I was sixty miles from my estimated position and it turned out to be Andrott Island. The anchorage was not sheltered enough to leave the *Majmaa* in the prevailing bad weather. I went in close enough to see the beach lined with local inhabitants, obviously wondering what apparition was looming out of the murk. I headed back to Kadmat Island, arriving the next evening, having averaged about one and a half knots.

Kadmat Island lies north-north-east / south-south-west. It is about six miles long and only three cables wide, lying to the east side of a coral atoll, which extends two cables to the north. The village is situated in the centre. The east coast, clear of the narrow fringing reef, is steep to, as is the west coast, clear of the atoll. Once I had made Kadmat, I slow-steamed in the lee of the island overnight, the smooth water making a welcome change. There was still quite a swell, even in the lee.

I called up the casualty on the VHF, wondering if she was still manned, or had been abandoned.

'The generator is still working and the engine room is dry,' reported the master.

'Are you loaded,' I asked, hopefully.

'No, in ballast, we are a reefer ship,' came the reply.

'What happened?' I asked.

'No sights and the cyclone: we ran aground at her full speed of 15 knots. The waves were breaking right over us,' he told me.

'OK, I will try and come on board tomorrow,' I told him.

'We are very pleased, very happy you are here,' he said.

What he thought I was going to do, with a sick tug towing a 40,000-ton storage tanker, I did not know – but I would worry about that the next day.

I plotted the position he had given me. The *Pacificoeverett* was on the windward, or west side of Kadmat Island, exposed to the full force of the southwest monsoon. What the cyclone had started, I thought the monsoon would finish off. I was not hopeful of a successful salvage. No wonder I had not seen her on the reef, for we had come up on the opposite side of the island.

The next morning it was still raining and blowing hard. I studied the north end of the island through our powerful binoculars, having timed our steaming in the lee to be

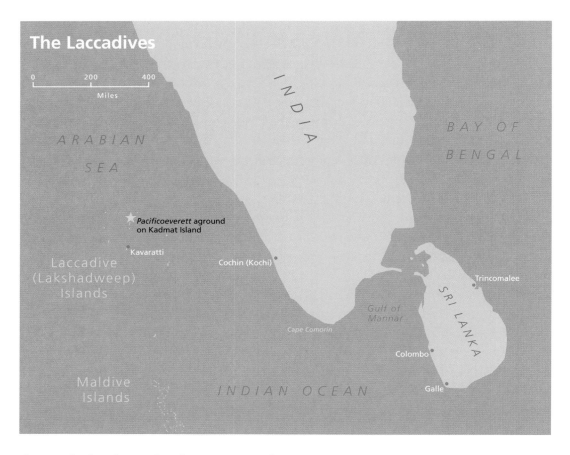

The Laccadives

0 200 400
Miles

INDIA

ARABIAN

SEA

BAY OF
BENGAL

Pacificoeverett aground
on Kadmat Island

Kavaratti

Laccadive
(Lakshadweep)
Islands

Cochin (Kochi)

Trincomalee

SRI LANKA

Gulf of
Mannar

Cape Comorin

Colombo

Maldive
Islands

INDIAN OCEAN

Galle

there at daybreak. Towing the *Majmaa* with turns every two or so hours required constant vigilance and tending of the tow wire. It was essential to keep it well greased, so it was not damaged. Luckily, I had an excellent crew.

A passage was reported through the reef, but I could not see any break in the very heavy surf. The only thing to do was to go and have a look in the Z-boat. The only way I was going to be able to get on board the casualty was from the reef itself. There was no way we could approach from the windward or outer side of the reef.

I called for volunteers, and took one fitter to look after the outboard engine and two divers, making four including myself – quite enough in the prevailing conditions. The Z-boat was launched when the tug and tow were back in the lee of the island. It was still raining, overcast, gloomy and blowing, but it was reasonably warm. Jesus the mate was left in charge and I headed for the reported position of the passage. The *Majmaa* looked huge from sea level, a great black hulk.

The heavy ocean swell swept round the edge of the reef, which projected north of the island, causing very heavy surf on the lee side. We could hear the thump, like artillery fire, as the waves hit the reef and broke in a seething cauldron of white, swirling water. It looked ominous in the murky weather. The soft-bottomed Z-boat was not the best craft in which to play around a reef; a hard-bottomed boat would have been much better and safer. But we had to make do with what we had.

We found what we thought might be the passage. There were occasions when a wave did not break, and every now and then a smooth, unbroken patch would appear with surf on either side. It seemed to be about every six or seven rollers, but it could not be guaranteed. Sometimes it happened, sometimes not. However, after watching for half an hour, I decided it might be possible. Had I got it wrong it would be curtains for us all. If the Z-boat was swamped and we were swept onto the reef, we would be torn to pieces by the coral.

'I'm going to have a go,' I informed my crew. 'Does anyone want to go back to the tug?'

There was no answer from anyone.

'OK, we will try,' I said, my voice thin with tension. It was not quite fear, otherwise I would not have attempted it, but I was apprehensive that I might get it wrong. If I got it right, I knew we would be OK.

I waited just outside the surf line, with the thump and crump of the waves breaking on the reef loud in our ears. The air was full of spray, blown back by the monsoon. There was no shelter from Kadmat Island itself, only the reef protruding north of the island, and the Z-boat lurched up and down in the heavy swell.

When the right moment occurred, I opened the throttle of the 50-hp Johnson outboard wide. The Z-boat leapt forward and I headed in towards what I thought was the passage at full speed. The Z-boat spun along the swell, her hull planing on the water. My heart was in my mouth and I could not see the faces of my crew, only their tense backs. The water ahead looked quite good, a smooth patch among the surf. I then made a mistake: I looked astern. A great surging, breaking wave was following us, the white spume bursting from its crest. It was too late to turn back – we had to outrun the wave or die.

Then, quite suddenly, the boat was in the smooth water of the lagoon and the crew was whooping and laughing, the men slapping each other on the back. Everything seemed bright, as though the sun had come out, but it was still raining and overcast.

'We've done it, Cap,' laughed one of the divers.

I throttled back, almost sick with relief.

'I don't know how we get out again,' I said.

The cloud-covered sky and rain made it extremely difficult to see the coral shoals in the lagoon. I posted a lookout standing in the bow, holding on to the painter, and headed for the now-visible *Pacificoeverett*. She was sitting almost completely high and dry on the edge of the reef. Every now and then, a wave would hit the hull, the spray leaping high over the bridge and accommodation. She was a conventional ship with three hatches forward and two aft of the bridge, with a single funnel situated in the middle of the white superstructure.

My heart sank. Even if I found a way to ditch the *Majmaa*, I did not see how I could make a connection. She was on a dead lee shore, almost inside the surf line. There was a heavy sea and swell running and I only had one engine working. On top of that, she seemed to be miles out of her draught and her captain had told me she was in ballast, so there was no cargo to jettison. The situation appeared no better the closer we approached, and the boom of the waves hitting the hull was more pronounced.

It became too shallow for the Z-boat some distance from the casualty. I did not want to risk piercing the hull or wrecking the propeller. We had to be able to get back to the tug. We found a suitable spot and anchored her in a sand pool, clear of the coral.

We walked the rest of the distance to the casualty in the shallows over coral and sand. It was deeper close by the ship and the water swirled around the bow as the waves hit her, causing a strong current to run aft back into the surf. The crew was lining the bulwark by a pilot ladder, and a lifebuoy attached to a line floated abaft it. I swam the short distance across the channel, starting well forward. I did not want to miss the pilot ladder and be swept into the surf astern. I reached it safely and climbed aboard, followed by my crew.

Spray was sweeping the foredeck as I was led into the accommodation and up to meet the captain. I instructed my men to sound round the ship over the sides for the depth of water.

The captain was very pleased to see me and told me about the grounding, the waves beating against his cabin windows. Looking out, all I could see through the rain was the angry sea, the rollers capped with white and falling onto the reef. She had discharged her cargo in the Persian Gulf and was on her way back to the Philippines. It was night. They had not had sights for days. It was very rough, the cyclone being quite close. There had been a heavy rain squall so nothing had shown up on the radar. One moment they were steaming at full speed, the next there had been a terrible crash and she suddenly stopped, high and dry on the reef. As the captain spoke, sipping his tea, the ship occasionally shuddered as an extra-large wave hit her.

The captain told me that two double-bottom tanks were flooded, the coral having pierced the hull. However, the holds and engine room were dry. When my divers reported their findings, I realised the ship was doomed. There was no hope of refloating her. She was feet out of her draught; it was almost as if she had surfed in on a huge wave. It would require more than 1,000 tons to be offloaded, but there was nothing to discharge except a couple of hundred tons of fuel and water. It would be incredibly difficult, if not impossible, to connect a tug, even a manoeuvrable one, in the present conditions. The bottom was already holed and with the pounding she was taking from the southwest monsoon, it would not be long before the tanks were breached and then, perhaps, the engine room.

I made encouraging remarks to the captain as we made our inspection of the holds and engine room. The freezer insulation dulled the noise of the waves hitting the hull. I wanted to keep up his morale while I reported back to Singapore and decided what best to do. On the bridge, the view was spectacular, with the reef stretched out ahead, culminating in the green of the palm trees on the island. To seaward was raging water. The rain had stopped.

It was almost noon when we headed back to the Z-boat, and there was the first break in the clouds for many days. What a difference the sun made. I thought it prudent to make my number with the village headman, so headed for the centre of the island. It was much easier to see the coral dangers in the sunlight.

We landed on a sandy beach backed with coconut trees, the palms rustling in the wind, a tropical paradise. People had gathered on the beach to watch us. As I walked up the beach from the boat, people kept touching my bare arms. Something held me back from telling them to stop. There was an odd look in their faces, which I could not fathom – a look of wonder, almost of awe.

'What's it like to be Jesus Christ Superstar?' asked Elmo, one of the divers.

'What are you talking about?' I said, surprised.

'Don't you realise? They don't seem to have seen a white man before,' he replied.

And so it turned out. I was the first white man to have landed on the islands for over thirty years – since independence, in fact.

We were taken along a path through the coconut trees, brown hands still touching my white skin, to the village. I explained why I was there to the headman, who spoke English. He had received a radio message about us. The administrator of all the Laccadive Islands lived on Kavaratti, some fifty or so miles southwards. He was due to visit Kadmat on the monthly supply ship.

The sun was fully out when we made our way back across the lagoon to the passage. The bright sunshine lifted our spirits. At the entrance to the boat passage, I turned against the strong current flowing out of the lagoon to watch. It appeared much worse than when we came in, the surf dazzling in the sunlight. It was continuous. Every wave was breaking. There were no gaps. We were trapped.

After watching for half an hour, I decided to land on the northern edge of the island. We found our way into the beach and pulled the Z-boat ashore. It was essential I got back to the tug. We started to carry the boat and engine along the beach to see if we could find a way to the sea in the lee of the island. While carrying the dinghy, some people came out from the coconut trees and greeted us, offering to help carry the boat. I accepted gratefully, for it was heavy work carrying her, loaded with the engine and fuel. We all shook hands and they grabbed hold of the boat.

'Who are you, and what do you do,' I asked.

'We are lepers and live at this end of the island,' the leader of the group replied.

To my eternal shame, I dropped my hold on the boat and, followed by my crew, ran into the water. The boat landed on the beach as the lepers all fell about laughing.

'Don't worry, you won't catch anything,' they cried.

Returning from the water we all, laughing and joking, carried the boat about half a mile along the coast. The lepers took us to a spot where there was a gap in the reef and we launched and returned to the tug, grateful for their help. The *Majmaa* did not look so formidable in the sunshine. I was extremely glad of a hot shower, cold drink and air conditioning while reflecting upon my experiences of the day. It was something quite outside the realms of fantasy, the island and its people in a time warp, my tug with all her modern comforts.

I wrote out a long report justifying why I thought the *Pacificoeverett* was a total loss and why she was not a salvageable proposition. It was sent by radio to Singapore. I also asked the question, 'What do we do if we have touched lepers?'

The reply was 'Don't touch,' which was not very helpful.

Selco confirmed that *Salvanquish* was on her way to assist me. There were suggestions that we transfer an air compressor onto the casualty to blow the flooded tanks. However, I knew she was finished and did nothing.

The weather moderated and it was possible to use the boat passage both ways. I visited the casualty every day and each time the situation was worse, another tank breached. Finally, there was a leak in the engine room and the captain was visibly drooping as he realised his ship was finally doomed. There was nothing he could do to save her.

Salvanquish

One evening, a longboat built of wood and propelled by oars came out to the *Salvaliant*, which was still towing the *Majmaa* up and down in the lee of the island. Two smartly dressed policemen with highly polished boots came on board and inspected the tug. After permitting me a suitable allowance, they put a seal on the bond. After tea and a chat (it was amazing how, in the middle of nowhere, people spoke English), they told me I should come ashore and visit the administrator. He had arrived on the monthly supply ship, which was hanging off the island. It was too deep for her to anchor. I changed into suitable gear and went with them.

Even in the lee of the middle of the east coast, there was surf. An occasional star appeared through the clouds as we were rowed ashore. Near the reef, the helmsman with the steering oar held the boat off until a suitable moment occurred. He then gave a sharp order. The men all rowed at full strength, straining at their oars, digging the blades deep into the water. The boat leapt forward as a wave lifted her stern and she surfed in over the reef. The helmsman kept her pointing at the shore so she did not broach, until she landed on the beach. The oarsmen all jumped out into the water and lifted the boat, carrying her up the beach with me still on board. I stepped onto the dry sand.

I was taken to a hut where I met the administrator, a charming and well-educated man. He had been to university in Paris. It seemed utterly unreal to be talking about Paris on a tropical island hundreds of miles off the Indian coast, surrounded by people whose only life was the island and where anyone under the age of 30 had never seen a white man.

Over suitable refreshments, which I had brought with me, we discussed, and I obtained permission to abandon the *Pacificoeverett*. I enlisted the islanders' assistance for evacuating the crew. After a most enjoyable evening, I returned to the beach. It was dark, but the moon was up. I was invited to climb on board while the boat was still on the beach. The crew then lifted and carried her into the water on the reef. While one man held the bow, the crew boarded and shipped oars, the helmsman standing in the stern. The helmsman gave the order and the men all pulled. A wave lifted the bow, and the bowman climbed on board. Another order, the crew strained at the oars, and then the boat shot out and was clear of the surf before the next wave broke.

As we rowed out, the crew began singing. One man sang a verse and the rest joined in the chorus. They kept perfect time, the oars dipping in unison and the boat riding the swells.

'What are they singing about?' I asked.

'They are singing your praises, how skilled you are to have brought this great black monster to the island and are going to save the men on the ship,' was the reply. I felt I had got into H G Wells' time machine and gone back a hundred years. It was something straight out of Kipling. The craft had not changed in centuries, nor had the method of propulsion.

The *Majmaa* looked huge and ghostly in the moonlight as we approached the *Salvaliant*. I said goodbye to the crew and they left for the shore, the sound of their singing diminishing as they drew away.

A week later, the *Salvanquish* arrived with the elderly surveyor from the insurers of the *Pacificoeverett*. She had called in at Cochin to pick him up. I joined the *Salvanquish* and Peter the captain steamed the tug round to look at the casualty from the sea. It only served to emphasise the extreme difficulty of making a towing connection in the prevailing monsoon. Once back in the lee of Kadmat Island, I took the surveyor in the Z-boat to the ship. I accompanied him on his inspection and, within the hour, he had declared her a total loss. We told the captain to prepare to abandon the next day.

We went to the village and arranged with the headman, the administrator having continued his inspection of the islands in the supply ship, for the evacuation.

The next morning, when we arrived at the casualty, the abandonment was in full swing. Half a dozen boats were close by and the crew and islanders were loading luggage. The crew was taken to the landing by the villagers and their luggage carried across the island to waiting boats on the other side, from where they were rowed out to the *Salvaliant*. I

The divers temporarily sealed the leak, while I entertained the jovial harbour master. He was particularly partial to my dwindling supply of Mateus Rosé – and luckily the divers finished before the supply ran out.

Mogadishu was utterly chaotic and I had to take a taxi everywhere, it not being safe for a European to walk. My crew enjoyed the night life, despite the chaos, but I was glad to get away to Mombassa.

Nobby had flown over from Singapore, and with the help of the local salvage company, who no doubt wanted us away as quickly as possible, managed to have the *Salvaliant* dry-docked. Permanent repairs were made and the hull cleaned and painted. I spent a few very enjoyable days sailing a hired dinghy round the harbour, and then we left to continue the voyage to South Africa.

Mahavel
Failure on Europa Island

FROM *LLOYD'S WEEKLY CASUALTY REPORTS*, 1976

Mahavel **(French) – Reunion, July 28** – Trawler *Mahavel* grounded Europa Island 0500, July 19, and abandoned the same day by crew. Shipowner and Administrator of Maritime Affairs flew to Europa in a military aircraft on July 23 and returned to St Denis July 24 with skipper and crew.

I was approaching Europa Island from the north and it was early morning. The star position I had just plotted on the chart told me I still had thirty-odd miles to go. The radar was on, but I could see no sign of the island, not that I expected to until I was about fifteen miles off. I settled down, wedging my chair against the heavy movement of the tug in the rough conditions, to re-read the pilot book.

Europa Island, position 22 20 S, 40 21 E, is a French possession in the Mozambique Channel about sixty miles southeast of Bassas da India, a submerged reef with two wrecks on it, and 160 miles from the western coast of Madagascar.

There was no large-scale chart of the island, but from the largest-scale chart available, Lourenço Marques to Durban, it appeared like a one-clawed crab, the northern claw missing. It was about four miles by four miles, making for an island circumference of about 11 miles. I was not too worried about the vegetation, being more concerned with the reef, which encircles the island. The pilot book states, 'A coral reef, which dries, extends up to half a mile from the northern coast of the island: the reef is fringed by a narrow bank, with depths of from 11 to 14 fathoms seawards, of which the depths increase rapidly. A six-foot shoal lies two cables off the edge of the reef, one and three quarter miles northeastwards of Pointe Nord Ouest.'

I felt quite nostalgic reading the French name for North West Point. Memories of a meal at Henri's (the old Hotel Normandie for the uninitiated) or the Café de Paris in Cherbourg floated across my mind, and I had to re-read it. There was such a heavy swell running that I was pretty certain it would break at any depth too low for the tug, so I was not too worried about the shoal – but of course one could never be absolutely sure.

The pilot book continued: 'The western side of the island is rocky and appears to be steep to; the eastern side consists of low, steep cliffs, and also appears to be steep to. The southern side is low, and the limits of the fringing reef are little known; as it is usually a lee shore, it should be given a wide berth.'

Well, I thought, not exactly a yachtsman's paradise. I felt rather like an explorer, and I was pretty certain I would have to go round onto the south side. The currents were also reported to run strongly, according to the pilot book, 'causing ripples, eddies and, in some places, almost a race, and are very variable, both in direction and rate, rendering constant observation necessary to check the vessel's position. HMS *Flying Fish* in 1875 found the current setting northwestwards.'

Here I am, relying on information that is 100 years old, and the Americans are exploring Mars!

The pilot book continued:

> There is no secure anchorage off Ile Europa. It is possible, however, to anchor near the edge of the reef fringing the northern coast of the island, sheltered from a southerly swell, in a depth of around 11 fathoms, but there is no room to swing in the event of a shift in wind, and the holding ground is very poor; this anchorage is approached with the flagstaff bearing 180 degrees ... these anchorages are precarious, and a vessel using them should be prepared to weigh at any time.

In other words, make a small mistake and end up a casualty yourself.

After reading these sobering remarks, with the wind blowing force seven from the south, the old tug labouring, pitching and rolling in the rough sea and heavy southerly swell, seas breaking over the foredeck and spray over the bridge even though I was at half speed, I felt like quietly heaving-to and giving the whole thing a miss. One has to be absolutely certain that there are not going to be any breakdowns when playing around on lee shores in rough weather and strong currents. An engine or steering failure would be fatal and, of course, we were completely on our own. No assistance of any sort was available.

Remembering that we were a salvage tug, and warming to the bright, fresh day as the sun came up, I increased speed to go and have a look in the lee. The least I could do was have a quiet lunch. I had not been given the position of the fishing boat that was aground, but I was pretty certain it would not be on the northern shore – that would be too easy!

I duly picked up the island on the radar, where it should be, and headed for the northwestern side, where the flagstaff and huts for the meteorological station were situated. I slowed down as I approached the reef, the swell rapidly going down as I steamed into the lee. I took the tug in close to the reef at slow speed and saw the French flag flying through the big binoculars. The northern shore was calm, although there was light surf breaking over the reef. I continued skirting the reef.

Pointe Nord Ouest was a different matter altogether. In a heavy, southerly ocean swell, we suddenly came upon a reef perpendicular to a depth of 1,700 fathoms, and the effect was startling, yes, even awesome. There was no gradual build-up. From a swell it dramatically and immediately became a great breaking, rolling surf, the top falling over itself and surging across the reef in a cauldron of white spume and spray, finally spending itself high on the beach. Nothing could survive that moving mass of water: once in surf like that, it would be the end. The spume and spray severely restricted visibility on the reef, so I had to move in close to the surf to look for the fishing boat.

The wind was southerly, so on this part of the coast, in the event of a breakdown, I would float clear – hopefully. I was close enough to hear the continuous roar of the breaking water on the reef and the heavy gun-like thump as each swell fell on the reef, a continuous reminder of the danger the tug was in. There appeared to be a strong current flowing along the reef but I felt pretty certain that the current would not set me onto, but along the reef. As long as I remained outside the line of breakers, the tug was OK.

The echo sounder was on all the time and continually watched by an officer, but I recorded no depth anywhere along the coast, excepting the north. This meant of course that, in an emergency, the anchors would be no use, and the tug would be into the surf and onto the reef before the anchors touched bottom. If I found the fishing boat, this presented big problems in making the connection. The tug being single-screwed, it was not possible to hold her in one place for very long. I would have to get close enough to the casualty to get a line across (too far, and

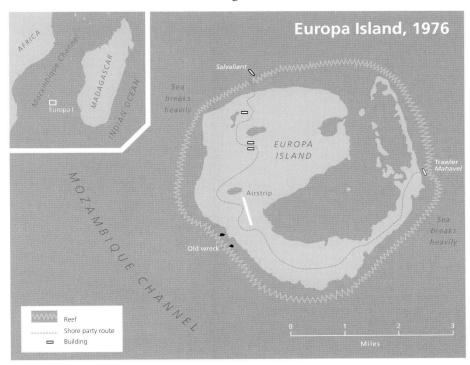

the weight of the tow line would be too much to haul across by hand), but far enough off to give a little time to drift while the wire was pulled across. I could not be too close; if the head fell off I would need room to stop the swing, because if she became broadside-on there would be no room to turn before entering the surf. There was the ever-present danger, during all this, of getting the line round the propeller. If I could have anchored it would have been just too easy, with no danger of getting the line round the propeller. My mouth felt dry, and lots of little butterflies were working in my stomach as I thought of the prospect, and wondered if I was not some sort of lunatic.

However, everything was working and the usual familiarity with the situation breeds not contempt, I hoped – for I had an ever-increasing respect for the sea – but an attitude of 'It's not so bad, I might as well have a go.' I steamed closer until I was just outside the line of breakers, close enough to see the pit-like effect of the swell on the edge of the reef; the undertow must have been tremendous. At times, where the reef jutted out, the tug was inside the line of breakers. Before hauling out, I could see the whole mass, the moving wall of water in a line, with the top curling over in a sheet of white, the wind blowing the spume of the breakers ahead of the surf itself. It was an incredible sight and I wished I had invested in a good camera and zoom lens.

I had the best man at the wheel, for I was on hand-steering – the gyro compass had packed up some months ago and so the automatic pilot did not work. The magnetic compass was difficult to see in daylight, being one of those Japanese periscope types; we had to rig a box around the periscope so the card could be seen. The 'oohs' and 'aahs' of the two officers on the bridge with me as a particularly large swell came thundering in confirmed that the whole thing was not just my fevered imagination.

I followed the configuration of the coast, altering to port all the time to keep close. On the south coast I pulled off just a little, a couple of hundred feet, as the wind was blowing right onshore. We saw the first wreck on the beach, a shapeless mass of metal partly obscured by the continuous mist generated by the surf. Then we saw another, further to seaward, on the reef itself. The reef here was not very wide, maybe a few hundred yards. We were still too far off to distinguish exactly what they were, but if one was the fishing boat, she was finished.

As soon as I was close enough, I slowed to dead slow and had a good look through the big binoculars. It was not two wrecks, but one. She was heading straight onto the beach, or at least the stern was, but the whole forecastle was 200 feet away to the west. It was on its side, jagged plates sticking out where it had been torn off the vessel and flung high onto the beach. It must have been some storm because, bad though the surf was, it was not breaking over the forepart now and, as I discovered later, it was about half-tide. She must have gone aground at night and the crew must have had a rude awakening! She had been a fishing boat but was quite obviously not salvable.

Maybe there's another one, I thought, as I increased speed to continue the search. The south and east coasts of the island were totally exposed to the southerly, or more like south-south-easterly, swell and wind. It was still blowing force six and *Salvaliant* was rolling heavily, occasionally kicking up dollops of spray to remind me she was still alive, not a series of broken, twisted and tortured lumps of metal strewn on a barren and inhospitable shore.

Along the east coast, the reef extended further out from the shore, about half a mile. There was nothing on the reef but about halfway along it curved into the shore and close inside the line of breakers there was a fishing boat – and in one piece too. She was a typical French deep-sea fisherman, the sort we see off the French coast steaming at full speed to and from the fishing grounds, with a great, long, rounded forecastle, square bridge and accommodation.

I continued altering to port along the edge of the reef. There was a faint possibility that she was not too badly damaged. Where the reef curved northwestwards to a distance of about 100 yards off the shore, it formed a small bay, which gave some – not much, but some – protection. Also, she was not yet broadside on but at 45 degrees to the prevailing swell.

I did not know how long she had been there, but it did not look too long, so there seemed to be a chance.

I slowed right down and headed in towards her. I had strictly instructed the officer watching the echo sounder (the wretched thing was placed in the chartroom, so I was unable to watch it myself when manoeuvring in close like this) to shout the second he saw anything resembling a sounding. If it shoaled, it would shoal quickly. The fishing boat appeared almost high and dry until a large swell came in, broke on the reef edge and

The trawler *Mahavel* on the reef at Europa Island, from *Salvaliant*

whirled along the starboard side, the top just going on board. She rolled. Before the swell she was listing about five degrees to starboard, but when the swell hit her she came almost upright and then, as the swell spent itself on the shore, she rolled back to her original position. I was now close enough to hear the slam as she rolled back, her two fishing derricks, which were swung out, rattling along with the unlocked doors.

'Well, that's it,' I said to no one in particular, 'she won't have a bottom left.'

'It looks like sand,' said one of the divers.

'Maybe, but she cannot last long pounding like that,' I replied. 'We'll go and have a look.'

'We can't land in that surf,' said the youngest diver in a strangled voice.

'No, you'd be walking,' I replied.

I closed as near as I dared, still with no sounding, the sound of the surf loud in my ears, the bang, rattle and thump of the dying fishing boat an all-too-continuous reminder of disaster. At last I'd had enough and went hard a-starboard and full ahead to haul off. About half a mile off I stopped and let her drift. I had not lost all hope and I wanted to see whether it was going to be possible to make a connection. The wind slowly blew the tug onshore, while the current pushed her south at first, then stationary, and finally, when close to, north. Though the current, as I thought, did not appear to push onshore, the wind did, and not being able to anchor would mean that making a connection would be very difficult. However, if the wind and swell went down a little, I was quite hopeful that I could do it. I felt quite certain that, once connected, I could pull her off. Unfortunately, there was not much point in pulling her off if she promptly sank, so the next task was to find out how badly damaged she was. If only one or two compartments were flooded, it might be possible to tow her round with pumps on board and beach her on the north coast. There was no possibility of doing much patching where she was unless the swell dramatically reduced, and there was not much chance of that happening. No real attempt had been made to batten her down, and the accommodation doors were open, so no doubt the water had damaged the interior. An attempt had obviously been made to get gear off, as some of it was on the shore.

The shoreline consisted of first a reef, and then a low rocky cliff. There was no beach as such. A tripod arrangement had been rigged ashore, and it looked as though they had removed some of the stores by a breeches buoy system. The stores had been left, because I could see them. A deflated life raft lay just above the high water mark, and further up there were the remains of a lifeboat.

I had seen enough. I could not make any further decisions before I knew the state of the hull, and I was not very hopeful, even if she was on sand. In fact the whole thing seemed like a washout. Even if I did get her off, I would have a long tow through possibly bad weather before reaching South Africa. There would not be much point in taking her to Lourenço Marques or Beira in Mozambique: the newly installed Communists would not be very interested, and there was always the possibility they would throw me in jail on some pretext. The Prime Minister of Madagascar had just been killed, so I did not think much of them either. That left South Africa, which at least had repair facilities, but it was a long way. The salved value of a fishing boat would not be very large, but it might be just worth it if the hull was not too badly damaged.

I continued round the island along the north coast, where it was calm. I searched for a suitable beaching place, but there didn't seem to be anywhere that was even half-suitable. There was one place off the entrance to the lagoon, which would be worth investigating in the Z-boat. There was a small bay in the reef.

The lagoon was enclosed by the crab claw and its seaward entrance was sealed by the reef. There was no opening at all along the north coast, so it would not be possible to enter the lagoon except by Z-boat across the reef at high water. This was disappointing (although not surprising from my perusal of the pilot book), because there was no safe place to anchor, let alone beach a casualty.

I closed the reef with the white hut of the met station bearing 180 degrees true, just drifting in. I could see the edge of the reef quite clearly as suddenly the echo sounder showed 20 metres when I was about a hundred feet off. The wind was offshore, so I was pointing at right angles to the reef, heading into the now light breeze.

I went astern and gave the order to let go the anchor. They were not quick enough, and the anchor fell off the edge of the reef. I tried again, with more success.

I was finally anchored, with the engine on instant notice. The sun was out, it was warm on the lee side of the bridge, the white sandy beach looked inviting, and obviously the mating turtles close by thought it was a nice day too! No sooner were we anchored than the first fishing lines were over the side: the fishing would be good. If nothing else, I would spend a pleasant and interesting day. Not many Englishmen have been to Europa Island.

I enjoyed my pre-lunch aperitif sitting in the sun, watching the tug. The crew was getting the big Z-boat ready. The vessel seemed quite safe, her bow pointing into the reef and the wind strong enough to overcome the slight east-going current. If there was any change, I would have to move out quickly as there was no room to swing and it would not be very helpful to put the stern on the reef.

After lunch, I went ashore. Although it looked calm enough, the swell on the reef was surprisingly large, and the one thing I did not want to do was damage the boat or the engine. As soon as we were in wading depth, I jumped out with one crew and sent the boat back to the tug. Looking back, the tug seemed large, anchored so close in.

We waded ashore across the partly exposed reef to the beach. The reef was dead and the coral life was not interesting. We walked up to a large concrete hut-like structure, but no one was in the radio room or mess hall. The hut stood on a small hummock and, looking inland, I could see some square barrack-like buildings and two men outside playing *boules*. We followed the track to the encampment but the two men were intent on their game.

'*Parlez-vous anglais?*' I asked politely in my best schoolboy French, when we were close.

'*Non,*' one of the men answered, continuing with the game.

Not very friendly, I thought, as Europa Island was hardly a usual port of call.

'*Où est votre capitaine?*' I asked.

The one who had answered pointed to a hut, so we set off to walk the short distance. The two had been so intent on their game that they had not even looked up. We could have been Martians for all they knew or cared.

I was about to enter the hut when another half-naked Frenchman (rig of the day appeared to be bathing costumes) saw me and called me inside. We were led in and sat down at a table laden with the remains of a meal. The *capitaine* spoke no English and my schoolboy French is pathetic, to say the least. However, the following story emerged.

The island was manned permanently by three meteorologists, who did fifty-day stints. Sometimes thirty or forty military personnel were landed for a thirty-day maintenance tour for the airstrip and buildings. There were no officers, and I assumed the man in charge was the equivalent of a sergeant. The Army and Met men did not seem to mix much, and the Army people appeared to be having a good time. The island is a prohibited area, but permission had been given for us to land (not that I knew anything about it). All personnel changes were made by air, using the airstrip in the middle of the island. No ships called, and there were no boats of any sort on the island.

The *Mahavel* had gone ashore at night at full speed on 18 July; it was now 31 July. The sergeant had produced some *anisette* to lace my coffee while Edgar, my first officer, who drank very little, was given a cup of neat whisky. The French military had been over to the wreck, to get the booze on board, I suspect, and the sergeant said the bottom had a hole in it. Evidently a supply boat had turned up on the 22nd but had not landed anyone, spending only a couple of hours before departing. A director of the company owning the fishing boat had arrived by air and left again, taking the crew with him to La Réunion. He had obviously not thought much of the chances of salvage, but the sergeant thought it would be quite easy to land from the sea.

He obviously did not know much about the sea. I offered to take him round to have a look from the sea on the tug, if he would take me by land the next day. He agreed but intimated that, as he was a military man, it wasn't difficult for him as he was used to walking, but he did not think I would make it! I said I would take my chances, and suggested we go to the tug then so that we could be back before dark. I steamed at full speed round to the *Mahavel*.

We arrived back at the anchorage just as the sun was setting and got the French ashore before it was dark. It was high tide now, and the Z-boat was able to go over the top of the reef to the beach.

By the time the Z-boat was back, it was quite dark. I was sitting on the bridge enjoying the quiet of the evening, the stars shining brightly in the deep blackness of the night sky. The air was crystal clear and clean. Close as we were to the shore, it was just possible, though difficult, to make out the shoreline in the starlight. The sea was calm and there was no swell in the anchorage. Half a mile to the west, off Pointe Nord Ouest, I could just see the whiteness of the surf and faintly hear the roar as it broke on the reef.

I retired for dinner and an early bed, enjoying half a bottle of Mateus Rosé with my freshly caught red snapper, chicken to follow, and a selection of Grieg on the tape recorder to remind me of Norway.

I came onto the bridge at 0400. It was calm, the sky was clear and the stars were still shining brightly, Orion and his belt with Sirius, one of the brightest stars in the heavens, clear to the southeast, past Madagascar to the wild open wastes of the Southern Ocean and Antarctica. The sea was mirror-calm and the tug was steady. Standing on the bridge wing, I could just see white, but it was not surf, it was the almost pure white beach that stretches along the whole northern coast of Europa Island. I could just hear the surf on Pointe Nord Ouest, very faint in the early morning quiet.

At 0600 I heaved up the anchor, and we made our rather leisurely way round to the wreck. High water would be just after 0700. There were no tide tables, but having been off the island for nearly 24 hours, it was not very difficult to make my own predictions.

Once clear of the east point of the island, we were up in the swell, but it was much reduced. I was surprised at how quickly the ocean swell had gone down. Once off the wreck, I stopped the engines and let the tug drift. There was no wind, and with the reduced swell it would be quite possible to make a connection. It was now high water and it quickly became evident that the hull was flooded. She appeared to be at her light draught, or a little less. She rolled with the bigger swells hitting her starboard side, the water rushing over her decks, through her accommodation, and cascading down her sides as the water withdrew and the next swell came whirling in. She rolled, but with that sluggish, waterlogged roll that told me she was dead. All that was left now was to find out how badly the hull was damaged and whether she was worth patching.

I was not very hopeful. I steamed back to the anchorage, breakfasting in the warm sunlight once anchored.

By 0900 a light breeze was blowing from the west, which meant the anchorage was exposed. There was a poor forecast for Durban East, which was south of us, and I felt I should not leave the tug for some six hours. Our walkie-talkies were also out of action, which meant that I would be out of communication as well. It would be quite possible for it to blow up and then I would not be able to get back at all. There was no question of swimming as the crew had caught sharks, some of which were over six feet long. Accordingly, the chief officer volunteered to go overland, and I would bring the tug round. They went off dressed in a variety of colourful clothing and hats, knapsacks filled with food, looking more like a bunch of pirates than respectable salvors.

Just after noon, I picked up the anchor and slowly steamed round to the *Mahavel*. It was still blowing gently from the west, so it was calm enough. I steamed as close as possible to the reef, relying on the colour changes rather than the echo sounder to warn me of shallow patches. The small bay I had noticed before looked quite promising providing the wind remained in the south or west.

I arrived off the wreck just after 1300 and the shore party appeared soon after. It was a lovely day, the sun was warm, the sea rippled in the light westerly breeze, which made this shore a windward one. The swell was still coming in from the south-south-east but was down even more since the morning.

I watched Edgar and two of the divers climb on board the *Mahavel*, using lines which were hanging down from the bow. I don't think they even got their feet wet! I went in as close as I could, stern-first and just one swell clear of the reef, hoping that Edgar would have the sense to take a photograph.

After about half an hour I departed back to the anchorage, and at sunset a very bedraggled looking party turned up, having had to walk all the way back. They were stiff from having employed unused muscles but had brought back a lot of gulls' eggs, of which I am inordinately fond, as they were.

Edgar told me that the engine room and all the other compartments were flooded and stank of diesel, the keel had been ripped out and some of the bottom plating was missing.

'OK, she's finished,' I said, 'let's get under way.'

So we picked up the anchor and slowly steamed clear of the island in the dark while the tug battened down. The next day it blew hard from the southeast.

The rest of the voyage to Cape Town was uneventful – but the ensuing weeks were not.

Ville de Mahebourg
A first in the Southern Ocean

FROM *LLOYD'S WEEKLY CASUALTY REPORTS*, 1976

Ville de Mahebourg **(Mauritian)** – Capetown, Aug 13 – *Ville de Mahebourg*: Understand vessel disabled with steering problems at 1630, Aug 11, in lat 36 S, long 18 E. Position at 1330, Aug 12, lat 47 44 S, long 16 48 E, 240 miles SW of Capetown. Vessel presently heading SW at 9 knots without steering control. Salvage tug *Salvaliant* left Saldanha Bay at 1730, Aug 12. – Salvage Association Surveyors.

'I am a European Englishman,' I concluded my arrival message to the agents, Ellerman Lines in South Africa. So many people in new ports came on board assuming that Captain Tew from Singapore must be Chinese or Asian. I did not want any confusion in apartheid South Africa!

I cleared in at Cape Town. The doctor came on board to minister to the 70% of the crew who had caught something from their beautiful, silk-skinned Somali girlfriends. I retired to the Mount Nelson Hotel for a good dinner and a quiet night after the rough weather from Europa Island. I was not feeling 100%.

When leaving the port, I was sick over the pilot's feet. He was not very impressed. I was feeling distinctly ill and contemplated going to the doctor. However, in Saldanha Bay, which is north of Cape Town, I felt a little better and started preparing for the long tow to the Persian Gulf. I expected to be at sea for at least fifty days. The *Salvaliant* was contracted to tow a dredger.

I was feeling ill again and plucked up the courage to go and see the doctor. He said I had flu and gave me antibiotics. Someone turned up and told me a ship was in trouble south of the Cape of Good Hope. It was overcast, cold and dismal weather, but I perked up at the prospect of salvage and made preparations to leave, despite running a high temperature. I phoned Singapore and Alan Bond agreed I should leave on speculation and he would investigate the rumour. It would be a coup for Selco to perform a salvage on the coast of South Africa.

I steamed out of the harbour and ran down the rocky coast past Cape Town. There was indeed a ship in trouble, but so was I, feeling very ill, and I stopped eating as I was unable to hold anything down. Once south of the Cape, the *Salvaliant* was almost in the Roaring Forties, the westerly winds that sweep round the world causing huge seas and bad weather. Tasmania was the next stop to the east, and Tierra del Fuego to the west. The *Ville de Mahebourg* was without a rudder, heading towards Antarctica, holding her bow up into the weather. I raced south at maximum speed, the old girl running in the cold water at over 15 knots, swooping and dancing over the swells, or so it seemed to me. Five hundred miles off the Cape of Good Hope, deep into the Southern Ocean, the sky was overcast and the sea grey. It was dark when I came up on the *Ville de Mahebourg*, slowly making way southwards, and a huge swell was running.

'Do you agree Lloyd's Open Form?' I asked the master on the VHF.

'*Oui*, yes,' came back the reply.

That was sufficient, I had a contract. I had a Lloyd's Open Form in the Southern Ocean. I was elated, as this was a Selco first. Mr K would be pleased, even Mr Bond would be pleased, and I would have one up on Captain Hancox! I just had to be successful.

I would not normally make a connection at night in such bad conditions but I was feeling so odd and ill and light-headed that I decided to try. It was a big, big risk, but I was frightened that if I waited the weather would deteriorate and I might pass out completely.

I was feeling so ill I could barely stand up, and I had not eaten since Saldanha Bay. The captain of the casualty did not want to stop for fear of rolling too heavily when he swung beam-on to the huge swell but I told him he would have to while I connected. I told him I would be as quick as possible and it was up to him to heave in the towing gear fast.

I climbed heavily onto the monkey island and told Edgar, the chief officer, to come

Ville de Mahebourg in the Southern Ocean, seen from Salvaliant

up with a chair and stay with me. Loretto, the second mate, should man the radio. I felt awful, sick and dizzy, but I was determined to connect and tow the *Ville de Mahebourg* to safety. The tug was shipping heavy seas on the tow deck, rolling and pitching. Tough, dependable Javier Patani, the bosun, and wild Pacito de los Reyes, the diver, were standing by on the aft hatch with the crew, looking at me and then at the rolling and pitching casualty.

It was dark, the sky was leaden and gloomy, and I had to get a move on. I decided to take even more of a risk: I knew I could depend on my crew and I guessed I could depend on the crew of the casualty. The question was whether I would last out, sitting in my chair, braced against the movement of the tug. I crossed the bow of the now drifting ship less than 20 feet off and a heaving line thudded onto the tow deck. In a trice, it was made fast to the polypropylene messenger and, with the French crew heaving like madmen, it flew out over the side and up onto the heavily rolling *Ville de Mahebourg*. I gave a kick ahead on the engine, turning the tug parallel to the casualty, the propeller away from the line.

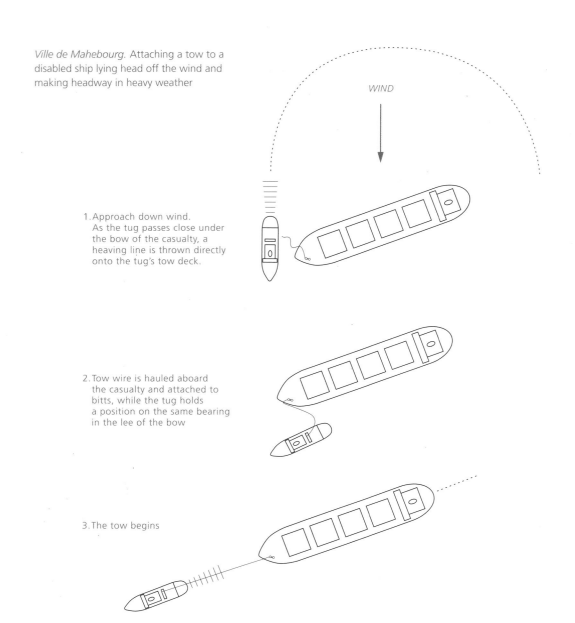

Ville de Mahebourg. Attaching a tow to a disabled ship lying head off the wind and making headway in heavy weather

WIND

1. Approach down wind.
   As the tug passes close under the bow of the casualty, a heaving line is thrown directly onto the tug's tow deck.

2. Tow wire is hauled aboard the casualty and attached to bitts, while the tug holds a position on the same bearing in the lee of the bow

3. The tow begins

The wire pendant forerunner slid over the well-greased gunwale, followed by the nylon stretcher. The tug was still very close to the ship and the wire pendant disappeared through the fairlead on the fo'c'sle of the casualty. Shortly afterwards, the French signalled that they had made fast.

There was a cheer from both tug and tow and I steamed ahead, paying the tow wire out to almost its maximum length. I needed the catenary in the heavy swells. I increased speed and turned north, and when the French told me they had backed up the mooring bitts on which we were towing, I increased to maximum power. The *Ville de Mahebourg* went out to one side and stayed there and we made good speed. The *Salvaliant* being a heavy-displacement tug, it did not matter that the tow was out on the beam. I catnapped in the captain's chair on the bridge, feeling very ill indeed. The connection had taken it out of me and I was having difficulty holding down any liquids so was becoming dehydrated and, at times, hallucinating.

I perked up a bit two days later when I saw Table Mountain, the flat plateau above Cape Town dominating the city, capped by cloud. It was cold and had started to rain when the pilot and tugs came out. I insisted on remaining connected and towed the casualty on short tow to the berth, assisted by the harbour tugs. Once the crew had disconnected and recovered the towing gear, their wet gear dripping with water, I wearily climbed on board the *Ville de Mahebourg*. The captain signed my termination letter, offered me refreshment, which I refused, and I returned to the tug.

I had radioed ahead to the agents for a doctor and he came on board. He agreed that I did not have flu but took some blood and said he would let me know the result the next day. I retired back to the Mount Nelson Hotel for the night.

The next day he confirmed a serious internal problem, and said I should go immediately to hospital. However, this was not possible until my relief arrived. I sailed shortly afterwards for Saldanha Bay and let Edgar take charge, retiring to my bunk. I managed to be on the bridge entering Saldanha Bay and, once alongside, I took a taxi to the local hotel and went to bed. The doctor was called and he confirmed that I should go to hospital straight away. I refused until the relief turned up.

Edgar turned up for instructions, coming into my bedroom. The wife of the owner of

Salvaliant towing *Ville de Mahebourg*

the hotel said that he could not stay: he would have to stand in the corridor because he was coloured. I lost my temper, shouted at her to call the police – Edgar was staying and he was worth a hundred people like her. She retired hurt, but I had no more nonsense. Various crew members turned up to wish me well and told me how much fun they were having in South Africa.

Ebullient, intense, talkative Hughie Murray turned up from Singapore. He was a retired commander from the Navy and mad as a hatter, a bit like a bull in a china shop. However, he was intelligent and got things done, but trod on many toes along the way. I was exceedingly glad to see his large figure, and departed in an ambulance to hospital in Cape Town.

Two months later, I flew back to England.

'What were the riots like?' my mother asked. 'I was worried.'

'What riots, Mum?' It's amazing how the press distort the news.

FROM *LLOYD'S WEEKLY CASUALTY REPORTS*, 1976

Capetown, Aug 16 – Motor vessel *Ville de Mahebourg* lost steering at 1310 Aug 11, and accepted services of salvage tug *Salvaliant* on Lloyd's Open Form, which connected tow at 0015, Aug 14, and arrived Capetown at 1230, Aug 15. Diver inspection shows rudder missing ... Salvage Association's Surveyors.

Città di Savona
Collision in Singapore Harbour

FROM *LLOYD'S WEEKLY CASUALTY REPORTS*, 1976

Vessels in collision at Singapore

Singapore, Oct 27 – *Città di Savona* (fully loaded crude oil) and *Philippine Star* (fully loaded crude oil) were in collision today. *Philippine Star* sustained damage to the bow. It was not known how much crude had leaked from *Città di Savona* but the sea in the vicinity was badly polluted. After the collision *Philippine Star* was in collision with steam tanker *Esso Spain*, empty. A Port of Singapore Authority spokesman reported that *Esso Spain* sustained only superficial damage. Anti-oil pollution craft from the authority, oil refineries and salvage companies went to work immediately. United Press International.

I flew back to Singapore on 17 October 1976 on a strict diet with no alcohol, and instructions to take it easy. It started well, living in a hotel and going to the office each day. I gave evidence to the lawyer for the *Showa Maru* salvage. It was OK if he was in a good mood but not much fun if he was not!

One Sunday, the Chairman, Old Man K, asked me out for lunch in the Mandarin Hotel, which was fun. We then took the Selco motor yacht *Salvalentina* out or, put it like this, the yacht picked us up. We went out to look at a job Selco was doing – an oil rig was being put on a large barge for repairs – and then we went to look at a ship that a Selco tug had towed in. All a bit different from the Solent!

The easy life did not last long.

Thursday 28 October 1976

'Three Tanker Collision: Oil Peril,' screamed the headline on the front page of *The Straits Times*.

> Singapore's pollution fighters scrambled into action again last night in an all-night vigil to mop up the oil gushing out of one of three tankers involved in a collision at the Eastern Anchorage.

> Specialised craft from the PSA and oil and salvage companies were out in full force to prevent threatening oil patches from being swept inward onto Singapore's shores by the currents.

In Darkness

But the unyielding darkness of the night made the operation, carried out with searchlights and the feeble glow of a crescent moon, extremely difficult – and an estimate of the extent of the pollution well-nigh impossible.

Still, the battle continued relentlessly as crew from the various craft placed booms round the fully loaded 36,708 tonne *Città di Savona*, the leaking Italian tanker, to arrest the oil flow.

The triple collision between the *Città di Savona*, the loaded *Philippine Star*, 39,929 tonnes, and the *Esso Spain*, 49,123 tonnes (empty), occurred at about 1630. Only the Italian caused pollution.

The master reported 'My tanker has a massive oil leak. My number five port side tank was ripped open. We are making attempts to patch up the damage.'

On the front page of *The New Nation* was a picture of the *Città di Savona* with a group of people standing on deck above the holes. Included in the group is me, dressed in a boiler suit and boots, hands on hips, head up and looking very satisfied. The female chief officer, wearing a hard hat, is next to me (she was the first female ship's officer I had ever met of any rank – how times have changed!).

Now I will tell you the real story.

It all started one evening at about 1700. Charles Deeney, one of the shore-based salvage officers, just back from study leave in the UK, came into my office – well, the office I had been using.

'There's been a collision in Eastern Anchorage,' he said. '*Salvista* reports that a tanker is leaking oil.' *Salvista* was the old Selco salvage and mooring vessel.

Emergency stations.

Selco's base was on the west side of Singapore Island, so it was about an hour's run to the Eastern Anchorage. Within twenty minutes we were under way at full speed of 15 knots in the Selco crew boat *Salvital*, the tropic night fast drawing in as we rushed through the harbour.

The *Salvista* was on location, and we sent one of the new Selco tugs, *Salvigilant*, to the tanker as well.

Once round at Eastern Anchorage, we could see the tanker, which was pouring out oil as it steamed into the anchorage. When we were up with her, I called the master on VHF channel 16.

'This is Selco Salvage and I offer to salve your ship on the terms of Lloyd's Open Form, no cure – no pay,' I told him.

'No, thank you,' he replied.

'Can I come aboard, please?' I asked.

'OK, you can come on board,' he consented.

We were now close to the green-painted tanker. I could see the collision damage and oil pouring out at the waterline. We could smell the crude, which was running to the east on the tide towards the South China Sea.

'Quick,' I said to the *Salvital* captain, 'go round the other side so I can get on board. We've got to beat Smit's.'

The gangway was down on the undamaged side, but there was no light. The ship was anchoring as the skipper put the *Salvital* alongside. There was a surge of water rushing forward along the side of the ship from the astern movement of the propeller. It was dark. I hurriedly stepped from the deck of the crew boat onto the gangway, but did not see the bridle holding it. I hit my head on the bridle and almost knocked myself out. The bruise was still there three weeks later.

I made my way up to the bridge, where I met the Italian captain. He said we could discharge cargo from the damaged tank, still pouring out crude oil, into a barge, but he would not sign a Lloyd's Open Form. It was rather like a farmer telling the vet to save his cow without payment.

The view from the bridge was a bit different from what we had seen from the *Salvital*. The foredeck of the tanker, with its myriad pipes, looked quite normal, illuminated by the deck lights. Ships at anchor, all lit up, were nearby. On the port side, looking over the bridge wing, I could see the oil gushing out. Over all was the stench of crude oil, which spelled real danger. One spark and there would be an explosion and the ship would be engulfed in flames.

I went to work on the captain, telling him what a fantastic salvage company Selco was, the danger his ship was in, all the equipment Selco had, including an oil barge, and that he must act as though uninsured and do the best he could for his ship, cargo and crew.

It worked and, after about half an hour, the master signed the Lloyd's form I had brought with me, albeit reluctantly.

I immediately informed base on my Motorola and Selco swung into action. I was feeling particularly pleased with myself: hospital in Cape Town, losing the *Salvaliant*, being a drain rather than an asset to Selco for months, convalescing in England and then still recovering in Singapore. I had now proved I was still an asset. To obtain a Lloyd's form in Singapore's Eastern Anchorage on a loaded tanker was quite a feather in my cap.

Selco's crew boat, *Swallow*, later renamed *Salvital*

And now for action. I was in charge. Selco was sending the oil barge, divers, oil booms and everything else anybody could think of. The plan was to discharge the damaged tank into the Selco oil barge.

The ship was still leaking crude. The leak was on the port side, just abaft amidships. The oil was being swept aft by the tide and so the whole aft part of the ship, which included the engine room and accommodation, was covered by gas. You could smell the stench from the bridge. The gas was highly inflammable and there was the ever-present risk of an explosion. I don't think the captain, or most of the others on board, realised the danger the vessel was in.

I immediately instructed the master to stop all smoking and batten down the aft accommodation.

A few minutes later the master said he had been instructed not to sign Lloyd's Open Form, but it was too late; I had sent the form down to the *Salvital* with Charles Deeney and it was on its way to the *Salvista*.

The Italian captain was in a very agitated state. He could of course have terminated my contract, but he chose not to. One side of him was grateful that Selco was there and that I had assumed responsibility for salving his ship, but the other was worried about his position with his owners.

In many ways the mechanics of the salvage were perfectly routine. There was not a great deal we could do until the oil barge arrived to start the transfer. I made sure all the fire precautions were taken. The *Showa Maru* salvage had taught me a lot and I must have appeared to know what I was doing because everybody did as I told them. I then thought what could be done. The captain had told me none of the cargo could be transferred internally, so the only way to get the oil out of the tank was to discharge it. Of course, if the hole could be plugged, that would also solve the problem.

It was still warm on deck in the tropical night. I arranged for a ladder and staging to be rigged over the leak. Together with one of Selco's men, I started to plug the hole at the waterline with wooden wedges.

Luckily, the divers from base arrived and they took over. Standing on the staging, I was up to my waist in oil and water from the wash of passing ships in the Singapore Straits. The water was quite warm, being so close to the equator. Later on that night I discovered that cargo could in fact be transferred internally, so I instructed the master to start immediately.

By the next morning, the hole at the waterline had been plugged by the divers, together with eight more which were under water. The level of oil in the tank was now below the waterline, and the leak had stopped. The ships in the anchorage took form in the gathering daylight, with the high buildings of Singapore Island as a backdrop.

The captain refused to let us start discharging into the oil barge, which had arrived in the early morning. He wanted us off – to get rid of us. Eventually, he signed us off and that was that. We had a valid Lloyd's form and a termination, so we would get something even though the services were short. The tanker was completely discharged later without our aid. However, there was subsequently a very nasty argument about what we did.

We said that we prevented a very serious situation becoming a disaster, while they said that the ship was only leaking and that all we did was to plug the holes. It was quite interesting from a lawyer's point of view. There was considerable legal argument, not over the validity of the Lloyd's form, which was agreed to be valid, but over the amount of the award. In due course I received a bonus – so the amount must have been reasonable.

But I was pleased with myself one way and another: it had been an exciting night and I had got the Lloyd's form signed. I felt I had fully recovered from my illness and if I was fit enough to save a loaded tanker I was fit enough for anything!

The next excitement was the grounding of the fully laden 215,000-ton tanker *Kansei*.

On day in early November I arrived in the office at Jurong at about 0900. A few minutes later I was told there was a ship aground. Within twenty minutes I was under way on *Salvital* out to the Esso single-point mooring buoy, where she was aground in the Western Anchorage.

Although it is comparatively sheltered amongst the islands and reefs of Singapore, it was quite rough, and it was difficult getting on board the supertanker. On the bridge I found the captain, the opposition salvage company (the world-renowned Dutch Smit's), the port master and two pilots. The master refused my offer of Lloyd's Open Form. I told him that Selco was mobilising all their available tugs, but he pointed to the five tugs already pushing.

It seemed quite clear to me that the Port of Singapore Authority was in charge and they had no intention of letting it slip through their hands. It was always a problem with a casualty in a port. I gathered information, kept base informed, and waited.

There was still plenty of wind, but it was a fine morning. It was hot in the tropical sun on the bridge wing, out of the air-conditioned wheelhouse, with a terrific view of the surrounding area, reefs and islands.

When I found out that they were going to try and get her off without sending divers to look at the bottom and assess the damage, I decided to do something. She had grounded at low water and was barely moving at the time, so it seemed to me that she should come off quite easily – and there was not much in it for Selco except a diving survey. But Smit's had divers too.

I got hold of the port master in a quiet corner of the bridge. I persuaded him that it would be the height of folly to attempt to move the ship until Selco had made a diving survey. If she was aground aft, she could be damaged by premature efforts. He agreed, so it was easy to persuade the master. The divers came and, just as they had finalised their survey, the ship came off.

The end of *Salvaliant* – in the breakers' yard

A few days later, just as the *Salvaliant* was arriving back from the Persian Gulf (the dredger tow from Saldanha Bay had taken 55 days), we received a report of a tanker on fire in the Malacca Straits. I agreed to go as salvage master and, within 45 minutes, was away on the new tug *Salvirile*. The panic lasted only two hours. Selco chartered an aeroplane to go and have a look, but it did not find anything, so we returned to Singapore.

I resumed command of the *Salvaliant* on her return, but before long she went for a complete refit. That was the last of my time in her, and a few years later, after ripping her bottom out on a salvage operation, she was scrapped.

Barge *Pastee*
Looting and riots in Colombo

August 1977. It had been hot in the Gulf, hot and hazy, and I was glad to be out and on the way to Singapore. In Bahrain I had taken over command of the *Salvanquish*, the company's largest single-screw tug, but it had not been all plain sailing. The main engine was giving trouble, starting trouble. Once the engine was running, no problem. But in order to manoeuvre the propeller had to be stopped, and being straight drive that meant the engine had to be stopped. So once stopped there was no way of knowing it would start again, which made going alongside a nightmare.

We had anchored off Muscat, which is outside the Gulf, to enable the chief engineer to sort out the problem, but without success. It was near where the *Dara* used to anchor, and the barren bleak sun-baked rocks with ships' names painted on them still looked the same. I agreed to continue to Singapore, notwithstanding the heavy weather brought by the southwest monsoon, and hope for the best.

In the Arabian Sea it was rough and unpleasant with rain and overcast skies. Star and sun sights had been unobtainable so our position was uncertain, but I was not worried. Head towards Bombay and down the Indian coast, I thought, and if the engine gave out assistance would not be far away. That would mean a role reversal, given that *Salvanquish* was a salvage tug and we were normally the assistor rather than the assisted!

It had been decided to try and sort out the engine problem in Bombay, and my friend Nobby Halls had flown up from Singapore. We spent a week or so in dock but Nobby had not been able to find out what had gone wrong. I agreed to sail for Singapore and hope for the best. Manoeuvring in the docks had been a nightmare, never knowing if the engine was going to start again, even though we had a tug in attendance – very *infra dig*. The number of white hairs on my head increased, and I was not yet thirty-five!

During the afternoon of 3 August 1977 I was having a quiet cat nap, the coast of India on our port side, when I was woken up by the radio officer, who handed me a message:

For Master *Salvanquish*
Please proceed into Colombo and await instructions stop
Regards AB

My pulse quickened. A salvage, I thought, or maybe a tow, although I did not fancy towing until the engine had been fixed. Still, if it was a salvage tow, one way or another it would be done. I was slightly surprised by the word 'please' in the message. Alan Bond was a man of few words, and the fewer words the better for a voice radio message.

It was not until the next morning that the suspense was relieved.

For master *Salvanquish*
On arrival Colombo please assist *Salvigilant* with salvage of *Pastee* barge stop do not remove main engine cylinder heads stop
Regards AB

A salvage, a bonus, I thought, and told the radio officer to let everyone know what was happening, which would be a good boost to morale. The monsoonal weather was very depressing. The *Salvanquish* arrived off Colombo that evening and anchored for the night, rolling in the swell from the southwest monsoon, not very comfortable.

The next morning, which was overcast but dry, I was instructed by the pilot station over the VHF radio to enter Colombo harbour and the pilot would board inside. The anchor was weighed and after numerous attempts the engineers managed to start the engine. I entered the port, my heart in my mouth, not stopping while the pilot boarded – 'a little problem with the engine,' I told him. I berthed alongside the passenger terminal with the assistance of one tug, which in the event was not necessary because the engine started

Salvanquish

first time going astern! It was with a sigh of relief that I rang off Finished with Engines on the telegraph.

Shortly afterwards the *Salvigilant* moved from her berth alongside the breakwater and berthed alongside the *Salvanquish*. Her master came on board and gave me his salvage report of the barge *Pastee*, and quite a story it was as well.

The barge *Pastee 1802*, 400 feet long and 100 feet wide, was aground on a reef outside Colombo to the south. Three weeks earlier in bad weather he had managed to make a towing connection to the grounded barge, loaded with timber, and started towing at full speed. The tug was rolling and pitching in the heavy swell and rough sea, water continually sweeping the towing deck. He found himself too close to the reef and slowed down to manoeuvre clear when suddenly the starboard engine stopped. He was in real danger and quickly let go his starboard anchor, but it dragged and the tug was drifting closer to the reef. He let go the port anchor and the effect of both the anchors was to stop the drift, but the port engine stopped as well. The *Salvigilant* was now in a perilous position with both engines stopped in heavy weather on a lee shore, the stern close to the breaking waves on the reef. There was a very real risk that the tug would be lost and some of the crew as well.

The chief officer was ashore directing operations on the barge and was in radio contact with the tug. The master sent him into Colombo to see the agents, who acted with commendable speed, and just before sunset two divers arrived in a motor boat. The boat was rolling heavily in the rough sea, but in the gathering monsoon darkness they dived on the rolling and pitching tug and found both propellers entangled in the nylon towing rope. It took skill and bravery and two hours of diving to clear the starboard propeller, a fine feat. The much-relieved master heaved up both anchors and proceeded back to Colombo on one engine. It had been a frightening experience for him and his crew, but they had done well to save the tug. The port propeller was cleared the next day, but he made no more refloating attempts. Since then they had been trying to offload the cargo by hand.

During the afternoon, after all the entry formalities were completed, which included ingratiating myself with the customs, I was taken by the agent in an old Morris Oxford to inspect the barge. The road led out of Colombo, and the main traffic was Morris Minors and three-wheeled taxis. It was overcast and grey and hot and sticky.

The barge was aground to seaward of Bambalapitiya railway station, a dilapidated and dirty place about four miles from the docks. The gate bypassing the station was locked so we had to cross the railway line, keeping a sharp lookout for any trains. A wall, about fifteen feet high, protected the station from the sea, and the barge was behind the wall on the reef. There was a narrow ledge between the wall and the sea. A barricade made from bamboos had been erected at each end of the wall in an attempt to keep out the looters. Looting of the cargo was a serious problem.

The barge was aground about 200 feet from the shoreline, which was a man-made embankment. She had a ten-degree list to starboard and the afterpart, which was clear of cargo, was continuously under water, being washed over by the swell. A reef extended about fifty feet from the embankment, and then sand. About nine hundred feet from the shore the swell was breaking on the outer reef. The *Pastee 1802* was lying at an angle of about thirty degrees to the shore line, with her bow pointing shoreward.

Although the weather had moderated from the time the *Salvigilant* made the refloating attempt it was still the height of the southwest monsoon. Heavy rain and gale-force winds could be expected at any time.

The cargo consisted of planks of sawn timber. It seemed to me that the best way to salve her was to remove the timber, fill the tanks under the main deck with compressed air to blow out any water, and use the *Salvigilant* to pull her across the outer reef into deep water, where the *Salvanquish* would be standing by with more compressors. The compressors on shore would have to be hired due to customs difficulties. It was not going to be easy with the monsoon blowing, the restricted area on the embankment, the railway lines to cross, the looters, and customs difficulties. Some timber had already been landed by hand using shore labour.

I phoned Mr Bond in Singapore that evening and he agreed with my plan. He told me that after the refloating attempt the barge had been sunk in her present position by two Selco divers sent from Singapore, to stabilise her and prevent damage from pounding on the reef.

I decided to use as many of the crew of the two tugs as possible to assist and direct the shore labour previously hired. The engineers on the *Salvanquish* were working on the engine, otherwise everyone was volunteered except one AB and one officer for each tug. One cook would accompany the shore party to look after the food and coffee on site while the other would remain on the tugs to prepare the meals. The salvage party from the two tugs was ready at 0730 the next day but the transport did not turn up until 0800. The time had not been wasted, however, because the customs required a list of all items we were taking to the barge. This included consumables like nails and screws, as well as all the food, pots and pans and kettle. The intention was to charge us duty on anything we did not bring back, but the problem was solved by the judicious giving of cigarettes and whisky.

We set out, once the customs were happy, in an old Holden pick-up truck and a Volkswagen van. Neither was in its first youth and the Volkswagen had starting problems besides the doors not closing and having to be lashed. Still, my crew were salvage men, and problems were there to be overcome!

Import controls were very strict, and anything mechanical or manufactured unless made in Sri Lanka was very expensive and difficult to obtain. The only thing that was cheap was manual labour, but a lot of it was needed to make up for the lack of mechanical equipment.

We arrived at the railway station before 0900, and found it to be busy, Colombo rush hour. Crossing the line necessitated a good lookout for trains, always fully laden with additional passengers on the roof and hanging on to the sides of the carriages. There were always crowds of people watching us, including the looters, hence the barricades.

On site I found four gangs waiting. They had been there all night as security. Each gang consisted of ten men, and there were two foremen in attendance. They had been hired from the stevedores with whom the agents normally dealt, for working cargo in the port. Although at first the cost of labour seemed very low, all sorts of hidden extras appeared. If the gangs were knocked off they would not come again and new gangs took time to recruit, hence the need, apart from the security considerations, to keep them on at night.

There was one ten-inch nylon rope from the bow of the barge to the shore, but it was not really suitable as a safety line so we rigged one from the middle of the barge. It was neap tides and the rise and fall was only 0.3 metres. Although the outer reef broke the main force of the swell there was always a considerable surge around the barge and over the inner reef, especially at high tide. At times it could knock you off your feet, and the inner reef was difficult to cross, as it was uneven and had channels and holes.

I crossed over to the barge for an inspection, getting soaked in the process, but at least the water was warm. It was a grey and dismal day. The inshore side of the barge was buried in sand up to a depth of about four feet, while the seaward side was under water, with spray coming over the stacked timber. The timber was in metal banded bundles stacked about twelve feet high. The barge had steel posts at intervals of about ten feet, and the cargo was further secured by wire lashings tightened with bottle screws. A lorry crane was stowed at the forward end.

The two Selco divers were on the barge. They told me that they thought four out of the six tanks on the port side were holed, and that there was a crack in the bulkhead between number one port tank and number one starboard tank. Number one was the only tank they had been able to get into, but they had sunk the barge by loosening the tank lids and no air had come out of the port tanks. The tank lids on numbers one, two, three and four port tanks had been removed and fitted with air and valve connections ready for blowing with compressed air. The idea was to blow air under pressure into the tank, which would blow out the water in it. They thought the starboard tanks might still be tight but it had been impossible to get at the tank lids due to the swell on the seaward side of the barge. They said some of the looters had lost toes and fingers.

At 0915, watched by the usual crowd of bystanders and looters, with the *Salvanquish* and *Salvigilant* Filipino crew on the barge and in the water, aided by the Sri Lankan port labour, discharge commenced by hand, piece by piece. The timber was thrown into the surging water and manhandled ashore over the reef and up the embankment, where it was stacked. It was slow and dangerous. The men would lose control of a piece in the swell, and it would then hit anyone not watching carefully or off balance. Crossing the reef was difficult enough without trying to carry pieces of timber. We tried various experiments, passing the pieces from hand to hand, two men carrying a piece ashore, but none was successful.

It seemed to me the best way would be to get hold of a crane, or failing that to rig a breeches buoy system. The timber did not all float, and a considerable quantity had sunk around the stern of the barge. Looters surrounded the stern, diving to recover the timber, then floating it ashore in rubber rings. They continually tried to remove timber from the barge itself but were beaten off by my crews. It was quite surreal to be fighting off looters in broad daylight beside a railway station with crowds of people watching, and I momentarily wondered if I had slipped back a century in time.

I went ashore when I saw Mr Mack, the shipping director from our agents, come on site. I asked him about the possibility of hiring a crane but he was most doubtful. They were in short supply and even if one could be found it would be difficult to bring onto the embankment. He said he would investigate. I then suggested getting hold of a powered or a mechanical hand winch with a tripod or sheerlegs, but again he was doubtful, although we could have sheerlegs made.

I suggested we do a deal with the looters, who were most resourceful and obviously willing and able to land the timber. He pointed out that the looters were selling their pieces for between thirty and forty rupees, and what could we offer that was better? The police were involved, apparently being paid off. Instead of stopping the looters crossing the railway lines and taking the timber away, they were allowing them to do so, although the customs had impounded three lorry-loads of looted timber. It was a complete bonanza for the poor and out-of-work fit workers, and they were making the most of it to make money while they could – not that I saw it in that light.

There was a small hand winch on site, and Mr Mack informed me that another could be obtained. I asked him to send down the second winch so that we could rig two breeches buoy systems, using the winches to keep the wires tight between the barge and the shore. Anchoring the winches was going to be a problem due to the nature of the embankment, which consisted of bricks and sand, and the proximity of the high wall. The wall was the obvious anchor but it was old and crumbling and we thought it would fall down if any weight was attached to it. I did not think the railway authorities would be amused if I pulled down their wall! The winch already on site had been staked down, but the stakes had moved and the winch was loose.

During lunch hour, noon to 1300, the port labour left the site to obtain food, while my crews ate the food which we brought with us together with the fresh fruit I had purchased. Immediately after lunch the crew re-staked the winch and lashed it to a railway line that was embedded between two concrete blocks, which in turn were embedded in the sand. The wire was made fast to a suitable securing post on the barge and set up tight.

At 1315 discharge resumed, utilising a shackle as the traveller along the wire. It did not work very well so I sent one of my crew back to the tugs to obtain a roller shackle which I knew to be on board. I split the crews so that slinging of the timber on the barge was done by us, while a couple remained ashore to stiffen up the shore gangs. Between four and six pieces of timber were slung with two pieces of rope, which were then attached to the shackle on the wire. When the barge was ready they signalled and the shore labour would pull the timber ashore along the wire. The load would come to rest at the bottom of the embankment and have to be manhandled up to the top and stacked. The embankment was not smooth but had big rocks sticking out, which made handling the timber very difficult – especially at high tide, when the men at the bottom were swept by waves.

At 1440 the bosun of the *Salvanquish* returned with the roller shackle. This was a great improvement, and made pulling the timber ashore much easier and quicker. I decided to bring two snatch blocks in the morning, as they would be even better than the roller shackle.

In the middle of the afternoon the lorries I had asked the agent for arrived. The timber which had been brought ashore had to be taken down to the docks for storage under customs supervision. The shore labour was split and part of the gang started loading the lorries, which were parked in the railway station yard opposite the gate. The key was obtained from the station master and the gate was opened. The men carried the timber along the shore, through the barricade, across two railway tracks, and so to the lorries. The trains normally hooted well away from the station so there was plenty of warning. We were not the only people on the lines. The looters for one, and sightseers, and the track seemed to be used as a pedestrian highway by a considerable number of the local populace.

After tea the second winch arrived, and by the time darkness fell we had manhandled it across the railway lines and positioned it alongside the first winch, which had been re-secured in line with the wire connection to the barge.

The Selco crew departed back to the tugs in the port for the night. On board the *Salvanquish* I instructed the welder to make two pulleys as travellers on the wire for the breeches buoy system. I was hoping to have both winches working the next day.

I returned after dark to see how the lorry loading was getting on and stayed until it was finished and there was no more timber at the station. The shore labour remained overnight as security against the looters. The agent told me three truckloads of timber which had been looted from the shore had been seized by the customs and delivered to our cache in the port.

The next day was Sunday and the agent arrived very early, at 0545, with the transport. Unfortunately the duty customs officer was in bed and although supposedly on duty did not take kindly to being woken up. However a suitable 'present' was given and we were allowed to proceed, picking up the two Selco divers *en route* from their hotel.

Discharge started immediately with the first winch while the second was secured and the wire to the barge made fast and tightened. When it was ready, discharge with the second winch commenced.

I had a major operation in progress outside the railway station. There were eighty Sri Lankan port workers, two foremen, fifteen Selco salvage crew and myself. They were split up as follows:

- 12 shore labour on the barge

- 6–8 Selco men on the barge

- 25 shore labour to each winch

- 2 Selco men to each winch

- 12 shore labour to load the lorries

- 6 shore labour to discharge the lorries in the port

- 1 Selco man to look after food and coffee, and guard personal belongings

- 2 Selco divers assisting as required, in charge of cargo lashings and tank fittings

- Myself or my chief officer in overall charge

This system was used throughout the operation. The two Selco divers were backed up by the two *Salvanquish* divers as required.

The cargo lashings on the barge were rearranged as discharge progressed to prevent the cargo being washed overboard, where it would be stolen by the looters. When everything was working well the discharge was quite speedy and I felt pleased with myself, so I took myself off to a hotel near the railway station for a short break. It had a telephone, which was useful for talking with the agent, and served cool drinks, which were most refreshing!

When I was back at the winches I heard shouts and screams behind the station wall. There was a strange thudding noise and I discovered that gangs of looters were fighting. One gang had caught a man from a rival gang and were beating him with iron bars. When the fight was over he was taken to hospital, where he died four hours later. Both his legs had been broken, one arm was smashed, his skull was fractured, and he had internal injuries.

The agents made a statement to the police concerning the involvement of a policeman in the looting, and he was going to be prosecuted. I thought on the one hand it was a good idea there should be no truck with corrupt police, but on the other it was almost certain to cause us trouble. I was told the police would not prosecute us if we injured or killed anyone while protecting the timber. I sincerely hoped it would not come to that; it was bad enough that the looters were fighting and one man had already died. Others had lost fingers or toes on the barge, the lure of money overcoming any sense or caution.

In the middle of the morning the lorries arrived and we loaded them. The customs had now decreed that the loading was to be done under their supervision, as the timber had been classed as an import. When the lorries were full no customs officer had turned up so they had to wait. This sort of delay frequently occurred, but there was nothing that could be done even though a suitable 'present' had been given. Discharge stopped for lunch and continued all afternoon without major incident, just a few cut feet on the men carrying the timber up the embankment.

The shipping manager from the agency turned up on site in the early afternoon and took me to see the Port Commission chief engineer. I had a change of clothes with me so I could look respectable. We wanted to hire a crane to speed up the discharge, but apart from being prohibitively expensive the engineer thought it would not be possible to get the crane opposite the barge. I said that if he could find a crane I could find a way, but despite prodding the agents nothing more was heard.

I stopped discharge from the barge an hour before dark and set all hands to loading the lorries. A considerable crowd were watching from both barricades and I wanted all the salved timber cleared from the station. All the equipment was loaded onto one of the lorries and spent the night in the driveway of one of the directors, guarded by a watchman. One loaded lorry remained in the station yard overnight, the customs officer departing before it was finished. Two gangs were left to guard it.

It was quite obvious to me that with the present methods the discharge was going to take three weeks to complete. I had to speed it up. As I could not obtain a crane then the only solution was to build a tripod or sheerlegs to lift the wire above the embankment, so the timber could be landed straight ashore, not carried up the embankment by hand. And if I could obtain suitable lighting we would be able to continue work at night. I asked the station master if we could plug into his power supply, but he refused, so I would have to find a generator. We had portable generators on board the *Salvanquish* but I doubted if the customs would let us bring one ashore.

The agent told me the police would patrol the site during the night, but I am afraid I thought they were more likely to assist rather than deter the looters. Although I was concerned at what had happened on the station today between the rival gangs, I was not too worried about my men. So far we had not been affected, and there had been no violence against them.

Although it was not raining the next day it was still overcast and very muggy. The station and surrounding buildings did not look so drab and unkept in the early morning light when we arrived. Of the forty men supposedly guarding the timber only a handful remained. There had been a raid overnight and a lot of timber had been stolen. So much for the police patrol!

The day's activities are best summed up in the message I sent to Alan Bond in Singapore.

1. Have week long open dated port clearance. [This meant both tugs could leave the port at a moment's notice if there was a ship in distress at sea.]

2. Cargo discharge continued as well as could be expected with about 100 tons discharged in last three days leaving about 550 tons to go.

3. Considerable pilferage last night and police no help, rather they assisted looters so have appealed to Government Minister in charge of police.

4. Have therefore hired additional guards with knives and found a generator and lights which have hired in attempt stop looting.

5. Ruled out self and crew to guard barge at night because if fight it would be foreigners versus Sri Lankans which not good politically.

6. Am having sheerlegs made which should increase rate of discharge.

7. Mechanised winch not available but still investigating possibilities.

8. Am trying to get lorry crane which part of barge cargo to work.

9. Have investigated possibility of floating barge and towing inside reef but there is no exit so still consider complete discharge of timber only way to salve her.

On the next day, Tuesday, the sheerlegs arrived in the morning but we found it impossible to secure them satisfactorily and we could not use the wall. I needed a welding set.

Although Aitken Spence, our agents, had an engineering works they did not have a suitable welding set. Eventually I was taken to a decrepit back-street workshop where I was shown a small welding set which was mounted in the back of a jeep. The jeep was at least twenty-five years old, and the welding set, which was run by a series of bands off the crankshaft, was at least ten years old. I had the *Salvanquish* welder with me. He borrowed a battery, pulled at various pieces of wire, fiddled with the magneto, started the engine with the starting handle, tested the welding set, and pronounced it workable. I hired it.

I remained with the jeep to encourage the owner to get on site as quickly as possible. Eventually we set off, and I had a hair-raising five-mile journey through Colombo because the jeep did not have any brakes. The vehicle arrived at the railway yard in one piece, but my nerves were in tatters. With all the labour and the use of timber we managed to get the jeep on site behind the wall, where we put it to work.

There were old railway lines lying around, so we welded the winches onto them. This made a much more secure foundation for the winches and enabled us to stake them much more firmly to the ground using three-foot-long metal stakes. We secured the sheerlegs by digging a three-foot-deep hole close to the wall, welded the railway lines together, welded a metal stake to the railway lines, welded the back sheerleg to the metal stake, put the lot into the hole and then filled it in with rocks, bricks and sand. This held quite satisfactorily, and with the winch secure it worked well. We had rigged up lighting during the day – a light on the barge and floodlights mounted on the wall, driven by the hired generator – and the entire location was well illuminated. While all this was going on discharge had continued, so at 2100 when I retired to the bar for a pick-me-up I felt well pleased.

The little local hotel I used as my headquarters was very small and the staff spoke only limited English. But we got along fine and the beer was cold and the phone worked. What they thought of me I don't know because I would often come in dressed in shorts and shirt, wet through, and change in the lavatory.

On Wednesday we were on site shortly after daylight and discharge continued all day. The sheerlegs were stiffened up with additional piping and another hole dug for the second set which arrived in the afternoon. One of the Selco divers was thrown by a wave against a metal stanchion and injured.

There were no more disused railway lines outside the wall but I found some more along the track, so went to the station master. He kindly agreed that I could borrow them, and we used four railway lines for the second sheerleg, welded together and put in the hole. Like the first one it worked well, and the discharge rate improved.

At 1800, just as it was getting dark, all the labour was arrested by the police on a charge of trespass. The complaint had been taken out by the station master. I never found out the complete truth, but it appeared the police from the local police station put pressure on him to make the complaint in retaliation for the agent's prosecuting the policeman for looting. It was noticeable that no effort was made by the police to prevent the looters transporting their loot over the tracks! From now on there were considerable delays caused by the railway officials refusing to open the gate and preventing us crossing the lines. The other possible reason – or maybe it was a combination of the two – was that the police wanted to frighten our labour and security so the looters, who were paying the police in kind, could raid the barge and the site. The agent managed to have our labour released, and the shipping director appealed to the railway transport manager to have this nonsense stopped.

Thursday proved to be an exciting but frustrating day, and I still wondered sometimes which century I was in. When we arrived on site early that morning I found the looters raiding the barge and landing the timber by our sheerlegs. They ran when we approached but the foremen and our shore men had been threatened with knives. Our security, who had been armed with knives themselves, had departed at daylight leaving the location wide open, the barricades being no deterrent for determined men. The police on site had not tried to stop the thieving – instead, they prevented my men bringing our equipment across the lines.

I lost my temper with the policemen, who retaliated by threatening to have me 'beaten to a pulp'. However, the agent persuaded one of the policemen to visit the station master, who agreed to let us take our gear across the lines but not to bring back any timber! Permission for this would have to be agreed later. Disgusted, I departed to fix a winch.

Later in the morning the agent's shipping manager arrived with the railway transport manager and we went to see the station master. He was instructed to allow us to carry on with the discharge and not to hamper our work. They then went off to the police station, because it was the police rather than the station master who were causing the trouble.

I told Singapore in my daily message that I had introduced an incentive scheme for the shore labour which would improve matters provided we were not interfered with by police, railway officials, looters or customs, and as long as we had no transport problems and the weather held.

The weather, though dull, hot and humid, had been good as far as the wind was concerned – and that is what mattered for us. The swell was down and it was a little easier working on the barge. The injured diver was back at work. I was hopeful of completing the discharge in five to seven days. Near the end we would lose timber as the swell would sweep over the barge, no longer protected by the cargo which had been discharged. The port tanks were ready for blowing with compressed air but not the starboard. My intention was to move the *Salvigilant* from the port and have her anchor outside the reef off the barge. She would connect to the barge with her towing gear, we would blow the tanks, and hopefully the barge would be pulled across the reef. The *Salvigilant* would have to connect her compressor to the barge to keep it afloat while she towed it into Colombo.

So far I had spent 45,000 rupees, excluding Selco costs, and had landed 5,700 pieces of timber, which were in the port. I was hoping to discharge the remaining 16,000 pieces for about 80,000 rupees. About 6,000 pieces had been looted, so the looters had been more efficient than me!

The incentive scheme speeded up the discharge, but permission to cross the railway lines was still withheld so we could not load the lorries. I had decided to work nights now we had lighting and split the Selco crew into two, working six hours on and six off. I spent a considerable amount of time with the shipping manager trying to obtain permission to bring the timber to the lorries. I paid the bonuses every eight hours so was on site at midnight.

On Friday morning I was on the barge and saw that the sand configuration around the middle part of the barge had changed. More work was needed on the manhole covers to the tanks to enable us to blow them. The remaining cargo on the barge was becoming loose and needed more lashings on it.

A quick change of clothing in my HQ and I went with the shipping director to see the Receiver of Wrecks, who was also the Master Attendant of Colombo and so in charge of the port. In his smart air-conditioned office we requested his assistance to prevent looting. It seemed a far cry from the railway station and the embankment with waves breaking over the barge and crowds of people watching, not to mention the looters in the water.

We read the relevant section of the Merchant Shipping Act concerning trespass etc and assisted in drafting a letter to the Commissioner of Police, Colombo. We also drafted a letter appointing my agents as deputy to the Receiver of Wrecks, which enabled them to act on his behalf and delegated his powers to them. Letters were also written to the General Manager Railways and to the station master, Bambalapitiya railway station.

I went with the shipping manager to the police commissioner, but he was not in his office. We left the letter with a senior officer who promised to place it on the commissioner's desk.

After lunch on site, where the discharge was going well but there was still no loading of the lorries, I returned to the agent's office. The letter from the Receiver of Wrecks had arrived, appointing one of the agents helping us as his deputy and empowering him to take whatever steps were required to protect the timber. Under the Act the Receiver of Wrecks, and by delegation his deputy, was empowered to use violence to protect the wreck and her cargo, and anyone employed by the Receiver who killed anyone in so doing was not liable to prosecution. Serious stuff, enabling me by delegation to do what I liked. The letter went on to require the station master to assist us. Under the Act the Receiver was allowed to cross any land or property, either private or government, and anyone preventing him was liable to a substantial fine.

I returned to the barge site and at 1600 permission was at last granted to cross the lines. Loading of the lorries started immediately and all the labour was utilised. I dismissed the welding jeep as we no longer needed it.

Just after midnight on Saturday I was at the station, where clearing the site of timber continued. The delay in loading the lorries had severely delayed the discharge. The lorries were supposed to be loaded as the discharge continued, to keep up a continuous operation.

I was back again just after breakfast. There was a bigger swell, which did not bode well, and I was keen to work as fast as possible. Some of the list had come off the barge with the reduction in cargo and it appeared there might be some buoyancy in the starboard tanks. I sent some crew back to the tugs to bring more lines to make the barge more secure.

Later in the day the barge moved and broke one of the sheerlegs, which was a blow. The list had almost completely come out and the barge visibly moved in the biggest swells. The broken sheerleg was discarded and the old system used, but of course it was much slower. The divers continued working on the manhole covers.

A compressor had been found and apparently hired, but it had still not arrived, although promised for the previous day. I wanted to start blowing the tanks and if necessary get the *Salvigilant* on site to hold the barge and prevent it drifting further ashore.

On Sunday morning it started to rain, and cargo discharge stopped at 0300. The timber on the barge was starting to move despite the lashings. Later on it was still raining but with the crew change discharge resumed, there being less movement at half tide. At 0800 it stopped raining, and I organised the re-anchoring of the bow line of the barge to stop the movement. A hole was dug, as for the sheerlegs, and railway lines lashed together with wire were placed in it, to which the bow line was made fast. This held well. The labour were distinctly unenthusiastic about working, complaining that the barge was unsafe and too difficult to reach. I must admit it was not fun on the barge: the swell had increased further, and waves were sweeping over it and breaking against the embankment. But I eventually managed to persuade them to carry on.

I went out to the barge a little later to give moral support to the Selco men, and to tell them where to discharge from and to place more lashings. The timber was moving on the barge, and if we did not improve the lashings we were going to lose a lot. There were many more looters, both in the water and on shore, and it was a full-time job for four men to keep the thieves off the barge. The sand on the inside of the barge had been further washed away.

In the middle of the morning I went to the house of a man with a compressor, which I hired. The owner would tow it on site with his jeep. When I returned I found a quantity of timber had been washed overboard, which is what I had feared might happen. The crew on the barge were putting more lashings on the remaining timber, but it was difficult. Loose timber was swirling around on the barge in the swell, making working very dangerous.

There was a complete riot ashore. Our own labour were picking up some of the cargo as it washed ashore, but quite literally hundreds of looters had come through the barricades and were stealing the timber. The Selco crew ashore, our security people, and myself managed to clear the looters from the winch area, and I went to get the police. Two policemen accompanied me back and using their batons, which made a distinctive thud as they hit human flesh, they soon had the riot under control, with looters outside the barricades. Unfortunately the police refused to stay more than a couple of hours.

The long-awaited compressor finally turned up and we manhandled it across the railway lines and onto the embankment. The hoses to the tanks on the barge were connected up and we started blowing the tanks. The compressor broke down. Our resourceful *Salvanquish* electrician found out what was wrong, took a piece back to the tug, and had it running again by mid-afternoon.

There was continuous looting all day after the police had gone, though mainly confined to timber which had previously washed overboard and sunk.

Once the compressor was going again the discharge stopped. The barge lifted slightly as the air was pumped into the two forward tanks and the bow line slackened. The bow line was kept tight, thus moving the barge slightly closer to the shore. Just before dark a loose plank broke the valve on the port tank and I stopped the compressor. The divers disconnected the air hoses, opened the valves and let the barge settle back on the bottom to prevent it pounding in the swell.

I decided to cease all discharge, jettison the loose timber forward and secure the remaining bundles. I would instruct the *Salvigilant* to come round from Colombo in the morning and make a towing connection by floating her towing wire ashore on 44-gallon drums. Hopefully the compressor would work long enough to blow the tanks and we would pull her off. I had hoped to discharge all the timber before attempting to refloat, but with the rougher weather and the troublesome looting I thought it better to try as soon as possible.

An hour and a half before low water the Selco crews went onto the barge and secured the remaining cargo under the floodlights. They finished at 2120 and I left four Selco men on watch together with our security and four standby gangs.

The customs were difficult the next morning so I had to smuggle out a portable walkie-talkie in order to keep in touch with the *Salvigilant*. On site, looting was continuing. The Selco crew were attempting to stop it, the gangs and security being ineffective until reinforced by our arrival. The looters were beaten back and departed in a rain of stones. The police were intermittently in attendance as there was a big crowd of many hundreds of people, colourful in their local dress. It seemed only a matter of time before people were either injured or killed.

The *Salvigilant*, rolling and pitching in the swell, arrived in the middle of the morning and anchored off. She was an immediate attraction and even bigger crowds built up at both barricades. The looters redoubled their efforts, as it was obvious a serious attempt was being made to remove their bonanza. The police were nowhere to be seen, having told

Salvigilant

the thieves two pieces of timber for you, one for us. It meant there was no crowd control and many more people joined in the looting. It became a kind of frenzy. There was much shouting and cheering as timber was brought ashore. It was quite frightening, but the Selco men behaved well.

The hired compressor only worked for one hour before breaking down, and the other compressor I thought I had hired had not turned up, so I decided to abandon the attempt. I instructed the *Salvigilant* over my smuggled walkie-talkie to return to Colombo. The swell was bigger again today and sweeping over the barge so there was no further discharge, although I kept the gangs on for security.

I returned to the agent's office and told the shipping director to put up the necessary guarantee to the customs so we could take our own compressor to the barge. In the event, despite our offering a 100,000 rupee bond, the customs refused, saying we had to pay import duty.

On site, additional mooring lines were put on the barge and secured ashore with railway lines dug into the ground. I harassed the agents, and persistence paid because another small compressor turned up in the evening. This was carried over the railway lines and onto the embankment ready for the morning.

On Tuesday when we reached the site I found some of our equipment had been stolen. So much for our security! The *Salvigilant* arrived during the morning but I sent her back to Colombo. We had been blowing the tanks with both compressors and it was clear the barge was much more seriously damaged than we had thought. I decided there was no point continuing until a bigger compressor could be found. There was an even bigger swell running and it was not possible to work cargo. I therefore ceased operations, dismissed the shore labour but kept on the security gang, and the Selco crews returned to the tugs.

Persistence again brought its rewards, and another large compressor turned up on Wednesday evening.

On Thursday I sent the following message

1. Having made two unsuccessful attempts with all three compressors to regain sufficient buoyancy necessary to pull barge over reef due more extensive damage than first thought including leaks in the deck consider barge to be a total loss.

2. Will therefore attempt move barge closer inshore to expedite discharge of timber and save more from looters.

3. Will continue work with utmost dispatch especially in view of communal disturbances as one town within 50 miles of Colombo was placed under curfew last night and deteriorating weather.

There was a tenseness among the crowd of watchers, no longer smiles, and I had a real sense of foreboding that something was in the air. The sooner we were finished the better. I did not wish to be involved in any communal rioting. We moved the barge closer to the shore during the day, using air in the tanks from the compressors. The weather was getting worse and it was becoming very rough. I dismissed all the hired equipment in the evening and the crew took all the Selco equipment back to the tugs.

On Friday morning we started jettisoning the cargo, and as it floated ashore our re-hired shore labour picked it up in the water and manhandled it ashore. Unfortunately it started a riot, and I was in the middle. The main looters were at the Colombo end of the embankment, and they started to advance through the barricades. I was between them and our people, dressed in brown trousers and white shirt and wearing white gloves. Behind me were the Filipinos from the tugs, together with the Sri Lankan shore labour and security gang. Ahead of me were the advancing looters, intent on stealing the timber.

To seaward of me was the barge, the reef and rough sea. To landward was the fifteen-foot wall. I was stuck and could not escape.

Suddenly a stone whizzed past my head, thrown by the looters. Another stone flew back from the opposite direction. My people were throwing as well. I could see the eyes of the advancing gang and knew I could not retreat. There was something in their eyes, a sort of glazed look, and I knew if I flinched I was lost.

'Come back, Cap!' One of the divers had run up to me. 'Its not safe.'

And he ran back to the safety of our people. I knew I could not move, let alone retreat. Stones were flying in both directions with increasing intensity and I knew I was in deep trouble. The looters advanced, my gangs advanced. What I was seeing in the eyes of the looters was blood-lust. I could not run away. I had to stand my ground. If I retreated it would be a signal of weakness and the looters would attack. I felt quite calm but incredibly tense – things seemed to be happening with extraordinary vividness and clarity and in slow motion. It was only a matter of time before blood was drawn, which would have been the spark for a full-scale riot. I knew that it was my own actions alone that would determine whether I lived or died.

I put my white cotton-gloved hands up in the air, and facing the looters I shouted, 'Stop! Stop, I say!'

I half-turned and shouted to my people, 'Fetch the police!'

'Stop, I say!' I continued to face the looters with my hands in the air like a traffic cop. My people stopped throwing stones, and then miraculously the looters stopped. Armed police arrived on the scene and suddenly the near-riot was over and the embankment was clear.

'That is it,' I said to my people. 'We are off.' And we departed back to the tugs.

That evening a curfew was imposed due to communal rioting with much killing and looting. We happened to have been involved in a salvage operation at the start of widespread rioting across the whole of Sri Lanka, arising from the long-standing tension between Tamil and Sinhalese. The troubles continued for some weeks, and many people died and were injured.

FROM *LLOYD'S WEEKLY CASUALTY REPORTS*, 1977

Colombo, Aug 22 1977 – Following spread of anti-Tamil rioting, curfew imposed on entire Sri Lanka from 1700, Aug 20, to 0400, Aug 22. Some loss of life and injuries and damage to private property reported. Colombo, 25 people died.

Colombo, Aug 23 – Many Tamils stayed away from work for fear of being beaten up.

Colombo, Aug 24 – Island-wide curfew in force effective 1800 today until 0400, Aug 25. Embarking refugees to Jaffna tonight, resulting no work Queen Elizabeth Quay night shift.

3 SALVANGUARD

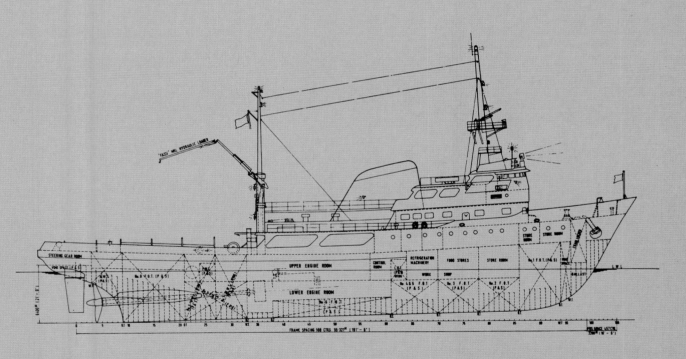

SALVANGUARD

The *Salvanguard* was a twin-screw motor salvage tug built in Japan
in 1966 of 1,167 GRT and 183 NRT. She had a length of 64.4 metres, a beam
of 13.4 metres and a loaded draught of 6.7 metres. She was powered by four EMD
diesel engines, which were coupled in pairs to twin, controllable-pitch propellers. Her
indicated horsepower was 12,000, which gave her a maximum speed of 17 knots.
Her navigational aids included radar, gyro compass, autopilot, echo sounder,
automatic direction finding, wireless telegraphy, radio telephony,
VHF, and telex over radio.

The *Salvanguard* was equipped with a 150-ton, double-drum electric towing
winch, which carried two towing wires, each 1,097 metres in length, one with 6.5 inch
circumference and the other with 8.5 inch circumference. Using all four engines, her
bollard pull was of over 100 tons. She was equipped with one 6-ton derrick
and one 5-ton hydraulic crane.

Her salvage firefighting equipment consisted of two dual-purpose Angus
foam/water cannons, mounted on a fire monitor platform on the foremast, and one
water cannon, fed by two Mather & Pratt centrifugal fire
and salvage pumps.

The *Salvanguard* had fully air-conditioned accommodation for 28 people, tanks
holding 115 tons of fresh water, and a range of 60–70 days, at a fuel
consumption of between 6 and 28 tons per day.

Mare

'Please I follow you to Aden'

FROM *LLOYD'S WEEKLY CASUALTY REPORTS*, 1978

Mare (Panamanian) – Singapore, Nov 3 – At 1854 GMT Oct 25, MV *Mare*, bound Aden, fully laden, was reported aground in position lat 27 34 48 N, long 33 53 18 E. Lloyd's Open Form signed by master of *Mare* and master of salvage tug *Salvanguard*.

Selco were expanding, and Mr Kahlenberg had bought the powerful United Towing tug *Statesman*, of Cod War fame. I was appointed to her command, and flew to the UK with Nobby Halls to take her over. We had to get her out of Hull quickly due to industrial troubles, and I sailed her down to Southampton with a scratch crew including my brother Donald as chief officer. Once she had been painted in Selco colours – renamed *Salvanguard* – and I had a full salvage crew on board we sailed for Singapore.

We transited the Suez Canal, always a thrilling experience for me, more than a hundred miles through the middle of a desert country. It was especially so the first time in command of my own ship. It had been an uneventful voyage and salvage-wise a complete disaster, nothing. My dreams of my very own *Amoco Cadiz* had eluded me.

It was October, so the weather was not hot in the Gulf of Suez. We were making our way slowly southwards, keeping a sharp lookout in this crowded gulf. A good portion of the world's shipping passed through it, and it seemed as though ships were passing us in a continuous stream in both directions. The barren desert and sand dunes were brown in the autumn sunlight, the sea unusually calm.

I was on the bridge in the evening when I saw to starboard two red lights, one above the other. Vessel not under command, I thought, but she was close to the reefs, as I was, keeping the tug out of the main traffic zone. I took a bearing, looked at the radar to measure the distance, and went into the chartroom.

'Keep an eye on that ship,' I ordered. 'She might need assistance.'

I carefully plotted her position on the chart, tense with excitement. Yes, I thought, thrilled, she is aground.

'Action stations,' I shouted to the mate on watch. 'She is aground. Launch the Z-boat.'

I rushed back into the wheelhouse and moved the twin control levers to neutral to slow down the tug. The chief officer ran down onto the boat deck while I manoeuvred the *Salvanguard* close to the casualty, keeping clear of the reef. It was dark now and I could not see it visually, only its outline on the radar. A diver came onto the bridge to pick up a walkie-talkie and went off in the Z-boat with the chief officer.

Some time later I heard the mate's excited voice on the radio, 'Cap, Cap, he's prepared to sign.'

I was elated. 'Send the Z-boat back and I will come over with the LOF.'

I packed a Lloyd's Open Form and – making sure I had a pen – made my way off the bridge.

'Keep three cables north of the casualty,' I told the second mate. 'You are in command while I am away.' He grinned.

My elation waned a little on arrival at the casualty. She was smaller than my tug. However, a salvage was a salvage, and it was mine. I had found her and the office knew nothing about it yet. It was my show: I was alone with the tug in Egyptian waters far from head office in Singapore. Even after four years in salvage, it was still exciting. I told the mate to take a look around and sound round the casualty.

The elderly Turkish master greeted me like a long-lost friend when I arrived on his minuscule bridge. He was fat and jovial, kissing me on both cheeks as he gave me a bear hug. I could see the open hatch over his shoulder, and there were cardboard boxes. Thank heavens she is loaded, I thought.

'Thank you, thank you, thank you for coming,' he beamed. 'Much trouble,' he continued. 'Come into my cabin, you like tea?' he asked.

The *Mare* was a small coaster of 837 gross tons, only 228 feet long with a beam of 29 feet, and she was 25 years old. There was one large hold forward of the bridge laden with 74,718 cartons totalling 976 tons of canned goods for Aden. Must be value in the cargo, I thought.

Over tea, the captain told me he had run aground at full speed and been on the reef for three days. Egyptians had come out in boats and tried to take his cargo, but he had resisted. They were most unpleasant and his crew were very frightened. His main radio did not work so he had not been able to tell anyone, and his VHF was very weak.

'Did you hear me on the VHF?' he asked. 'I have been calling all the time.'

'No,' I replied, 'I saw your not-under-command lights.'

'Many ships pass but no one reply.' He looked sad.

'Have you had any leaks in the tanks or hold?' I asked.

'No no no my ship very good no leaks,' he gushed.

'OK, very good,' I said. 'You sign my Lloyd's form and I will salve you, I will tow you off. I have divers as well.'

'OK, OK, OK, I sign, no problem,' he beamed as I filled in the LOF on his table. I gave him my pen and showed him where to sign. He signed with a flourish and I signed as contractor. I felt very pleased with myself. Now to get him off without leaving the bottom of his ship on the reef, I thought. I had contracted Selco to a Lloyd's form purely on my say-so. I was well aware of the responsibilities but it was a heady feeling.

The mate had taken her draughts, sounded round and confirmed with the crew that there was no leakage. She was well out of her draught forward, more than three and a half feet, which was a lot for such a small ship. We would have to wait for daylight before the divers could take a look at the bottom. Just hope the weather remained fine. It looked as though we would have to jettison some cargo. I did not want to damage the bottom when

I pulled her off with my powerful tug. The last thing I wanted to do was to have to take her to an Egyptian port. The less the Egyptian authorities knew the better. Just pull her off and send her on the way to Aden.

Salvanguard

I walked round the little ship with my chief officer. The mooring bitts aft were too small to take the strain of my big tug so I decided to rig a wire round her hold. All the time on board the *Mare* I kept looking at the *Salvanguard* to make sure the second mate was keeping clear of the reef. It is always an unnerving experience to see one's command in the hands of another.

The weather was fine, a bright starlit night, the hills ashore dark against the sky. I said good night to the captain and told him we would be back at dawn to rig the towing gear. I would leave one of my ABs overnight with a walkie-talkie in case there were any problems.

Back on board the *Salvanguard* and a good dinner consumed, I composed a suitable telex which the radio officer sent to Singapore, via Berne radio. I spent the night dozing on the bridge of my tug, making sure the officer of the watch kept clear of the reef and did not stray out into the stream of traffic steaming up and down the Gulf of Suez. It was too deep to anchor.

Just before dawn the AB on the casualty called me up and said he was hungry, there was no food. I arranged with the cook and the salvage crew took his breakfast with them when they went over to the casualty in the Z-boat. The salvage gear included the wire to secure round the hold and a pelican slip-hook. I told the mate to find out what the food situation was on the casualty. The more I could help the captain, the better the award for Selco.

As soon as it was light enough the divers made an underwater survey and reported to me with a neat sketch. 'She's aground from forward to about amidships. Propeller and rudder are undamaged and clear of the reef,' the senior diver said, pointing to his sketch. 'The reef falls away sharply, and there does not seem to be any damage. It's soft coral and the bow itself is clear of the reef. If you pull her off the way she came on I don't think there will be a problem.'

The *Mare* was aground on the northern edge of Abu Nuhas reef. She had been heading south, so if I towed her north she should come clear. I would have to be careful with my powerful tug on such a little casualty.

The weather was fine and I enjoyed my breakfast sitting on the bridge in the bright early morning sunlight before the heat of the day. The mate reported on the radio that he was ready and I could come in and make the connection. He had put timber where the wire went round the hatchway so it did not damage the wire or cut into the steelwork. The hatch was battened down and all was ready. I studied the draught aft of the casualty and it was deeper than previously reported, which coincided with my tidal calculations. I was going to try without jettisoning any cargo.

I carefully manoeuvred the *Salvanguard* close to the casualty, mindful that my draught was deeper than hers. I placed my starboard quarter next to her starboard quarter and an AB threw a heaving line across to the *Mare*. The salvage crew heaved the line, which was connected to a messenger through the fairlead and back to the tug. The messenger was put onto the barrel of the winch on the tug and the towing forerunner was heaved over to the casualty, where it was connected to the pelican slip-hook. I had to hold the tug in position with her twin screws. It was important to keep the messenger and wire out of the water, to ensure they were clear of the propellers. I did not want to become a casualty myself.

'She's connected!' the mate reported at 0936.

The bosun slacked out the tow wire on the towing winch as I manoeuvred the tug clear and to the north of the *Mare*. It was a beautiful, bright morning and the white horses sparkled in the sunlight. The wind was rising.

When about 850 feet of wire had been paid out I told the bosun to secure the winch. I slowly increased power on the four powerful engines, the propellers automatically increasing the pitch and thus the pulling power. I ordered the helmsman to steer north and continued to increase the power.

'She's moving,' reported the mate.

I applied more power and she came clear and refloated. It was all over in twenty minutes. I was elated, just hoping I had not damaged the bottom. I towed her well clear, north of the reef but inshore out of the south-bound traffic. A large tanker thundering south had come perilously close despite repeated VHF warnings and displaying the correct visual signals.

Once clear, I held her as stationary as possible while the divers made a diving survey. They reported no damage, just a few scratches. The mate reported no increase in the tank or hold soundings. The master was happy.

'OK, slip,' I ordered the mate.

The towing gear was recovered while the radio officer typed up the termination letter. We went over together in the Z-boat, the second mate again in command of my tug.

'Oh thank you, thank you, thank you,' beamed the captain, giving me another bear hug and kisses on both cheeks, 'I am so happy.'

He signed my termination letter and we drank tea in celebration. The radio officer had not been able to do anything with the main radio but had been able to improve the range of the VHF.

'We've given your cook some bags of flour – good fishing,' I said as we departed in the Z-boat.

'Thank you, thank you, thank you,' he cried again.

While consuming a celebratory drink on my bridge I composed a suitable message for Singapore telling them of our success. I was well pleased with myself, my crew and my tug as I watched the *Mare* head south. Well that is the last I shall see of them, I thought, as we passed them heading south ourselves, waving and sounding the tug's siren.

Shortly afterwards I received a message from Singapore instructing me to shadow the *Mare*. They had not yet received security for my salvage. She was still in sight although a long way off, so I altered course, slowed down and stopped. She passed about two miles away, not going very fast. My chief engineer did not want to go too slowly, so I passed her again, steamed well ahead, and again stopped. Once she had got almost out of sight ahead I steamed on again, and so on.

In the distance behind, the great barren mountains of the Sinai Peninsula were seen, in the words of Adrian Hayter, 'giving a sense of timelessness, as if they had outlived their own souls.'

It was much more difficult to see the *Mare* at night and easy to mistake another ship's lights for hers. I put an AB on *Mare* watch, his only job being to watch her. We did not lose her, and the next day was fine as we slowly made our southwards down the Red Sea.

Just before beer time in the evening I heard a weak voice emanating from the VHF on channel 16, the distress frequency.

'*Salvanguard, Salvanguard, Salvanguard.* Please give position.' It was the *Mare*. I gave it to him.

'My compass is not working. Please I follow you to Aden,' the master said.

'OK,' I replied.

My mind was racing. Can I get a second Lloyd's form, I thought. If I lead him to Aden that is salvage.

'I am turning on my deck lights to make it easier for you to follow me,' I told him, and so instructed my mate.

Oh, thank you, thank you, thank you,' he gushed, 'I am so happy; my crew is so happy; thank you.'

I told him if we got too far ahead I would stop and wait, not to worry. We would give him the position every four hours.

'Oh thank you, thank you, thank you, Captain. We are so happy now.'

The next day the weather was still fine. I received a message from head office instructing me to call at Jeddah for bunkers. The *Salvanguard* burnt diesel fuel, which was very expensive, and Jeddah was one of the cheapest bunkering ports in the world. I told the *Mare* and instructed him to anchor outside port limits.

'OK, anything you say, Captain. We are so happy to follow you.'

The next morning, 29 October, I entered Jeddah, bunkered and left that evening, picking up the *Mare* on the way out. The captain reported he was running out of flour again so bread rolls and flour were transferred by Z-boat. I went over as well and the captain signed my second Lloyd's form. He was very pleased to see me and thanked me profusely.

The rest of the trip was uneventful and we were lucky with the weather. On 3 November I stopped outside the port limits of Aden and went across to get my termination letter signed. I was very pleased with myself. The *Mare* proceeded into Aden.

'*Salvanguard*,' called a voice on the VHF, 'this is harbour control, you must come into port and clear in.'

'Why?' I asked.

'You are in port limits.'

'No, I am not in your port limits,' I said, altering course for Djibouti and increasing to maximum speed.

'You are in port limits, you must come in,' the voice insisted.

I did not answer as the *Salvanguard* increased speed to 15 knots and Aden receded into the horizon.

And that was that.

I never knew what happened about the salvage until many years later when I got hold of the Arbitrator's Awards and Reasons. There were two Arbitrations, one for each of the two Lloyd's forms and, unbelievably for such small sums of money, two appeals. For the second, or escort salvage, the award was reduced. However the Arbitrator's Reasons were complimentary about me.

I visited Aden by land some ten years later and while in the harbour master's office I inspected the notice board. The name *Salvanguard* leapt out at me. She was still 'wanted' for unpaid port dues. Aden was communist and authoritarian so I kept my mouth shut.

FROM *LLOYD'S WEEKLY CASUALTY REPORTS*, 1978

Aden, Nov 6 – MV *Mare* and salvage tug *Salvanguard* arrived Nov 3.

Global Mariner

10,000 tons of grain for the starving

FROM *LLOYD'S WEEKLY CASUALTY REPORTS*, 1979

Global Mariner (Greek) – Massawa, Jan 18 – Understand salvage tug *Lloydsman* left
MV *Global Mariner*. New salvors signed to refloat vessel. All crew members of *Global Mariner*
abandoned ship and at present at Massawa ... Lloyd's Agents per Salvage Association.

After delivering the *Mare* and escaping from Aden's territorial waters, I took up salvage station in Djibouti. Djibouti is hot at any time of the year; hot and dirty and poor. There were a couple of trees in the main square, Place Menelik, otherwise it was barren and dusty. The further inland I travelled, the more lunar the landscape became – a bit like a hot Iceland. The overall colour on the ground is brown and the sky a pitiless blue. In the afternoon the town is dead as everyone is asleep. The one saving grace is that it used to be French and, although now independent, a lot of French still live and work there. There is a naval base, and the French Foreign Legion was in residence. As a result I could have a decent meal and, if I so decided, a night out in the honky-tonk bars. However, honky-tonk bars aside, salvage standby is very frustrating, always wondering when anything might happen, and when it does, hoping that nothing will stop a quick getaway.

Svitzer, the Danish salvage company, had been in the area for fifty years and did not like the competition from the interloper from Singapore.

Early in the new year (1979), I received a telex from Singapore instructing me to proceed to Assab in Ethiopia and then north to Massawa. There was a war raging between Ethiopia and Eritrean rebels and it was not clear whether Massawa was in government or rebel hands. Assab was in Ethiopia, hence the need to clear in there first and obtain permission to sail through Ethiopian waters. I was not feeling too well, suffering from an apparently blocked gut. However, I felt better sailing at full speed, leaving the Danes guessing as to my intentions! The *Global Mariner* was aground north of Massawa, and I was to salve her.

In Assab, the agent and lots of officials came on board for their honorariums. The agent had obtained permission for me to proceed to the Global Mariner. Massawa had been in Eritrean hands but it had just fallen and the government was in charge again. However, the rebels still controlled the coastal area opposite the position of the *Global Mariner*.

'You will be safe enough from the rebels,' the agent said. 'They do not have any boats or ships as far as we know. Only move during the day, otherwise the navy might shoot at you. Nothing is allowed to move at night, and the navy carries out regular patrols,' he continued.

This would be a first for me – into a war zone. The agent and officials left, but it was too late to make the *Global Mariner* before dark.

Although it was incredibly hot outside in the sun, the accommodation and bridge were air-conditioned. I was feeling better and, at first daylight, sailed without a pilot. The inside passage to Massawa, along the coast, was intricate and tricky. I watched the navigation like a hawk, posted additional lookouts, and proceeded through the reefs at full speed. I did not want to be moving at night and risk being shot at. The coastline was spectacular: barren, dry brown mountains rising steeply out of the sea into the blue sky – harsh, and no place for the weak.

I arrived at the *Global Mariner* in the evening, just as the sun was setting, and anchored off. The Z-boat was launched and I went on board the casualty.

'You take us to Massawa,' said the captain as I was received into his cabin.

'We will take the ship to Massawa when she is refloated, yes,' I answered.

'No, no, you take me and the crew to Massawa,' he said excitedly.

'Whatever for?' I asked. 'You are quite safe here and could help me salve your ship.'

'No, no, ship very bad, you no can pull off,' he shouted. 'One big tug, bigger than you, try for four days and then ran away. You must take us to Massawa.'

This was news to me. It turned out that the *Lloydsman*, the United Towing supertug, had made an attempt and then fled. She was the sixth-biggest tug in the world (little did I think that, within a year, she would be my command) and if she could not pull off the Global Mariner, I could not. Clearly, discharge or jettison would be required.

Many heated words were spoken and I made my feelings quite clear, but the Greek master was adamant. Basically, he would not allow me to start work unless I agreed to take him and his crew to Massawa.

I returned to the *Salvanguard* defeated and angry. Singapore told me that I did not seem to have much option: I had better take them to Massawa. I sent a message over to the captain telling him to bring his crew across at 0600 in the morning. He would have to use his lifeboats. I was in no mood to risk my tug alongside until I had made a full survey, neither was I in the mood to make it any easier for the Greeks.

It was only 58 miles to Massawa and at full speed it would take about four hours. If I was lucky I could get there and race back within the day. I called for volunteers to stay on the *Global Mariner* while I took the crew ashore. Nobody wanted to stay.

'It's only for the day,' I told them. 'We'll be back before dark,' I coaxed.

With great reluctance, three men agreed to stay, and I sent them across in the Z-boat with walkie-talkies. The Greeks arrived in a motor lifeboat, together with mountains of luggage. Once on board, I sent the lifeboat back to the casualty and picked up her crew with the Z-boat.

It was well after daylight when I set off for Massawa at full speed on all four engines. The *Salvanguard* kicked up a big wash at 15 knots and burned a dizzying amount of fuel, but I was in a hurry.

I steamed into Massawa without a pilot and found the port empty. I put the tug alongside the nearest wharf. Massawa had been under siege for a year and, although open for some months, the road to Asmara, 118 kilometres up-country, had only recently been opened. The Ethiopians, with the aid of the Russians and Cubans, had lifted the siege and the Eritrean rebels had been chased into the mountains. They were now fighting a guerrilla war. The whole area, including the adjoining sea, was a war zone.

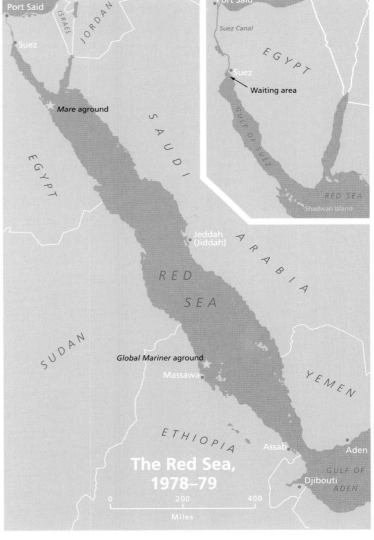

The agent did not seem pleased to see me, nor the numerous officials who climbed on board. The regime was communist, with its attendant bureaucratic controls and, of course, I was in a war zone. It appeared there had been some sort of problem with the *Lloydsman*, so I set out to be my most charming English self and finally won them over. I persuaded the Ethiopians that I was here to help and, in return, needed their cooperation. I won permission to land the Greeks, but it was getting late. The naval officer warned me under no circumstances to move at night. Anything moving was shot at by the patrol boats without warning.

I had set a deadline to be away by 1500. I reckoned the first hour of darkness would be safe enough near the Global Mariner. Just as I was about to leave, in a frenzy to be away and fulfil my commitment to my men left on the casualty, a political commissar turned up.

He obviously had a lot of power. All the Ethiopians deferred and bowed and scraped before him. I explained why I needed to leave but it cut no ice with him. I resumed my English charm and explained why I was here and that there was no political dimension. I was a 'doctor of the sea'. After some hours, the talk was more relaxed and he eventually agreed to let me sail. By then it was dark, so I left the empty port at first light the next morning.

The three men I had left behind were extremely glad to see their tug appear over the horizon, and were none the worse for their overnight stay. I anchored the *Salvanguard* close to.

The divers made an underwater survey of the hull and a sounding survey. The *Global Mariner* was hard aground on coral and two of her fuel tanks were open to the sea. She was fully laden with 10,000 tons of grain, a free gift from the European Community to the starving Ethiopians. There was not much fuel or fresh water on board. The weather was fine and pelicans were swimming in the vicinity. There was sufficient water to bring the *Salvanguard* alongside, which was very helpful.

We now commenced a long and arduous three weeks. We were completely on our own; my only outside resource was my telex communication with Singapore. It was quite clear I would have to jettison the cargo, or some of it. It was loose grain, but there were plenty of bags in the holds. What we really needed was a clamshell, rather than laboriously filling the bags with shovels. However, Selco telexed that they were sending a tug and barge from Jeddah and that I should discharge the cargo onto it.

Before discharging anything, it was important to secure the casualty on the reef. Fernando, my chief engineer, who had been on the *Salvaliant* with me, had managed to start the generators, so we had power. If necessary, I could refuel the *Global Mariner* from the tug. On the starboard side of the casualty there was just enough water for the *Salvanguard* to lie alongside. Consequently, it was reasonably easy to run the starboard anchor astern with it hanging off the bow of the tug. With twin screws and bridge control, she was very manoeuvrable.

The port anchor was much more difficult. We had to walk it back, using the derricks. The further aft we manoeuvred it, the heavier it became, dragging the chain. Eventually we got it far enough astern so it could be secured on the bow of the *Salvanguard* and then run out. Thus, with both anchors laid, the casualty would not move any further up the reef as we lightened her.

It was now necessary to hold the stern steady. I would normally just connect the tug and anchor off but I wanted her alongside. I also had proper ground-tackle blocks and wires on board the tug which, if properly laid, could be used for pulling – in effect another tug.

We managed to lift the spare anchor from the *Global Mariner* onto the *Salvanguard* and I used that as a ground-tackle anchor and laid it with the tug. The wire from the anchor was connected to the ground-tackle blocks laid on the deck of the *Global Mariner* with the block wires led to a winch and heaved tight. Thus within a few days the casualty was held steady and would not move while we discharged the cargo.

Meanwhile the divers had tried to patch the holes in the bottom, but without success. They could not get far enough under the ship: she was too hard aground. The salvage crew and fitters welded valves and blanks onto the double-bottom air pipes so we could blow out the water in the tanks, creating an air cushion. The portable air compressor was loaded onto the deck of the *Global Mariner* so the air operation was independent of the tug.

It was very hot indeed during the day in the holds. Filling the bags with loose grain was hard, thirsty and exhausting work. We were working eighteen hours a day. The bags were filled by shovel and then loaded on deck. When the deck was full, we kept the bags in the hold until the tug and barge Selco had chartered from Jeddah arrived.

It was strange to be out on a limb, completely dependent upon our own resources. To the west were the brooding mountains of Eritrean rebel-held territory, brown, bright and barren, shimmering in the heat of the blazing midday sun. They looked dark in the morning until the rising sun's rays lightened them, formidable in the evening as the sun dipped below the horizon and darkened their clear contour on the skyline, and finally black as they merged into the night. My overriding thought was that the rebels were there and would no doubt love to get their hands on the grain. I was grateful for the occasional naval patrol in the distance. To seaward there was a series of reefs, which did not give us as much protection as I would have thought and, when the wind blew, I had to anchor the tug. It was too rough to remain alongside.

The pelicans provided an excellent weather forecast. When it was fine, they swam and fished in the surrounding sea. When bad weather was imminent, they stopped fishing, disappearing completely when it arrived. As soon as the spell was over, they returned.

The small tug and flat-topped barge arrived direct from Jeddah in the charge of a Singaporean. We organised all the crew for the discharge and when it was full, some days later, we covered the cargo with tarpaulins. The tug then towed the loaded barge to Massawa, where no doubt the Ethiopians would be pleased to receive it.

The highest tide was on the last day of the month. The tug and barge had gone the day before. All fresh water had been transferred to the *Salvanguard*. The hold tanks were blown with air. The windlass heaved tight the two bow anchors while the winch did the same for the ground-tackle wire. The *Salvanguard*'s towing gear had been connected while she was alongside. An hour before high water (we had made a tide gauge and put it on the reef), I moved the *Salvanguard* out astern of the casualty.

The *Salvanguard* is a big, powerful tug and the utmost care was required to make sure I did not break anything. I was acutely aware that I was on my own. I increased to full power, the propellers causing a huge surge astern of the tug. There was no movement from the *Global Mariner*. The ground-tackle wire was bar-taut, as was the tow wire. I started to steer the tug to starboard, so she moved sideways through the water, heeling until water flowed onto the tow deck. The tow wire hummed and sang, lifting clear of the towing gunwale. I went as far over as I dared and then put the helm hard over to port, the tug swinging fast and heeling the other way, sweeping down through the water. Again there was no movement. I continued until the tide started to fall. I sent the divers down and they confirmed there had been no movement.

The pelicans had gone the next morning and bad weather set in, which kicked up quite a sea. I hoped this might help, and made another refloating attempt, but to no avail.

The tug and barge had been detained in Massawa and did not come back. I had some friends in Djibouti who owned two small coasters, which they traded round the Red Sea.

They knew Ethiopia well. Via my communications system, I got Selco to charter one of their coasters, to bring a clamshell.

While waiting for the coaster, we continued to fill the bags in case the tug and barge turned up again. The men were sullen when I went on deck early one morning to drive a winch. On the bridge front was painted, in large letters:

SLAVEMASTER, WE ARE NOT SLAVES

I would have laughed and taken a photo for the arbitration in London – the lawyers would have chuckled – but I was on my own and did not want any trouble. My excellent chief officer, Roger, who had taken over the tug with me in the UK, had gone on leave from Djibouti. The fat second officer had been promoted, but he was never going to set the world on fire. In general, the crew were pretty enthusiastic on a salvage, so I asked him what the trouble was all about. If Roger had been there, I would already have known and we would have sorted it out.

He told me the crew was tired and wanted an additional bonus for discharging cargo. I must admit we had been working pretty hard for over two weeks, and it was dispiriting that our refloating attempt had failed.

'Why didn't you tell me earlier, before that not-so-subtle message was posted?' I asked.

He just shrugged his shoulders.

I had no one to consult. However, I was determined to refloat the *Global Mariner*, come what may. I called the crew together in the mess room to discuss their grievances. I finally agreed to pay an additional bonus for the cargo discharge and reduce the working hours from twelve to eight. I telexed Singapore and received a non-committal reply. Deep down I thought it all a bit of a joke, and I left the 'slave' wording on the bridge front for all to see.

That night, an Ethiopian navy gunboat came alongside the *Salvanguard*. We, in turn, were alongside the casualty. The commander, a lieutenant, came on board to ask how we were getting on. He was very handsome, looked smart in his uniform, and spoke excellent English. I had seen armed sailors go aboard the *Global Mariner*.

'I don't want any armed guards on my salvage,' I objected.

'Don't worry, we're only here overnight,' he replied.

'Look, we've been here for weeks with no problems. I do not like armed personnel on board,' I said rather forcefully.

'Well, I'm staying overnight,' he said, returning to his ship.

Late that night I was shaken awake in my bunk by an agitated AB.

'Cap, Cap,' he said, 'there's trouble on the casualty.'

I rushed on board and found the Ethiopian navy had broken open the bonded liquor store and a lot of them were drunk, including the armed guards. I went absolutely ballistic with rage, knowing the Greeks would accuse us of looting. I had enough troubles of my own without drunk, armed sailors running amok amongst my Filipinos. I shut the bond locker door and shouted at the sailors to get off my ship, pushing aside the rifles of the armed ones. I went back to the *Salvanguard* and onto the gunboat. I pushed past the armed sailor pointing his rifle at me and shouted at him to take me to his captain. He was so astonished at this raging, shouting, red-faced Englishman that he complied and took me to the captain's cabin. I barged in and awoke the lieutenant, ordering him to take his drunken men off my ship and take his gunboat elsewhere. I would complain to his High Command. He quickly dressed and came back with me to the *Global Mariner*. He saw the broken padlock on the bond locker, the empty bottles, and his drunken sailors roaming around with their rifles. The gunboat was gone within half an hour. I had no more trouble with my crew and no more gunboats.

The coaster arrived and I put her alongside the casualty; the pelicans were in residence. Work with the clamshell discharging the loose grain was quick and easy, much to the relief of my crew. The bags from the deck were loaded onto the coaster. Thank heavens for Fernando keeping the generators running so we could use the ship's derricks and winches. Once the coaster was full, I took her off the casualty and anchored her on the other side of the reef. At high tide, with the ground-tackle wire humming, the chains tight, and by throwing the *Salvanguard* around, the *Global Mariner* was refloated. With anchors down, it was just a matter of slipping the ground tackle, to be recovered later.

The anchors were recovered using the windlass and I towed the *Global Mariner* round to the other side of the reef, which was more sheltered. The cargo was reloaded from the coaster and she sailed for the open sea. I recovered the ground tackle with the *Salvanguard*. The divers patched the holes in the bottom, and then I took the *Global Mariner* and anchored her off Massawa.

I thought the Ethiopian officials would be overjoyed to receive free wheat with which to feed their starving citizens, but it was not so.

I left the *Global Mariner* outside and entered the now not-quite-empty port. The murdered emperor's yacht was alongside a wharf, as were some Russian landing craft. I went alongside a deserted commercial wharf and the few people I could see were not very fat. The agent, a nervous individual, drove me around in the only car I saw in the place. The shops were empty. The other side of the harbour, to the north, had been flattened in the fighting. It was just as hot but not quite as dusty as when I had been here before, aged seventeen, on the *Chindwara*, the BI cadet ship. Then it had been a bustling, busy port, now it was deserted apart from the Russians, who were loading their landing craft with cases bound, I was told, for Aden.

One hotel was open, with one course on the menu, spaghetti with precious little else to go with it. However, there seemed to be unlimited quantities of export Gordon's gin. I did not ask, and was not told, where it came from, I just consumed it. I was shown over the old emperor's yacht and the bath in which he was rumoured to have been suffocated. My brother Edward had been in Ethiopia with the Royal Engineers and had built a bridge for a leper colony. Emperor Haile Selassie had personally given him a medal.

I was in Massawa for four hot weeks. Every evening I took the tug out of the harbour and alongside the *Global Mariner*. Every morning I brought the tug back inside again. I made friends with the deep-voiced harbour master, who said I was welcome to bring the *Global Mariner* inside the port but that it was not his decision. I pointed out that it was food for the people, but he just shrugged his shoulders.

There were daily meetings with officials, many of whom were political, but they would not give me permission to bring the ship in. As soon as I thought I was making progress, the officials seemed to change. There was a lot of shooting at night and sometimes the harbour master whispered to me that the people I had seen on the previous day had been eliminated.

Funnily enough, I did not feel any fear for myself. My crew and I were allowed ashore. I spent time in the hotel while the crew was elsewhere. The soap stock on board mysteriously disappeared – obviously it had a high value amongst the female population ashore!

At the meetings, I offered to bring the *Global Mariner* into the port and put her alongside the wharf myself. I would sign a guarantee that Selco would pay for any damage to the wharf. There was a sunken wreck alongside one of the berths and I offered to move it. This was agreed. The divers attached wires and I towed it clear. I was thanked but still permission was not granted.

I offered to take a party to the Dahlak Islands, where the Russians had a base. This again was agreed. But just as I was moving off the berth with all the officials on board, an armoured car arrived at speed with the gun pointing at the bridge. The trip was cancelled by a higher authority and the officials departed ashore; some I did not see again.

I offered to do anything if they would grant permission, but it was not forthcoming.

Meanwhile, the grain started to go rotten and the people continued to starve. No other ship, apart from the Russian landing craft, came into or left the port all the time we were there. It had been made quite clear to me at the beginning that, if I tried to make a run for it, the Russians would be sent after the tug to bomb me. I believed them. Then one morning, out of the blue, the agent turned up with a port clearance and told me to leave. I did, picking up the riding crew from the *Global Mariner*.

It was very rough returning to Djibouti, once clear of the reefs, and one heavy sea came on board and sprayed down the funnel. The chief engineer was not amused. I was down to five knots and it was very uncomfortable. The feeling of relief to have escaped from Massawa was overwhelming. I had not realised how oppressive it had been to be under virtual arrest. The nightly shootings, and people I had dealt with disappearing. The empty streets and shops told their own story, but it was only after leaving that the enormity of the situation struck me.

I learned some years later that the *Global Mariner* was never discharged and the wheat never reached the starving people.

Back in Djibouti, there was no activity for weeks. I had the tug at anchor in the inner anchorage for ease of getting ashore, as it was not possible to remain alongside permanently. Anyway, it was cleaner at anchor. It grew hotter by the day and was frustrating after all the excitement in Ethiopia. I was friendly with the couple from whom we had chartered the coaster. One morning he came out in his speedboat to pass the time of day. On the way back he ran, at full speed, into an anchored coaster. I heard the crash and then saw the boat drifting with my friend slumped forward on the foredeck. I rushed down on deck, taking a couple of my men with me, and jumped into the Z-boat, which we kept alongside. I tore across at full speed. When I reached the boat my heart was in my mouth: I thought he was dead. There was blood on his face and he was covered in glass from the windscreen, which he had been thrown through. Luckily, he was only knocked unconscious. We got him into our Z-boat and took him ashore to the yacht club. There was a Frenchman I knew and I told him to take my friend to the hospital. I went back and towed the speedboat to the club.

I phoned his wife and she picked him up and took him home. We thought he had had some sort of mental blackout, because he had been playing around in small boats for a long time. It was a shock: one minute I was talking to him and the next he was out. It just goes to show one cannot be too careful.

One day in March, I rushed up to Jeddah, burning a mint of fuel on a wild goose chase. I was stuck and could not leave. Old Man K had got it wrong and others had to sort out the mess. It was doubly frustrating for me because, if a salvage job had turned up, I couldn't have sailed and we would have lost it.

We were in Saudi Arabia, so no alcohol was allowed – even though I was at anchor. I was reduced to drinking orangeade and Coca Cola and soda water. The last launch back from the shore was at 1500 and cost forty pounds.

Eventually we escaped and I returned to Djibouti.

The scene was Biblical. One Sunday I went up-country with the agent, his wife and two children. He had driven us to the hills, where there was scrub grass on the black soil. A young boy shepherd carrying a staff was tending his herd of goats, barefoot. It was the end of April and becoming very hot during the day, well into the 90s Fahrenheit. We had lunch in a restaurant 2,000 feet high, overlooking the Gulf of Tadjoura. On the other side of the gulf were the mountains of Ethiopia, mountains that only one European had walked through, and that was before the war. It took him four years. It is a harsh part of the world.

I was glad to eventually receive orders to take the *Salvanguard* to Singapore. It was still the fine northeast monsoon. I had always been fascinated by Minicoy Island, some 200 miles south of Kadmat, where I had made an unsuccessful attempt to salve the *Pacificoeverett* three years before. Minicoy marks the north side of the Eight Degree Channel (the south side being the Maldive Islands) and has a lighthouse on its southern side. I had spent many an anxious hour on the bridge of a merchant ship looking for that light in the southwest monsoon, after crossing the Indian Ocean without sun sights. This time I was close in, and waved to the people ashore standing on the beach. I did not quite have the nerve to stop and go ashore without permission. We arrived back in Singapore at the end of May 1979.

The *Safina-e-Najam* was a Pakistani general cargo ship of 9,415 gross tons, built in 1960. She was loaded with 9,750 tons of general cargo. She was bound from Manila to Chittagong. At 0525 on 29 June, running across the China Sea, she ran aground at full speed on the Northwest Trident Shoal, heading 240 degrees. Numbers three, four and five port double-bottom fuel tanks were leaking and water was flooding into number two hold. She had a list of three to four degrees to port. Refloating attempts had been made without success. The master was very concerned and his ship was banging badly on the reef in the rough seas of the southwest monsoon. I should hurry up to help him and his crew.

Receiving this information made me even more determined to risk going through the reef area, rather than round it, to reach the *Safina* as soon as possible. The weather was bad. It was overcast, raining and rough. The tug was pitching and rolling heavily and some of my crew were seasick. I was not feeling 100% myself and I was worried, very worried.

We rushed through the night knowing we would not see any reefs before the tug hit one, but it was the last eighty to ninety miles that appeared to really matter. I was prepared to take the risk, and spent a sleepless night on the bridge.

At daylight I posted lookouts up the mast and on the forecastle and the bridge wings. It was most unlikely we would see anything before we hit as it was still overcast and raining. I was not certain of the tug's position, not having been able to take a sight since leaving Vietnam (this was before the days of GPS). However, I knew where the *Safina* was in relation to my position as she was sending a DF (direction finding) signal every half hour, which my radio officer picked up.

The last sixty miles were very tense and the usually talkative Filipinos were silent. All eyes were straining to see anything through the murk. One officer was permanently watching the echo sounder while another monitored the radar. My course was shaped to pass between North Danger Reef to the north and Lys Shoal to the south. They might or might not show up on the radar, which was not working very well in any event. There were unmarked reefs and shoals abounding and steeply rising. My stomach was tied in knots and I was so tense standing with my hand on the bridge controls that I was unable to drink my tea. My eyes were glued to the revolving clear-view screen ahead of me and my ears were tuned for the first shout from a lookout.

Suddenly my second officer exclaimed, 'It's getting shallower, Cap!'

My hands started to pull back the engine control levers.

'Stop, it's very shallow,' he almost screamed, eyes peering at the stylus rising vertically on the revolving paper.

'Shallow water,' shouted a lookout.

My heart was in my mouth and I thought I was going to be sick as the tug slowed down.

Then, just as suddenly –

'Depth increasing,' said a relieved voice.

The *Salvanguard* passed over the shoal with only feet beneath the keel. My shaking hands slowly increased power again as I stood on shaking legs and we continued to speed through the rain. My crew started laughing with relief. There was no need to tell them to keep a good lookout.

At 1020 on 1 July, a faint echo on the radar showed up, distance eight miles. I did not know if it was a reef or a ship, except that it was on the correct radio bearing. It continued overcast and raining as I came up on the *Safina*, the tug rolling and pitching in the rough seas.

'I am very glad to see you,' said a Pakistani voice on the VHF.

I skirted around the north edge of the reef, on which the casualty was aground. We could not see any land, signs of shoals, rocks, coral or anything to indicate shallow water. The ship was stationary in the ocean. I decided to approach her on the same heading she had taken when she went aground, on the assumption that her draught, which was 27 feet against the *Salvanguard*'s 23 feet, would allow the tug to reach her. I slowly approached her stern. We could see the waves rolling down both sides of the ship, for she was heading into the southwest monsoon. The wind was blowing force six. Thus there was no lee under which the Z-boat could go alongside.

I knew that a lot of her cargo was heavy steel products in the hold, but there were motor cars on her decks. The captain told me the situation was much worse and that the deep tanks were flooding; there was oil in numbers four and five holds and salt water in the afterpeak. I could see that the engine room and accommodation were aft, and that all the derricks were stowed. She was listing four degrees to port as reported. It was quite clear that I would have to be quick before she broke up. Worse, bad weather was on the way, with a tropical storm approaching. The master, and I don't blame him, was urging me to connect immediately.

However, I had to assess the situation. He told me

Safina-e-Najam on Trident Shoal – the view as we approached in *Salvanguard*. The sea is whitened by disturbed coral

there was only 23 feet on either side of his ship so I could not put the *Salvanguard* alongside, especially in the rough seas. However, there was apparently 30 feet astern of him. Maybe I could get up to the stern and put some pumps and a compressor on board with our newly installed crane. It would be difficult and dangerous, given the sea and swell running, but it might be possible. It was too rough to launch the Z-boat. The overcast weather and rain made it impossible to see any shallows before we hit them.

About two cables off the stern, there was only ten feet beneath the keel of the tug. My heart sank, but I had to put a good face on it to encourage the crew and I continued in

Safina-e-Najam's crew take the messenger attached to our tow line. The double nylon stretcher can be seen on *Salvanguard*'s tow deck

towards the *Safina* bow-first. There was a real risk the bow would hit the bottom because at times there was less than five feet under the keel as the tug rolled heavily and pitched in the rough sea and swell.

I impressed upon the captain the importance of speed when heaving across my messenger line and then the towing gear. He had a big crew. I could see them lining the stern, and there was more than ample manpower to make a quick connection. He told me not to worry.

About 40 feet from the stern of the casualty, I turned the tug in her own length and started to approach stern-first. The *Salvanguard* was rolling heavily and it was very much one hand for oneself and one for the ship. I was manoeuvring from the stern position in the rain. The water continued to shoal and I was dubious about there being 30 feet at the aft end of the *Safina*. I decided to abandon the attempt to put any equipment on board and just make a connection. I was frightened that, if I continued stern-first and hit the coral, I would damage my propellers and rudder.

I cannot explain how tense I was. My heart was in my mouth. We were in the middle of the ocean with nothing but sea in sight, rough sea at that, and yet we were almost aground. I knew I had to make a connection because worse weather was on the way. I had a form of stomach cramp, perhaps as a result of the hours of tensed muscles.

I shouted through my loud-hailer to the *Safina* –

'Throw a heaving line!' – which they did.

My salvage crew made it fast to the messenger.

'Heave,' I shouted, 'heave like hell! Heave!'

The messenger was snaking across the water and up through the fairlead and then the forerunner was over the side and I could see the eye going through the fairlead.

'Heave, heave for your lives!' I shouted.

The tug was being set southwards towards possible shallow water.

'Heave!' I kept shouting.

There were enough men on the *Safina* to pull the tug, let alone the tow wire. I could not imagine what the problem was. The forerunner should have been made fast by now. Meanwhile, the tug was drifting further southwards on the current. I should have anchored, but it was too late now.

Suddenly I felt as though my whole world was collapsing around my ears. The tug struck. It is the most terrible sensation for a captain to feel his ship touch bottom. I felt a cold, icy fear in my tense stomach. It was not a touch, but a tremendous pound. I was almost knocked off my feet, and some of my crew fell down, the mast and radar whipping wildly and the radio aerials flying. I thought they were going to come crashing down. The noise was tremendous. The salvage crew on the after deck all looked up at me. We were now in a very serious and dangerous position. If I did not extract the tug quickly, she would become a casualty herself in the middle of the China Sea.

'Let go of the messenger,' I shouted through the loud-hailer to the *Safina*.

'Get a line on the forerunner and heave it on board,' I shouted to the bosun as the tug hit the bottom again with a tremendous crash, broken coral discolouring the water. It was still raining.

The tug continued to pound on the reef.

'What the hell are they doing?' I thought.

'Let go of the messenger. Cut the thing!' I shouted.

The messenger was holding the forerunner, which was holding the stern – and now the bow started to fall off. I was taking a huge risk using the engines, trying to turn the tug. As a result of trying to turn, more strain came on the forerunner and the nylon stretcher slipped over the side and round my port propeller. The *Salvanguard* was still pounding very heavily on the coral. I had to get her off. The chief engineer appeared on deck, looked at me and disappeared again. I went hard a-port and full ahead on the starboard engine, there being enough slack in the nylon left on board to allow the tug to turn, and I manoeuvred back to the starboard quarter of the *Safina*. It was a huge relief that the pounding had stopped. They had still not let go of the messenger and I had to hold the tug on one engine until they did. The tug was held by the stretcher round the propeller and then by the forerunner to the *Safina*. Eventually the Pakistanis let go of the messenger and I moved the tug into deeper water and anchored.

I felt awful: tired, wet and with a feeling of utter failure and despair. But I had to put on a good face, for my crew were all looking at me. I went down onto the tow deck, water sloshing over my feet as the tug took a heavy roll. The divers were on the hatch and I spoke with them. I knew it was extremely dangerous to dive as the visibility would be zero in the coral-filled and discoloured water, but I could not salve the *Safina* on one engine.

They agreed to have a go at clearing the propeller. They quickly donned their gear and went over the side, firstly with a line. This they attached to the forerunner by feel and the salvage crew recovered the wire and the end of the stretcher. Thank heavens the metal eye and shackle had not hit the propeller, otherwise it would have taken the blades off. The divers worked a miracle and, by cutting the 12-inch-circumference nylon, were able to unwind it from the propeller shaft. They reported that the propeller appeared undamaged. Of course, this was all done by feel in the zero-visibility water. It took them an hour.

I spoke with the chief engineer and he went below to stand by the propeller shaft. I tried the port propeller ahead and astern: the KaMeWa variable-pitch system appeared to work normally. No oil had been lost from the system and the chief engineer reported that all appeared normal in the engine room. The double-bottom tanks had been sounded and no change had been found in the soundings. It was a tremendous relief, and I thanked the good Lord who must have been watching over me.

I spoke with the captain of the *Safina* and he urged me to make another attempt. He admitted that it was now low water and emphasised the leakage into the *Safina*. I agreed to have another go and told him he had better get down on deck and make sure his crew got the tow wire on board quickly. He had enough men to heave it on board without wasting time by using a winch. Evidently the messenger had been badly handled and jammed round the winch. He promised he would be there and that the connection would be made in double-quick time.

It was late afternoon when I made the approach. I turned and moved slowly stern-first towards the stern of the *Safina*. The entire crew were on the after deck with the captain on the poop. They had backed up the after bitts. Just as the *Safina* crew were getting ready to throw a heaving line, albeit a bit far off, the *Salvanguard* struck the bottom. My nerve failed me and I went full ahead, back into deeper water, and anchored.

'OK Captain. Sorry. We'll try at midnight at high water,' I told him. 'Have all your crew ready then.'

'OK,' replied a dispirited voice on the radio.

It was a dark night with no moon and no stars visible, the low monsoon clouds blocking out the night sky. It rained intermittently. The tug lay serenely at anchor, occasionally rolling heavily, while the casualty remained aground with her accommodation lights visible.

By midnight, the wind had increased to between force six and seven and it was rough. The forecast was for worse weather. The anchor was heaved up and I slowly made my approach, standing in the rain at the manoeuvring position in the stern. The tug was now on an even keel as the chief engineer had transferred diesel oil.

I felt almost sick with apprehension as I approached the starboard quarter of the *Safina*. The Pakistani crew were out in force. Just before the first heaving line came aboard, the tug touched bottom, but only lightly. My nerve almost failed again. My crew made fast the heaving line and we all shouted –

'Heave!'

The Pakistanis made no mistake this time; the messenger disappeared through the fairlead followed by the wire forerunner. The eye was dropped over the bitts and the 'all fast' signal was made. I manoeuvred the tug ahead, watching carefully as the spare nylon stretcher went over the gunwale, followed by the tow wire. The bosun paid out the tow wire slowly and I kept tension on it. Two thousand two hundred feet of tow wire was out when I instructed the bosun to make fast and secure the winch.

I retired to the bridge and a dry set of clothes. It was with enormous relief that I drank my first cup of tea, feeling dry, and sent a one-word telex to Selco.

'Connected.'

The *Salvanguard* was in deep water – well, comparatively deep. The problem was to make sure that enough tension was kept on the tow wire so that it did not snag on any coral head and damage or even break the wire. Once I had built up to full power, and

Salvanguard, at full power, churning the sea in an attempt to pull the casualty free of the shoal. Note the angle of the tow wire

remaining on the reverse heading of the casualty, I called up the *Safina*.

'OK, go astern on your engine,' I instructed, 'I am at full power. Don't let your engine overheat.' Overheating engines were a common problem with grounded vessels.

I commenced a salvage sheer. I turned the tug to port, keeping maximum tension on the tow wire. The *Salvanguard* heeled to port until water came onto the tow deck and she moved sideways through the water, further and further to the north until almost at right angles to the *Safina*. I then went hard a-starboard and the tug swivelled on the tow wire, putting even more tension on the wire as the full weight of the tug, in addition to her power, came into play. It hummed and sang, lifting right off the well-greased towing gunwale, despite having 2,200 feet out. The tug moved quickly to the south with the current, until we were almost at right angles on the other quarter, the forerunner hard on the stern of the *Safina*. The echo sounder indicated

Salvanguard's wake, on our beam, as we are forced sideways through the water while towing at full power

Disturbed coral whitens a broader swathe of sea, as the reef's grip on *Safina-e-Najam* comes under strain

shoaling water and I quickly went hard a-port and moved back up to the north.

'The heading changed 24 degrees,' reported the master, 'but no astern movement.'

'OK, keep the fairlead well greased,' I said.

'We will.'

I made another full-power sweep but there was no change and I ceased the attempt at 0305 (2 July). I maintained a steady heading with about 70% power to keep the wire off the reef and sat catnapping in the captain's chair.

The cook brought me a substantial breakfast after daylight, which revived me. The weather forecast was not good and it looked as though the tropical storm Ellis was heading our way. I had to refloat the *Safina* quickly. The fact that she had changed her heading was encouraging, but the leaking tanks and water in the hold was not, and I could not get pumps on board.

At 0925 the captain called up.

'Captain, the ship is pounding on the port quarter,' he reported excitedly.

'OK, we'll make another attempt,' I said, 'but high water isn't until afternoon.'

I increased to full power and began salvage sheering.

'She's pounding on the starboard quarter as well,' called an excited voice.

'Don't use your engine,' I ordered. 'Your propeller will hit the coral boulders if you are pounding on both quarters.

'OK.'

I continued to twist and turn at full power, the tug heeling to port and starboard. I could turn the *Safina*, but she was held fast. She must be pivoting on boulders or a pinnacle of coral, I thought.

The *Safina*'s master kept urging me to pull harder. He was very worried about the continued pounding on the reef, and I must admit I could not blame him.

The messman had just brought me my elevenses coffee when the VHF crackled into life.

'She's moving,' shouted an excited voice.

'OK, keep me informed,' I said quietly.

I continued to salvage sheer, and the heading of the *Safina* continued to change. The tide was rising, the sea was rough and there was quite a swell running.

Two hours after the first reported movement, the *Safina* refloated. The crew on the

Salvanguard all cheered as I reduced power. I had to control the wildly swinging *Safina* and tow her into deep water.

I intended to change the towing connection to the bow of the *Safina*. I did not want to tow her stern-first in the prevailing conditions. It would further damage the rudder, and towing by the stern was notoriously difficult. Even towing the right way was not going to be easy because I could see the *Safina* was well down by the head.

Once clear of the reef, I instructed the chief officer to heave in the tow wire.

'We're sinking,' said a worried voice over the radio.

'It doesn't look like it,' I calmed.

'Water is in number one and two double-bottom and the water is increasing in number two hold,' he explained.

'Don't worry,' I said, 'she will settle down. Keep your engineers pumping. I'm going to change the towing connection to the bow and tow you up to the North Danger Reef, where I can patch your bottom and get pumps on board.'

There was a squall with heavy rain and the wind increased to near gale force, with the tops of the waves beginning to be blown off. It was difficult and dangerous working on deck, with the tug rolling heavily at times, water pouring onto the tow deck. The wind was blowing us away from the reef while we made the new connection.

At 1700 the new connection was made to the starboard bow of the *Safina*. It was comparatively easy to put the stern of the *Salvanguard* close to the bow of the heavily rolling *Safina*. She lay broadside to the sea and swell. I commenced to tow her westward toward North Danger Reef. The *Safina*, under the influence of her jammed rudder, went off to my port quarter and stayed there. It was deep water so the tow wire was safe.

Afloat again, *Safina-e-Najam*, with water in her hold, rolls heavily in the swell

I was now worried about tropical storm Ellis, which was definitely heading our way. I wanted to tow south and get out of her way. On the other hand, despite my words to the captain, if I did not secure the *Safina*, she might sink. She was obviously badly damaged. It was going to be a continued race against time to save the *Safina* and her crew.

Four hours later, in the darkness of yet another overcast night, through the rain, I saw the lights of another vessel – and a very welcome sight she was too. It was the *Salvanquish*, in command of Edgar, my ex-chief officer from the *Salvaliant*. He had been sent up to help me. It was a real relief to see her, partly, I suppose, because we were now not alone and could hear his confident voice on the radio.

The *Salvanquish* was in the lee of North Danger Reef and Edgar talked me into the lee. He had a problem with his engine and I towed the *Safina* up and down in the lee until the *Salvanquish* could get under way. It was too deep to anchor, the reef being steep to. The

Safina's master was not too happy but I told him to stop fussing as the *Safina* had stabilised, as I had told him she would, and he and his ship would be OK.

Further in amongst the shoals was another light, and I took it to be a fishing boat. However, something did not seem quite right and, through the powerful binoculars, I saw it was two vessels alongside each other and they were not usual fishing boats. I felt uneasy. It was eerie seeing other vessels inside the reefs in the middle of the sea. It was the time of refugees from Vietnam and I wondered. But they stayed where they were and I stayed outside the reef.

At 0530 on 3 July, the *Salvanquish* was secured alongside the *Safina*. Edgar quickly transferred two heavy-duty diesel pumps and fuel to run them, together with an air compressor and two air pumps. He left enough men to run them 24 hours a day and pulled off. The *Salvanquish* was ranging alongside the *Safina* and damaging herself, even though we were in the lee of the reef.

It was now almost daylight and I told Edgar to go and find a suitable spot to anchor the casualty so we could carry out a diving survey and patch the holes. Unfortunately, this proved impractical; the holding ground close by the reef was very poor and the anchor would not hold in the strong winds. In the end, I hove to in the lee of the Southern North Reef, which proved to be the best place. The two mysterious vessels I had seen the night before had disappeared. I was glad they had gone.

Safina-e-Najam yawing, under tow in worsening weather

At 1100 the divers from both the tugs went over to the casualty while the *Salvanquish* went alongside. It was calmer in the lee and she was able to remain there.

The divers sealed four fist-sized holes under number three port double-bottom with plugs and underwater epoxy resin. This epoxy was marvellous stuff because it sealed hard underwater, like concrete. Edgar got his crew organised and soon had the two diesel pumps pumping out number two hold. An air pump was used to pump fresh water from the forepeak to the domestic tank. The *Safina* engineers were able to reduce the water level in the double-bottoms, once the epoxy had hardened. Things were looking up. In fact I considered I could tow her safely to Singapore even though the weather remained bad. There had been frequent heavy rain squalls all day.

Shipping it green – seas bursting over Salvanguard's bow as she tows Safina-e-Najam

By dark, all was ready. There was a salvage riding crew on board to man the pumps

and keep the captain happy. The *Salvanquish* cast off and, at 1800, the tow to Singapore started.

The tow wire was let out and secured at 2,000 feet. I towed the *Safina* round the North Danger Reef. When well clear, I shaped a course for Singapore with the *Salvanquish* escorting. The *Safina* was feet down by the head and yawed out to the port quarter and stayed there. It was rough and we were heading into the wind and sea, so progress was slow, only about three and a half knots.

Aboard the *Safina*, the pumps were only needed intermittently and the man in charge of the salvage crew kept me informed via radio. They regularly greased the forerunner, so it would not be damaged. The next afternoon, the *Salvanquish* was dismissed and she sailed for Singapore. I promised Edgar I would not steal his equipment aboard the *Safina*.

The weather became worse, with the wind increasing to gale force. It was very rough and the *Salvanguard* rolled and pitched heavily, shipping water over the bow and on the after deck. It was very unpleasant. The *Safina* rolled and pitched heavily but followed well, albeit out on the port quarter, which meant I was dragging 2,000 feet of wire horizontally through the water – and this kept the speed down.

On 7 July, four days into the tow, my salvage crew reported a rise in the water level in the forward double-bottoms. It was too rough to do anything except tell the engineers to keep pumping.

On the morning of the 8th, the weather had moderated considerably. The water level was increasing in number two hold and I became quite concerned, as was the *Safina*'s captain. About 400 miles from Singapore, I hove to and sent the divers down. The underwater visibility was good and they found, plugged and sealed a crack in number two double-bottom, which stopped most of the water ingress. I sent the chief officer and chief engineer over as well and they made an inspection of the *Safina* while the divers were down.

The tow resumed just after noon. In the afternoon, a gale-force squall swept over us and it became rough again. Once the squall passed, the weather improved and the speed increased. On the 10th, in much calmer conditions, I again hove to while the divers made another inspection of the bottom. They found and sealed a crack in number four port double-bottom and re-sealed all the other patches.

The radio officer had sent a message to Singapore Radio with my navigational warning. This they broadcast every few hours. Despite this, we were nearly run down that night by a ship. VHF warnings and the use of the searchlight made no difference and she came straight at us. My navigational lights and towing lights were working perfectly. It was only at the last minute that she altered course. It was a hair-raising experience.

At 1300 on 11 July, Horsbrugh Light was passed. It was a fine day, a great change from the weather in the China Sea. The visibility was good. Singapore Radio was still broadcasting my navigational warning. A cargo ship, which turned out to be Japanese, was heading to pass my port side, but the starboard side of the *Safina* – in other words, between the *Salvanguard* and her tow. The *Safina* was out on the port quarter as usual. The proper daylight signals were being shown. I called up on VHF channel 16. The officer of the watch signalled with a searchlight. I sounded the whistle and told the *Safina* to do the

Concerned by reports of water rising in the casualty's hold, *Salvanguard*'s divers head off in the Z-boat, taking advantage of a lull in the weather to make an open-sea inspection of the hull

same. All was to no avail. I could not believe my own eyes. When I realised it was too late for the ship to alter course, I slowed down to lower the tow wire in the water, so as not to damage her. I must admit I was tempted to increase power, lift the wire, and take her propellers off.

The Japanese ship passed over the wire and then, to add insult to injury, turned round and re-crossed the tow wire. She then altered and continued west, passing on the port side of the *Safina*. There was no answer to my repeated calls on the VHF. I was left considerably shaken by the incident.

Singapore Eastern Anchorage was reached that evening, and I towed the casualty in without assistance. The forerunner was disconnected and I came alongside the *Safina-e-Najam*. I had towed her 900 miles. I went on board to shake hands with a very relieved captain, who thanked me for saving his ship and crew. My bunk was very welcome that night, and I had my first full night's sleep for many days. It was three years later that the salvage went to arbitration, and I was appraised of the arbitration reasons.

The arbitrator said that the *Safina* was saved from a situation of serious danger and, if not refloated, total loss. The weather worsened after our departure as tropical storm Ellis passed over the area. He said the services were meritorious, performed by leading professional salvors, and well performed in severe monsoon weather. He emphasised the risk to which I had subjected the tug, which was to be encouraged in order to salve property.

The initial award was appealed, but the appeal arbitrator adopted all the initial arbitrator's reasons and added some of his own: 'This was an outstanding service where property of substantial value is proved to have been exposed to a real risk of being totally lost and where dangerous services of unusual merit succeed in salving the property at risk.' It couldn't get much better than that, I thought. 'The connection was an extremely dangerous operation and was achieved with skill and resolution.' He increased the award. I felt that our efforts had been well recognised and it was very encouraging.

FROM *LLOYD'S WEEKLY CASUALTY REPORTS*, 1979

Safina-e-Najam (Pakistani) – Singapore, July 2 – *Safina-e-Najam* refloated approximately 1400, local time, today with tug. As vessel has cargo for Singapore, present intention to tow her here for direct delivery under Lloyd's Standard Form terms. Reported damage considerable, including broken rudder, broken propeller and several holes in hull. – Salvage Association's Surveyors.

Jane Stove
A sleepless night

The *Safina-e-Najam* salvage was the precursor to a period of intense activity for me. The *Salvanguard* lay alongside on the night of arrival but I took her away the next morning on a new salvage call. On our return, we were involved with the salvage of the Norwegian supertanker *Jane Stove*. She had been refloated, and was awaiting the full discharge of her cargo outside Western Anchorage port limits. I was the designated pilot to put the lightening tanker – once again, the *Uranus* – alongside the *Jane Stove* for the discharge. The night before, the *Salvanguard* was at anchor with *Salvain*, another Selco tug, alongside. I had gone to bed early to get a good night's rest before the berthing, so as to be fresh and alert. It was a major operation for me and I did not want to mess it up.

'Cap, Cap,' a hand shook me awake, 'there's been a fight. One AB very sick.'

Salvain

I was immediately awake. This was something I did not need just before my berthing operation. It was just after 0200. I got out of my bunk and quickly dressed, following the AB out on deck, out of the air-conditioning. It was a fine, starlit night and completely calm. He took me over to the other tug and into a cabin, and then left.

Jane Stove aground, with *Salviking*, *Salvortex* and *Salvanguard* in attendance

171

Salvigilant transferring hoses, in preparation for the lightening operation

'Wait,' I ordered, but he had disappeared.

On the bunk, a man was lying curled up in the foetal position. He was not wearing a shirt. He was only semi-conscious and did not respond when I asked him what was wrong. His hands were clutched around his stomach. I tried to move his hands and straighten him, and recoiled in complete horror.

His guts were hanging out. I almost went into shock myself but took a grip; after all, I was the Captain. I wondered briefly why I had been called and not the master of the smaller tug. I realised that I needed to get him ashore quickly and do something about his insides. I rushed back on board *Salvanguard* and called up base on the Selco network.

'Send *Salvital* fastest to take badly injured man to hospital. Get a doctor on the line now,' I ordered Operations. They were their normal efficient selves, and shortly afterwards I was talking to a doctor.

Berthing the lightening tanker *Uranus*, with Yokohama fenders, alongside the grounded *Jane Stove*

'Get a towel, push the insides back in and tie it up to hold them,' he instructed.

I realised that I needed help. There were crew members around, but they were keeping out of the way. There had been a knife fight. No one wanted to help because no one wanted to be involved.

Eventually I became angry and forced the second officer, Francisco, to help. Once he agreed, he was more than helpful. We returned to the AB and Francisco found a towel. It was very difficult to push the intestines back inside because they were so slimy, and there was blood all over the place. The AB did not make a sound as we pushed as much as we could inside and wrapped the towel round, secured by a rope, to keep them in. We put him on a stretcher, still curled, and carried him on deck. It had taken some time, and shortly afterwards *Salvital* arrived and took him ashore.

Jane Stove at anchor, completing full discharge after refloating

I did not return to sleep. The slimy feel did not leave my hands and I had to keep washing them. I am not normally very good around blood, let alone guts, but I suppose the emergency, and having to do something, overcame my natural repugnance.

Despite the unwanted excitement in the night, I successfully berthed the lightening

At the start of a tow from Labuan to Singapore. The chain bridle used in standard towing can be seen clearly at the bow of this ultra-large crude carrier – one of the biggest vessels on the South China Sea

And one of the smallest – a local **prau**

tanker. During my pilotage I received a message that the AB was alive and that we had saved his life. He had been on the operating table for four hours. As soon as she was fast, I returned to the *Salvanguard* and steamed at her maximum speed of 15 knots to Labuan, where a tow awaited us. I was glad to go to sleep once past Horsbrugh Light – it is 'stay on the bridge' time for a captain in the Singapore Straits.

There were many ULCCs (ultra-large crude carriers) laid up in Labuan Bay. I went alongside my tow, which was over 250,000 tons, and when all was prepared the anchors were lifted. It was a minor salvage operation in itself to lift the anchors using air compressors. I towed the ULCC to Singapore for refit. Not many ships of this size had been towed before, but the *Salvanguard*, with her power and clean towing gunwale, performed well and there were no problems. Once delivered, I returned to Labuan and towed a gas carrier to Singapore for the same reason. Shipping appeared to be coming out of the doldrums.

4 SALVISCOUNT

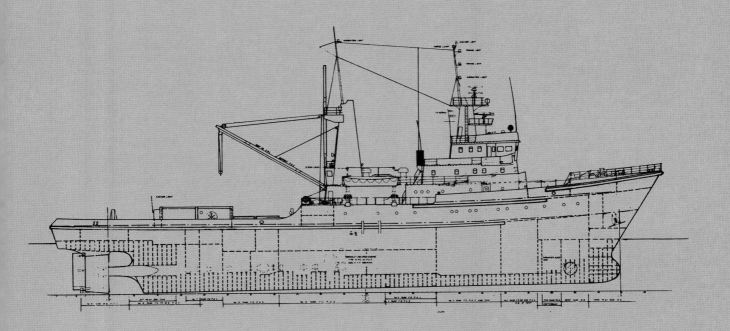

SALVISCOUNT

The *Salviscount* was a single-screw motor salvage tug built in Leith, Scotland in 1971, of 2,040 GRT and 307 NRT. She had a length of 80.2 metres, a beam of 14.2 metres and a loaded draught of 7.9 metres. She was powered by Two Crossley Pielstick 10-cylinder diesel engines, coupled to a single, four-bladed, controllable-pitch propeller in a nozzle. She was fitted with a 600-hp 7-ton Brunvoll bow thruster. Her indicated horsepower was 16,000, which gave her a maximum speed of 18 knots. Her navigational aids included radar, gyro compass, Loran, satellite navigator, autopilot, echo sounder, automatic direction finding, wireless telegraphy, radio telephony, VHF, and telex over radio.

The *Salviscount* was equipped with 150-ton and 100-ton electric towing winches, with towing wires 1,097 metres in length, one with 6.5 inch circumference and the other with 8 inch circumference. Her bollard pull was of 135 tons. She was equipped with two 10-ton derricks. Her salvage firefighting equipment consisted of three monitors and 20 tons of foam.

The *Salviscount* had fully air-conditioned accommodation for 36 people, tanks holding 135 tons of fresh water, and a range of 75 days, at a fuel consumption of between 8 and 30 tons per day.

Actuality
Storm in the Bristol Channel

FROM *LLOYD'S WEEKLY CASUALTY REPORTS*, 1979

Actuality (**British**) – **Hartland, Dec 16** – Lifeboat 70-003 launched to stand by MV *Actuality* drifting with no engine in position 2¹⁄₄ miles 320 deg from Hartland Point. *Actuality* will attempt to anchor. Lifeboat will continue to stand by. Tug arranged and expected to arrive position noon today. (Later) *Actuality* has now weighed anchor and with assistance of lifeboat is attempting to find better shelter from impending bad weather in Bideford Bay. – Coastguard MRSC.

M r K had been busy once more, and Selco had purchased another of the world's supertugs from United Towing. This time it was the *Lloydsman*, also of Cod War fame. When built in 1971 by Robb Caledon in Scotland, she had been one of the biggest tugs in the world. Little did I think when I joined Selco five years earlier that, in such a short time, I would return to the UK and take command of such a magnificent ship (and she was only 8 years old). I was extremely elated at the prospect.

I flew with Nobby Halls, who was a good friend, to Rotterdam. She looked huge when we drew up in a car on the quayside, her accommodation towering above us. Her tow deck had large rounded bars to keep the tow wire high above the deck and storehouse. The forecastle was also high and rounded, designed for working in bad weather. A rubber bar fender surrounded her hull and forecastle.

Also a little tinge of fear. Had I bitten off more than I could chew? I ruthlessly thrust such alien thoughts aside. Others had commanded her; so would I. But if she was such a magnificent beast, why sell her, a voice whispered in my head. Don't question, I thought, thank your lucky stars. She would be yours – one of the largest tugs in the world.

We were greeted on board by her captain. I was on the bridge when we sailed, her bow thruster making manoeuvring comparatively easy, compensating for the lack of side thrust from the single propeller in its nozzle. She seemed so high off the water, standing on the bridge, and the stern seemed a long way away.

The passage across the North Sea was uneventful. I familiarised myself with her accommodation, which would sleep thirty in comfort. Single cabins, mess room for crew and wardroom for officers. It seemed huge. Her motion was slow and easy, like a well-loaded large ship. Nobby and I were not unwelcome but I had the impression that the crew felt they were coming to the end of their road, whereas we were at the beginning of ours.

The captain told me, nay warned me, that it was essential never to let the tug take the ground. Her hull was completely cut away aft. If she grounded, she would fall over.

It was low tide in the Humber as we approached the lock gate. The tug stopped and quite literally fell over. She had touched bottom, albeit soft mud. She stabilised with a fifteen-degree list. It was most alarming, and gave me much food for thought.

We were met at the berth by the Managing Director of United Towing, Captain Gaston, who greeted us in his loud, deep voice.

'I'm taking you both out to lunch – and don't forget to tell Mr Kahlenberg, to whom you moaned that we never brought you lunch when you took over the *Statesman*,' he said.

I laughed as Nobby looked surprised. It was true: United Towing had never bought us a drink, let alone lunch. Obviously I had jokingly told Mr K when he had taken me out and I had described our previous visit to Hull. This time Mr K had told me to keep my mouth shut and not criticise anything, least of all the *Lloydsman*.

It was a good lunch!

There was industrial strife, and strike action was in the air. It was touch and go as to whether we were going to be able to dry-dock the *Lloydsman* for the purchase survey on the east coast. We might have to take her to Southampton or Falmouth first, which of course would cause problems. Nobby appointed me ship's husband as well as master, which meant I was entirely responsible for the tug.

In the event there was no strike and we stayed on the east coast. She was dry-docked in Middlesbrough at Smith's Dock. It was an illuminating insight as to why the United Kingdom had fallen behind the rest of the world, especially the east. The country seemed to be in another century compared to Singapore.

The men turned up for work first. They did nothing until the foreman arrived an hour later. They, in turn, were constrained because the white-collar workers and managers did not arrive until another hour had passed. They then knocked off for lunch at noon for an hour. They had no canteen, unlike the foreman. The managers ceased work at 1300 for pre-lunch gin and tonics. Silver-service lunch with wine was in the dining room at 1330. They arrived back in their offices replete and sleepy at 1430 or so. Everyone went home at 1630. It could not, and did not, last. Smith's Dock closed down shortly after we departed. I could not get away quickly enough.

I took my new command, the *Salviscount* (ex *Lloydsman*), in her smart new Selco colours to Southampton. It gave me a chance to get used to her, especially her size.

It suddenly struck me – this was not so much a tug in the conventional sense, this was a ship and I should think of her as such. She was bigger than most of the famous sailing ships I had spent a lifetime reading about, bigger than many warships. She had the loaded draught of a

Salviscount, during speed trials in the Solent

wartime Liberty ship (29 feet) and a single propeller which was as large as the *QE2*'s. She was almost as long as the cargo ship *Eastern Maid*, on which I had spent years trading on the liner run in the Bay of Bengal and across the China Sea to Hong Kong and Japan. The tug carried 1,500 tons of fuel, enough for more than fifty days' continuous steaming at full power, or a hundred days at economical speed.

This was no handy tug, to be thrown about in intricate manoeuvres. This was a supremely powerful being. She could tow the largest ship on earth on her own. I had thought the *Salvanguard* powerful and I had no problem towing empty VLCCs, but this was in a different league. It gave food for sober reflection, yet it was highly elating and exciting. My mind raced ahead in fantasy as to what I could do with her. She had shown herself to be no submissive mistress but a potentially wild thing to be tamed and mastered. She would try all sorts of tricks and I would have to be constantly alert, constantly on my guard. Little did I dream that in a few short months we would both be tested *in extremis*.

When berthing in Southampton, my wild surmise about my new command turned out to be not so wild. I felt perhaps she was testing me. The bow thruster packed up. No problem, you might think, but the single propeller, which was variable pitch, was contained in a huge fixed nozzle under the cutaway stern. When going astern, there should have been no kick one way or the other, it was masked by the nozzle – or so I thought. But the *Salviscount* would do what she felt like, which was to kick either way or not at all.

She was completely unpredictable. If the bow thruster worked, then berthing was simple enough. If it did not, then berthing was more of an art form. Somehow I had to feel what she would do, or if I felt wrong to have a plan to counteract the wrong move. When the bow thruster failed, berthing opposite the *QE2*, I was swinging the bow alongside. A quick touch ahead, with the rudder hard a-starboard to stop the swing, a quick touch astern to stop the ahead movement, and she was alongside. No harm done, I thought: I was still her master, but even more alert.

She got her own back. While in Southampton, Nobby converted the engine to burn heavy fuel and, when it was done, we bunkered. Unfortunately, there was a spill and a small quantity of fuel went into the harbour. Most of it was contained on board and the crew cleaned it up. The small quantity in the water was dispersed with detergent that was on board the tug. I rang the agent and told them to have more supplied immediately. Finally, I informed the port.

The law is quite clear. Putting oil into the water is a crime, and there are no extenuating circumstances. However, by the time the police turned up, the mess on the tug had been cleaned up and there was almost no trace in the water. The inspector noted the drums of detergent on the quayside and the spraying equipment, for the chandler had been quick. In my cabin he lectured me on the seriousness of my crime in front of the attending port official. I had the sense to keep quiet, for the master is always responsible, even for the sins of his crew – in this case the chief engineer. In fact I think it was the shore people pumping too fast. I thought at one stage that I might end up as a guest of Her Majesty but in the end, because we had cleaned up so quickly and been prepared, I was given a caution.

Diesel had become very expensive and, if the *Salviscount* was going to be competitive in the towing market, converting her to burn heavy fuel would make her so. It caused problems, not least that winter was coming on and the fuel would have to be heated.

Speed trials were conducted in the Solent. I had various friends on board for the day as guests; after all, I was very proud of my new command and wanted to show her off. *Salviscount* behaved magnificently. The 'I am undergoing speed trial' flag signal was flying as she achieved a speed of 18 knots over the measured mile opposite my mother's house. In her loaded condition, she kicked up a huge wash, much to the annoyance of a couple of boats out for a sail. At that speed, the massive power of the tug could be felt.

When all was ready, and the *Salviscount* was fully fitted out with her salvage gear, I took up station

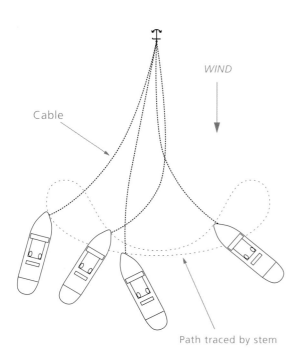

Salviscount yawing when anchored with a single anchor in a gale

WIND

Cable

Path traced by stem

off Yarmouth, Isle of Wight. In calm weather at anchor, the *Salviscount* was fine, but when it blew it was another matter. She yawed terribly, the wind blowing her high bow. At times, I had to put the second anchor down underfoot, which contained the yawing somewhat and stopped her dragging. Although there was a lot of bad weather that winter, nothing happened and we remained at anchor for some months.

I visited my mother in the Z-boat, the sea lying smooth along the shore, and landed on her beach. The crew cut a Christmas tree to take back on board.

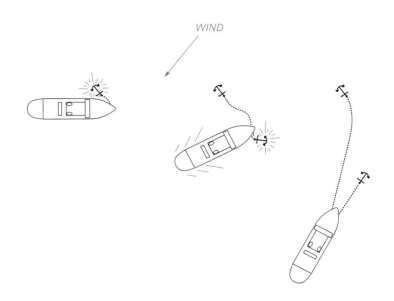

Using a second anchor 'underfoot', on a short cable, to prevent yawing

I bought my mother's black scow *Molette* and sailed her back to the tug, although there was not much wind. She was hoisted on board, much to the amusement of my crew.

In the middle of December, I took the *Salviscount* back into Southampton for stores and fresh water. I was fed up, as was my crew. Salvage station is most frustrating when nothing happens. My Filipinos did not like the cold and gloomy English weather, nor the seemingly incessant gales, and neither did I for that matter. My fanciful ideas of a salvage on the English coast had come to nothing.

It was blowing hard, it was dark and raining, and I was about to go home for supper, when the telephone went. It was Alan Scofield from Samuel Stewart, the salvage brokers.

'*Actuality*, Everard coaster, loaded, at anchor off Clovelly, needs a tow, engine breakdown,' he said.

'Where's Clovelly?' I asked.

'North Devon.'

'You mean the Bristol Channel?'

'Yes.'

'Seems a long way. Is there no tug any closer?' I asked.

'No, or at least not on offer,' he replied.

'Well, I'd better go. Offer Lloyd's Open Form,' I instructed.

'I've done better,' he said. 'They will agree a daily rate to reach the ship and, on your say-so, convert to LOF if you want.'

'I want. Tell them I agree and we are on the way. It's a foul night,' I said, putting the phone down.

'Action stations,' I shouted to Roger, my chief officer. The crew were electrified – salvage at last.

I called for a pilot on the VHF.

'It's blowing southwesterly storm force ten in the Channel,' a voice informed me.

I was elated. No problem for my tug, I thought. The pilot came on board.

'Take me out through the Needles, please,' I asked. 'It's the shortest distance to my casualty.'

'You must be joking,' he laughed. 'Have you any idea of the seas in the Needles Channel, especially with the ebb running?'

'Well yes, actually; I have lived and sailed here most of my life,' I said quite sharply.

'Well, I would never be able to get off,' he said. 'The pilot boat can't get out there in this weather.'

'OK, we'll go east about.'

The *Salviscount* was the perfect lady. The bow thruster worked fine and, despite the wind, she came off the berth with no trouble. It was a terrible night. No other shipping was moving. The wind howled and shook the wheelhouse in the gusts as we steamed down Southampton Water, becoming more intense rounding the Brambles, which are open to the Solent. It was raining, and visibility was restricted, but at least it was reasonably warm and dry inside the wheelhouse with the doors firmly shut.

The pilot disembarked before the Nab Tower, at Spithead. I increased to full speed. The full violence of the storm hit us once the shelter from the Isle of Wight was lost. It was right on the nose and very rough indeed, with seas being shipped green over the bow, the spray smothering the bridge. The motion of the big tug was comparatively easy, with a long, heavy pitch, but became violent when she hit a particularly mountainous sea

Salviscount towing *Actuality* in the Bristol Channel in storm force 10 conditions

and brought it on board, her huge propeller pushing her through it. I slowed down. There was no point damaging anything. The engines were working well on the heavy fuel; the chief engineer had switched over after the pilot was dropped.

I kept well clear of the race off St Catherine's and, bearing in mind Hilaire Belloc's warning, as well as that of the pilot book, stood well to seaward of Portland Bill. I did not see the lights.

It was a wild, dark night and I remained on the bridge. I had to slow down again after a particularly heavy sea smashed into the wheelhouse windows. I was mindful that the *Queen Mary* had her wheelhouse windows smashed by a huge sea in the Denmark Strait during the war. The *Salviscount* might not be the *Queen Mary*, and the Channel was not the Denmark Strait, but the seas seemed mountainous. It was dark, and it was only at the last minute that I could see a curling, white crest loom out of the murk, high above the forecastle, and crash on board.

The faint lightening of daylight brought it more into perspective and the seas did not seem quite so threatening. The weather improved marginally and I was able to increase speed. Off Penzance, I passed the *Scillonian*, making very heavy weather of it. I was surprised that she was out.

It was Sunday 16 December when we rounded Land's End and increased speed to 14 knots, now running before

A tug from Swansea takes over to tow *Actuality* into port

the sea with much water coming on board the towing deck. It was dark again and the midwinter daylight seemed awfully short when I came up on the anchored *Actuality*. The high ground behind Clovelly appeared dark against the clouds. The lifeboat was standing by. There was some sort of shelter because it was not so rough, although there were still storm conditions. The coaster did not seem much bigger than the *Salviscount*. I spoke to the captain on the VHF and told him of my plan.

The anchor party had to hold on to avoid being blown off their feet. I anchored the tug ahead of the *Actuality* and dropped back. I was able to manoeuvre the stern of the tug close to the bow of the casualty and the forerunner was heaved across. The towing gear was outsized for such a small tow.

Once connected, I moved ahead and held the *Actuality* into the wind while she weighed anchor. It was very rough indeed crossing the Bristol Channel, and the *Salviscount* rolled very heavily – a slow roll, which I thought would never stop. The conditions on the tow must have been appalling.

I towed up and down off the entrance to Swansea. I did not want to lock into Swansea so I arranged for a harbour tug to tow her in. It was still blowing hard in the morning while we waited – westerly force nine. The tug *Margam*, painted black, was rolling and shipping heavy seas when she came out, a helicopter hovering over her. A yellow pilot boat put the pilot on board the *Actuality* once the *Margam* was connected. *Salviscount*'s towing gear was slipped and the *Actuality* was towed into Swansea.

FROM *LLOYD'S WEEKLY CASUALTY REPORTS*, 1979

Actuality (British) – Swansea, Dec 18 – *Actuality*: *Salviscount* released tow Swansea Bay and *Actuality* docked Swansea 1623, Dec 17, with assistance of two harbour tugs. Main engine examination Dec 18.

Intermac 600
Adrift off the Lizard

FROM *LLOYD'S WEEKLY CASUALTY REPORTS*, 1979

***Gulf Majesty* (American) – Land's End Radio, Dec 25** – Following received from *Fort Macleod* at 1644, GMT: Following received from tug *Gulf Majesty*, WYH6873, on VHF: 'Position 49 12 N, 04 38 W, have extinguished fire in engine-room completely immobilised, batteries only, request tug tow to Falmouth.' Pan (urgency) broadcast being made by Land's End Radio.

Falmouth, Dec 25 – *Gulf Majesty*: Salvage tug *Salviscount* sailed Falmouth. – Coastguard MRSC.

Falmouth, Dec 27 – The unlit barge of *Gulf Majesty*, which was in tow of *Friesland*, broke adrift in approximately lat 49 57 N, long 04 45 W, at 0050 GMT, Dec 27. Securite broadcast being made. – Coastguard MRSC.

London, Dec 27 – A 500-ft barge was adrift off Cornwall early today after gale force winds broke her towline. Yesterday *Friesland* took in tow *Gulf Majesty*, which was towing the barge from the Firth of Forth to the Gulf of Mexico, after a fire in the engine-room immobilised the *Gulf Majesty*, which was adrift and without lights with the barge for several hours.

Falmouth, Dec 27 – *Intermac 600* has cargo of cranes and engineering equipment for offshore oil rigs ... barge tow parted 0048 Dec 27. Weather forecast wind southerly, force 9, occasional storm-force 10 ... Crew of *Gulf Majesty* airlifted by helicopter, all safe. Barge unmanned.

I had a free hand to take up station wherever I liked. No port clearance was required provided I did not leave United Kingdom waters, despite being registered in Singapore. I could enter any port that was large enough for my draught. It was all slightly surreal. I had joined Selco, a salvage company in Singapore, to salve ships in the tropics. But here I was, just having salved a ship in the middle of winter in the notorious Bristol Channel – a first for me and a first for a Singapore-flagged tug. I was in independent command of one of the largest tugs in the world and could do whatever I liked with no reference to anyone. I just kept Singapore informed of what I was doing and where I was. It was quite beyond my wildest dreams.

The closest port was Milford Haven, where the *Salviscount* could enter or leave at any state of the tide, so I went there. Inside, it was a relief to be sheltered from the storm-force conditions. The weather moderated and it became calm.

One morning there was a dusting of snow on the tug and the land nearby. The Filipinos were like excited schoolboys as they had never seen snow before; the cold was forgotten.

I did not like Milford Haven, so I steamed back around Land's End. I spent a day anchored off Mullion Cove, visiting the pub by Z-boat.

The weather forecast was bad again, with storm-force winds, so I decided to take up station inside Falmouth. I could get in and out at any state of the tide and it was a good station for the English Channel or the Atlantic, and included the Irish Sea. There were good facilities available as well.

Christmas Eve in Falmouth – *Salviscount*'s crew going ashore

I arrived in Falmouth on Sunday 23 December and anchored in Carrick Roads, surrounded by communist-bloc fishing factory ships. Fishing boats, heavily laden with fish, would go alongside and discharge. I went ashore and made my number with the coastguard operations room.

Early the next morning, Christmas Eve, a Bulgarian factory ship caught fire. My officer of the watch was alert and called me. The engines, which were on short notice, were put on immediate standby, the anchor weighed, and I went alongside. The foam-making equipment was all ready but the Bulgarians managed to put out the fire themselves and the *Salviscount* was dismissed. It was good training, if nothing else, and kept us all on our toes.

Christmas Eve was one of the few calm days of the winter. My Filipino crew, all Catholic, decorated the mess room and the Christmas tree they had cut at my mother's house. There was a new gale warning in operation.

On Christmas Day it was blowing a gale, low cloud making it very gloomy. The engines were on standby and the *Salviscount* was yawing heavily around her anchor. I was on the bridge, where I seemed to live, wondering whether I should put the second anchor underfoot. Suddenly I was electrified and all thought of Christmas celebrations went out of the window.

The tug *Gulf Majesty*, towing the barge *Intermac 600*, was on fire and required assistance. She was approximately 45 miles south-south-east of the Lizard, only about 60 miles from us. Falmouth is a compulsory pilot port for vessels the size of *Salviscount* and I called on the VHF for a pilot. None was immediately available, so I sailed without. If the buoys can be seen it is not particularly difficult to pass through the anchored ships and out past St Anthony's Lighthouse to the sea.

Outside it was blowing hard but I proceeded at full speed, sheets of spray flying over the bridge. I offered my assistance on Lloyd's Open Form, but it was declined. The Dutch tug *Friesland* took the tug and barge in tow and I returned to Falmouth and anchored back in Carrick Roads.

A full gale was still blowing and I spent a lot of time on the bridge. On Boxing Day it blew even harder. The engines were kept on standby and a second anchor was dropped underfoot to stop the yawing. It was wet and dismal, the low cloud obscuring the hilltops and making the daylight hours seem very dark.

That night I remained on the bridge. The wind had increased to storm force ten. The surface of the water was white where the wave tops were blown off and the air was full of spume, mingling with the rain. It was a worrying time because some of the factory ships started to drag. The deck lights of the anchored ships illuminated the storm conditions.

Early on the morning of the 27th the storm grew worse. The wind howled round the wheelhouse, the raindrops peppering the windows like pellets from a shotgun. At times the whole tug shook as she snubbed at her anchor chain, despite the second anchor. Thank heavens the radar worked – though sometimes I wondered if the scanner was going to be blown away. It was very tense on the bridge, making sure she was not dragging, and I resolutely pushed aside the occasional whisper of fear that curled around inside me. I had to maintain a cheerful pose for my crew, who had never been in weather like this before. It was getting as bad as the typhoon that passed over Hong Kong when I was on the *Hang Sang*, and broke adrift.

Once again, the situation was transformed from passive acceptance of the weather, grin and bear it, to action. The *Intermac 600* broke adrift from the *Gulf Majesty*. I offered Lloyd's Open Form and it was accepted. How, I thought, was I going to get out?

It was dark, the visibility was severely reduced and it was rough, even when sheltered by the shore, as we were. I could not see the navigation buoys. However, the anchored ships gave an indication of where the channel was. The radar was working. I had been in and out, so knew the way – not that I could see much now. I had called for a pilot but was told I must be joking.

The anchors were weighed, which was almost a feat in itself, to hold the tug up to the anchor and not let her head fall off. If I lost control for a second, I would be onto the nearest anchored vessel. Immediately the anchor was aweigh, I piled on the power, the big propeller thrusting the tug forward. I needed the speed quickly to be able to steer in the near-hurricane conditions. One side of me kept whispering that I was quite mad and would lose the tug and all on board. Her grounding at Hull and fall-over was ever in my mind. The other side was thrilled with the challenge and exhilarated by its execution. I must have seemed confident because no one queried what I was doing; all eyes were looking out through the wheelhouse windows, peering through the murk for the buoys and ships. The bow thruster assisted until I had built up speed. It was blowing so hard that I needed almost full speed on both engines to maintain proper steerage. I think the hand of God must have been guiding us because we reached the entrance without hitting anything.

Outside, and once clear of the land, the weather was appalling – a Biblical raging tempest. The conditions were quite the worst I have ever experienced at sea. The seas were huge, almost ocean mountains, but these were the comparatively shallow, strong tide waters of the English Channel and so the waves were exceptionally steep – they could not become mountains because they fell over themselves and broke. The darkness and water-filled air made it extremely difficult to see anything. It was only at the last moment that I would see through the swirling clear-view screen the next rolling, breaking crest hurling itself at the tug like some malevolent thing, trying to overwhelm her. The bow would lift, heave itself up and out of the water, the huge propeller thrusting her powerfully forward, and the crest would break on board, smothering the hump-backed forecastle. The bow would then plunge down, surging forward because of her power and then, before the bow had time to lift enough, the next mountainous sea came on board, heavy water sweeping across the forecastle and landing on the bridge windows, the tug shaking and shuddering like some human having a fit. I had to slow down, but not too much otherwise the bow would fall off. The ship pitched and rolled and plunged.

The view from *Salviscount*'s wheelhouse – the weather reports recorded hurricane-force winds

My hand was on the engine control, her heart; my eyes were her eyes, my brain her brain. I could feel her through my feet; my whole being was in tune with her. I felt instinctively when to slow down and when to increase speed; it was as though she was telling me what she needed. It required immense concentration to remain in tune yet conscious of the people around me, giving instructions and navigating towards the drifting barge.

After a couple of hours we found the barge, drifting fast.

I slowed down when close and ruined our night vision by turning on the searchlight. It could be controlled from inside the wheelhouse; anyone outside would have been blown away. The barge was a huge, black thing, loaded with oil-industry equipment and cranes. It rolled and pitched in the mountainous breaking seas, the crests falling on board and the motion quick and violent. All seemed to be in order and the cargo had not moved. I circled the barge, the tug rolling heavily, looking for the emergency pickup line.

We found it, but it was tangled and ensnared at the stern of the barge by the jacket launch slipway, not streaming in the water as it should have been. There was nothing we could do until daylight. I hove to, stern to the seas, and drifted down with the barge. The tug was quite comfortable, with only the occasional extra-large wave coming aboard and filling the tow deck with water.

The terrors of the night subsided with the dawn, a mere lightening of the darkness. It was a wild scene. The tops of the waves were blown off, the cloud so low that I felt I could almost reach out and touch it, dirty like a smoke-filled ceiling, scudding past fast to the east. The barge was huge: 500 feet long with a beam of 120 feet, depth 33 feet and a displacement of 30,000 tons.

Once it became light enough, we made an attempt to get hold of the barge. The only way was to pick up the emergency line. I held a meeting on the bridge, the wind still howling and moaning around the wheelhouse, which quivered at times.

Roger, the chief officer, went aft to the tow deck while I went to the enclosed after control position. In the open, I had to crawl on hands and knees as the wind just blew me off my feet. The tow deck was at times engulfed with water, but it was sheltered from the wind by the high bulwarks and storage house. The problem was to stand in the open. Roger had a harness on with a line tended by the bosun and ABs. He had a boathook with

Our view of the drifting *Intermac 600* in the first light of dawn – conditions not conducive to pin-sharp photography

which to try and pick up the line. The waves were at least thirty feet high at times, so the rise and fall between tug and barge on different waves was much larger.

I manoeuvred upwind of the stern of the violently rolling barge. It was drifting downwind, so I had to move stern-first to follow it. Roger stood on the towing gunwale, held in his harness by the bosun, the wind on his back. Thus he was able to use both hands to hold the boathook and prevent it from being blown away, and maintain his balance. I manoeuvred closer and closer to the barge but the entire pickup line was curled up on the barge; none of it was in the water. With the tug pitching and the barge rolling heavily, it was imperative I did not touch the barge. Apart from killing Roger, I would certainly badly damage both tug and barge. Try as I might, I could not quite get close enough; one minute the barge was above Roger, the next minute below, and he could not reach far enough to touch the line, right against the black barge.

After an hour or so, my nerve finally broke and I gave up. Back on the bridge, Roger said 'If we could get a helicopter, it could be landed on the barge.' He had been involved with the Vietnam War.

The *Gulf Majesty* and *Friesland* were in trouble. The *Friesland* had called for and obtained a helicopter to evacuate the crew of the *Gulf Majesty*.

I called the coastguard and explained the situation.

'It is essential that we connect to the barge and prevent it running aground,' I said.

'Sorry, *Salviscount*, the weather is too bad. All helicopters are grounded.'

That was the end of that idea.

The barge grounded inside Gribbin Head, off Fowey.

Meanwhile the radio officer had been sending my telexes to Singapore, explaining the situation and asking for shore assistance. Eurosalv were appointed and were sending men overland, but they would not be in position for some hours. It was essential I got a man on the barge as soon as possible to secure our position. Captain Gaston's son was on board as supernumerary chief officer and he agreed to go ashore if we could find a boat.

Singapore was talking to our Falmouth agents and a fishing boat agreed to come out from Mevagissey, which was comparatively sheltered from the storm.

I steamed round, rolling and pitching, water everywhere, and anchored off Mevagissey. The coastguard reported that gusts of hurricane force twelve had been recorded and the *Friesland* had reported waves over thirty feet high.

The blue-painted *Torbay Pol* made her way out across the white sheet of water, the tops of the waves blown off, towards the *Salviscount.* Even though sheltered by the land from the full force of the wind it was rough, and the *Pol* made heavy weather of it. It was very difficult to come alongside and they took half an hour to pick up the chief officer, damaging their vessel whilst doing so. Gaston went ashore and made his way overland to the barge while I steamed back to Fowey and anchored off.

Torbay Pol coming to pick up *Salviscount's* chief officer

By the next morning, Friday 28th, the weather had moderated. The *Salviscount* was anchored to seaward of the barge while Gaston was ashore to landward, together with the Eurosalv people. It was overcast but the cloud was high and it had stopped raining. There was still a ten- to twelve-foot swell running and I could see it breaking along the starboard side of the barge. At low water, the port side of the barge was high and dry and the shore gang could clamber over the rocks and climb on board. However, once the tide came in, they could not get on or off and initially it was not possible to get the Z-boat alongside. The problem was how to get the tow wire to the barge.

Intermac 600 aground near Gribbin Head after the weather had moderated

Intermac 600 aground, seen from the shore, with *Salviscount* standing by

The Fowey pilot came on board. He said the tug and barge were in the Fowey pilotage area. Like a fool, I believed him and accepted his services. In fact, it was not the case and I should have refused him. He later claimed salvage. At the time, however, speed was essential: it was vital to refloat the barge before the next, inevitable gale arrived.

Following discussions with the pilot, he returned ashore with the pilot boat. The shore gang had to find a way to slip the chain bridles, which were entangled on the rocks underneath the barge. I did not want them to be caught and interfere with my refloating attempt the next day. They had established that the barge was tight and that there was no leakage into the tanks.

Salviscount towing the *Intermac 600* into Falmouth

Saturday dawned fine and clear. It was a welcome change to see blue sky and it put everyone in good spirits. The pilot turned up with his boat laden with empty, sealed beer barrels. The pilot boat crew tied a line to the end of the tow wire and started towing the wire towards the barge while the winch operator slacked it off. Every few hundred feet or so the bosun and crew would tie on a beer barrel to keep the wire off the bottom. In this way, the pilot boat towed the part-floating wire towards the barge.

It was too rough for the pilot boat to go alongside the barge so Rene, my expert Z-boat handler, ran a line to the waiting crew on the barge. He had to be careful because the occasional wave broke alongside the barge and, if he was there in the Z-boat at the same time, he would be swamped and swept onto the rocks.

Once the line was on the barge, the pilot boat crew let go the tow wire and, making it fast to one of the beer barrels, assisted the men on the barge to heave in the tow wire. They had cleared the emergency towing forerunner and now connected it to the tow wire.

When all was ready, I picked up the anchor and started to tow. It was still an hour before high water. I did

Salviscount on a calm evening in Falmouth

not want to damage the barge so waited until high water before increasing to full power. As I increased, the bow of the barge started to swing and, shortly afterwards, full power was achieved and the *Intermac 600* refloated.

Once the barge party had made an inspection and reported all to be in order, Rene took them off in the Z-boat and over to the pilot boat. Gaston came back to the tug while the pilot boat took the others ashore.

I increased speed and towed the barge to Falmouth.

On Sunday, harbour tugs took over and towed the barge to Falmouth Dock. I anchored the *Salviscount* once more in Carrick Roads.

I was very pleased. *Salviscount* had behaved beautifully in, dare I say it, once-in-a-lifetime weather conditions. Everything had worked, my crew had responded brilliantly, and we had enhanced Selco's name with the *Salviscount* appearing on TV. A Singapore company had performed a major salvage on the English coast. It certainly made Smit and Wijsmuller, the world's great salvors, sit up and take notice. The only damage was to the funnel: the hurricane-force winds had stripped some of the new Selco paint off. The bosun soon had that put right.

FROM *LLOYD'S WEEKLY CASUALTY REPORTS*, 1979

Gulf Majesty (American) – Falmouth, Dec 29 – *Salviscount* towing *Intermac 600*, entered Falmouth Bay to anchor. – Coastguard MRSC.

Last independent command

The rest of our time on the coast of England proved a bit of an anticlimax. There was some fine, but cold weather. It snowed, which delighted the crew, but the cold did not. My mother turned up on a whim. The London lawyer arrived to take evidence about the *Intermac 600* salvage in preparation for arbitration.

The crew was getting restive. They had been reading too many UK papers about industrial trouble and more pay. Luckily, in late February 1980 I received instructions to sail for Toulon in the south of France, and entering the Mediterranean with better weather was a relief to all.

We had to tow a drill ship to Singapore, and it proved a bit of a saga. *Salviscount* was getting her own back for her good behaviour in all the bad weather.

The engineers were having problems with the two Pielstick engines. When they were both connected to the single shaft, one would be lazy and do no work, while the other one worked overtime. The balancing gear was not working. Nobby flew down to fix it while we prepared the tow. I enjoyed a few meals ashore in expensive restaurants.

Salviscount leaving Toulon with the drilling rig *Petromar V* in tow

I started the tow in fine fettle. The drill ship was fully manned, with the crew getting her ready for her next operation. However, things started to go wrong, and by the time we reached Port Said, not only were the engines not balancing, but one did not work at all.

In Port Said, my friend Sayeed Hassan, who was also our private agent, turned up on board. I told him what had happened. He told me to keep quiet, as the canal authorities might prevent the *Salviscount* from towing the drill ship through the canal, or impose hugely expensive assisting tugs. The master of any ship passing through the canal has to fill in and sign a form that, amongst other things, states that the engines are in good working order. Giving false information is a serious offence. I did not fancy the idea of an Egyptian jail. On the other hand, I wanted to get Selco's new supertug and her tow to Singapore. In the end I stated that the engines were in good working order. The canal transit towing the drill ship was made without incident and at the correct convoy speed, but it was a tense time for me. I was glad to get out of the Gulf of Suez.

Pielstick experts were waiting for us at the southern end of the Red Sea at Djibouti. The *Salviscount* remained at anchor with the tow still connected for four days. The drill ship captain was getting fed up with the delay, and I did not help by sailing my scow *Molette* in

Petromar V butting into heavy weather in the Mediterranean. Note the chain bridle

the afternoons. I claim to be the first and only person to have sailed a Beaulieu scow in Djibouti. I made sure not to capsize because, not far away, the biggest sharks in the world have been found.

The air conditioning had packed up as well and the accommodation was incredibly hot. Neither the portholes nor windows could be opened as no provision had been made for it going wrong.

It was cooler once we got under way again, the experts remaining on board. A few days later I received a telex instructing me to pick up and tow a fishing boat to Singapore.

The Japanese fishing boat was valuable and had a full catch, but she was only about one quarter the size of the *Salviscount*. The drill ship captain was most cooperative, and we quickly connected the fishing boat between his vessel and mine on a separate tow wire. She made no difference to the speed.

It was a bit tricky off Galle, Sri Lanka, dropping off the Pielstick experts. I wanted to

Through the Suez Canal on one engine

The tow has a baby – picking up a Japanese fishing vessel in the Indian Ocean

keep moving, albeit slowly, to prevent the drill ship running into my second tow and it took a little time to make the shore boat captain understand.

However, all went well and we reached Singapore without further incident. I was glad to get ashore into cooler accommodation.

The *Salviscount* was my last permanent command. In On 19 April 1980 I left the *Salviscount* in a launch off Penang. She was towing a large barge loaded with transformers bound for Saudi Arabia, in command of my ex-*Salvaliant* chief officer Edgar Selorio. I became based ashore in Singapore and elsewhere, mainly Djibouti, Egypt and the Gulf, as Salvage Master and Mr Fixit. For the rest of my years with Selco I lived in a hotel, when not on a salvage. My life took on a new turn, very different from command, which I missed. There is nothing quite like having one's own ship. I had been incredibly lucky to have had such a supertug and such freedom, even though she had been mine for only eight months. It was truly an independent command to finish with.

5 SALVAGE MASTER

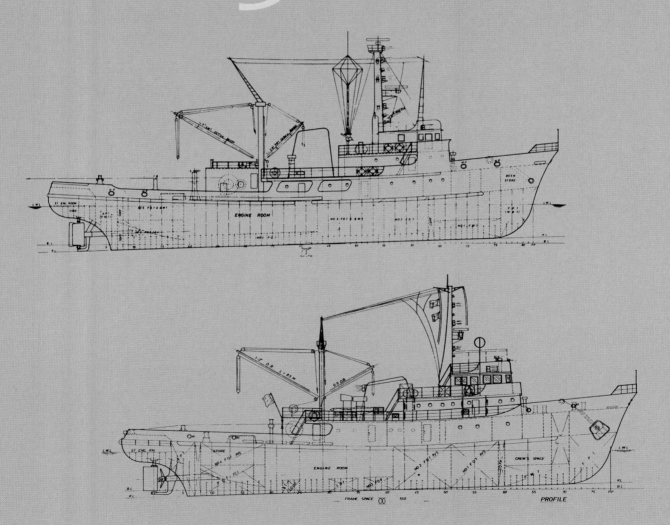

SALVERITAS

The *Salveritas* was a twin-screw motor salvage tug built in Kure, Japan, in 1976, of 493 GRT and 151 NRT. She had a length of 50.5 metres, a beam of 10 metres and a loaded draught of 4.5 metres. She was powered by two Fuji diesel engines, coupled to fixed-pitch propellers in Kort nozzles. Her indicated horsepower was 7,500, which gave her a maximum speed of 14 knots. Her navigational aids included radar, gyro compass, autopilot, echo sounder, automatic direction finding, wireless telegraphy, radio telephony, VHF, weather fax, Omega navigator and telex over radio.

The *Salveritas* was equipped with two electric towing winches, with towing wires 800 and 1,000 metres in length, 7 inches in circumference. Her bollard pull was of 71 tons. She was equipped with one 5-ton swinging derrick, and three firefighting monitors.

The *Salveritas* had fully air-conditioned accommodation for 20 people, tanks holding 101 tons of fresh water, and a range of 32 days, at a fuel consumption of between 8 and 16 tons per day.

SALVIVA

The *Salviva* was a twin-screw motor salvage tug built in Japan in 1972, of 495 GRT and 136 NRT. She had a length of 48.5 metres, a beam of 9.5 metres and a loaded draught of 4.35 metres. She was powered by four Yanmar diesel engines, coupled in pairs to two fixed-pitch propellers. Her indicated horsepower was 5,500, which gave her a maximum speed of 13 knots. Her navigational aids included radar, gyro compass, Loran, autopilot, echo sounder, automatic direction finding, wireless telegraphy, radio telephony, VHF, and telex over radio.

The *Salviva* was equipped with one double-drum towing winch, with two towing wires 800 metres in length, 50 mm in diameter. Her bollard pull was of 50 tons. She was equipped with one 2-ton swing derrick.

The *Salviva* had fully air-conditioned accommodation for 22 people, tanks holding 91 tons of fresh water, and a range of 35 days, at a fuel consumption of 13 tons per day.

San Juan
Salvage in Egypt

FROM *LLOYD'S WEEKLY CASUALTY REPORTS*, 1982

San Juan **(Greek) – Port Said, Jan 7** – MV *San Juan* grounded north of Shadwan Island and understand salvage tug *Salveritas* now alongside. – Lloyd's Agents per Salvage Association. (Note – *San Juan*, Havre for Jeddah with bagged barley, which passed Suez Jan 4, is reported to have grounded Jan 5.)

Singapore, Jan 7 – *San Juan* stranded in lat 27 34 54 N, long 33 55 36 E, Jan 5, *Salveritas* attending from 2145, GMT, Jan 5, and Lloyd's Standard Form signed with Selco Salvage Ltd at 0700, GMT Jan 7. Salvage master arrived Cairo Jan 6 and proceeding to casualty. – Selco (Singapore) Pte Ltd.

I n early January 1982 was staying with my mother at Thorns Beach, her house on the southern Hampshire shore. We had gone out for drinks at a friend's house when I received a phone call from my brother Donald.

'Telephone Singapore,' he instructed.

I asked for permission from our hostess to borrow the telephone, and dialled direct.

'Ship aground Gulf of Suez,' said Captain Hancox. 'I want you to fly to Egypt and take charge. *Salveritas* is in Israel and I am sending her immediately. Hopefully you can join her at Hurghada or Safaga.'

'OK,' I replied. 'It's evening here, I'll get a flight in the morning.' It must be just after two o'clock in the morning in Singapore, I thought.

'See if you can arrange a coaster,' instructed Captain Hancox, 'and good luck.'

I put down the phone and answered the questioning looks of my mother and her friend.

'Salvage in Egypt,' I said. 'Off tomorrow.'

My mother smiled away her disappointment at my imminent departure. I had not been back for long, and over the years not home often, so she enjoyed my visits when they occurred.

I was itching to get away, and my mind was already in Egypt amongst the voluble Egyptians and the ever-present sand, so utterly different from the drawing room I was standing in overlooking the upper reach of the Lymington river, scene of some of my boyhood sailing.

Early next morning, 6 January, I was on the telephone at Thorns, looking out of the window at the Solent. A coaster, just the right size but in the wrong place, was steaming westwards towards the Needles, past a dredger at work between Cowes and Newtown. It all looked so peaceful, the sea and the foreshore, green and pleasant.

Gellatly Hankey's office in Antwerp was open, and I spoke with the man in charge of the Djibouti operations, whom I knew of old. I told him to find a coaster, anything between 500 and 2,000 tons. Next I told my travel agent to get me on the next plane to Cairo, then on to Hurghada, and finally to book a room in the Sheraton Heliopolis Hotel, near the airport in Cairo.

It was 0940 and a yacht was running east with a fair wind, all sail set. Captain Hancox in Singapore said, 'Go! Check at the airport and I will relay any messages via the lawyers in London.'

'OK,' I replied. 'I should think we'll need the *Salvanita* from Djibouti, and fenders for the coaster. It can be pretty rough in the Gulf of Suez at this time of year. You'd better alert Port Said Navigation and Shipping.'

I said my goodbyes and drove fast to Lymington. The travel agents had my ticket to Cairo ready and were trying for the Hurghada leg. The telephone rang. It was Gellatly Hankey in Antwerp: my mother was telephone-efficient when she wanted to be. He said he had found a 650-ton deadweight coaster in the Red Sea which was available.

'OK – telex Singapore and copy me the details at the Sheraton Heliopolis,' I instructed.

An hour and a quarter later I was at the Sheraton Skyline Heathrow (it was in the days before speed cameras). I confirmed my booking for the Sheraton in Cairo, got rid of the car and went to the terminal. I rang Elbourne Mitchell, our London lawyers, from a pay phone (I always kept lots of change), and the message from Singapore was 'Go', although no Lloyd's Open Form had been agreed.

I checked in, confirmed my Hurghada flight, went through to the transfer lounge and boarded the plane. It was a relief to relax in my seat as the aircraft took off. It had been a busy morning.

Cairo airport was its usual hot, dusty, bustling self with crowds of 'helpers'. Thank heavens I had organised an agent to meet me and arrange for the necessary visa. Within half an hour I was out of the airport into the cool Cairo night with its distinct smell, so different from Thorns.

At the Sheraton the Port Said Navigation and Shipping representative turned up, so I had two agents. Not that it helped, because I was stuck. My Hurghada booking was lost in the labyrinth of Egyptian bureaucracy and I could not obtain a ticket until 0900 the next morning. But the flight left at 0730. I spent hours on the phone, helped by the hotel operator, but without success. I could not even get through to my friend Sayeed Hassan, who owned the Port Said Navigation and Shipping Agency.

Thursday 7 January was a most frustrating day, but I had put on my Middle Eastern hat: don't do today what you can leave for tomorrow and don't get angry. There was no point losing my temper: the only person who would suffer would be myself, and my cause would as likely as not be hindered rather than advanced. The phone did not work. I had telex communication with Singapore, but no telephone communication within Egypt.

In the end I gave up on the flight to Hurghada – in any case there were none on Friday – and arranged for a car and driver for the 700-kilometre desert journey. Thank heavens for the Sheraton, with its pool, bar and reasonable food.

I was up and ready to go at 0600 on Friday, the Muslim Sabbath, but no car arrived. I was livid, but kept my Middle Eastern hat securely on my head. I managed to get through to Onsy, the Port Said representative, who arranged for a hotel taxi. He would organise payment.

It was a fine cool day and I enjoyed the run across the desert. Just past Suez, the car slewed across the empty road and stopped. It was not surprising, I suppose, with the deep potholes. The driver changed the wheel and we continued. However, just before noon the wheel fell off and that was that. I abandoned the taxi and its crestfallen driver in the desert, where the car had fetched up, and sat in the middle of the road on my luggage wearing my suit.

I was lucky. At noon a 'Santa Fe' truck pulled up in front of me. I had not moved, and a suspicious driver asked me what I wanted. I thought it was pretty obvious, and he reluctantly agreed to give me a lift, dumping me an hour later outside the police station near Ras Gharib.

The police were helpful and organised a taxi. I sat on my luggage in the road and read a book. It was a fine day but cool enough to need my jacket. An hour later the taxi turned up and we set off, only to discover he was short of petrol. We ran out just outside the gates to Ras Shukheir oil terminal, where, after a little present changed hands, a jerry can of petrol was obtained and my much-interrupted journey resumed. At 1630, ten hours after leaving Cairo, I arrived at the Hurghada Sheraton, a rather one-eyed beach hotel. Not bad time, considering the various problems!

But now the real problems started. I had no communications. The telephone at the hotel did not work, and I later found out that the only telephone communication was at the Hurghada post office. Selco's appointed agent, the Canal Shipping Agency, was at Safaga, over an hours' drive away, so I went there by taxi.

The agency, with whom I had not worked before, was housed in a dirty wooden hut which contained four unshaven dirty unhelpful men. My heart sank. I was in their hands. I had to obtain both permission and transport to get out to the *San Juan*. Keeping my Middle Eastern hat firmly tied to my head, I cajoled and persuaded. It did not help that it was Friday, the Muslim Sabbath.

Eventually I obtained cooperation and we all piled into an ancient car and returned to Hurghada, where the immigration officer lived. He was not at his office so we went to his house and persuaded him to come to his office and issue me with a pass.

He pointed out that the whole place was a military area, and that there were mines and bombs. I was not under any circumstances to land on Shadwan Island, and he was going to confiscate my passport to ensure I returned. I agreed. Anything for a pass. I would worry about any complications after the salvage. My sole aim was to get out to the *San Juan* and salve her.

The agents said there was no transport out to the casualty and we could not get into the port that night. I suspect they did not want to try and wanted to go home. To add to my trials there was no room at the inn and I had to return to Safaga. The hotel was no Hilton, not even a beach one, and it had neither telephone nor telex. But I was not that unhappy with my efforts. I had managed to get myself to the right area and had obtained permission to go out to the ship, even if my passport had been confiscated.

On Saturday the agents arrived early for breakfast on my account, asking for money to pay expenses. I carried a certain amount for emergencies but I was certainly not going to give it to my agents. Agents are for obtaining money from, not for giving it to! I knew it would be sorted out in the fullness of time, but time was the thing I did not have at the moment. I was in a fever to get out to the salvage.

The agents drove me through the dusty town to the stevedores' office in Safaga. They told me there was no boat available to take me out to the reef where *San Juan* was aground. We returned to the hotel for refreshments. I eventually persuaded them to take me to Hurghada port, where we arrived just before noon. The armed guards at the gate stopped us from entering despite my pass. While the agents entered into a wild argument with them I walked into the small port. The sand was swirling in small whirlpools at my feet as I walked out onto the quay, half expecting to be shouted at, or even shot at, by the armed guards. It was blowing hard and there were small white horses on the water in the gusts. There was a supply boat belonging to the German company OSA alongside, the *Maritnum*, and I went on board.

On the bridge the helpful German captain let me use his VHF radio, and I called up the *Salveritas* and the *San Juan*. There was no answer from either vessel. I looked at the chart and saw that Abu Nuhas Reef was only 22 miles away. But unless I could find a way out it might as well have been 220 miles. The captain said he was sailing shortly but he could not take me out. I would have to obtain permission from the oil company and he doubted it would be given. He wished me luck as I went ashore.

From the bridge of the *Maritnum* I had noticed a rather elderly-looking large white motor yacht moored in the port. I walked out to the *Gabriella* and introduced myself to the owner, who also turned out to be German. We chatted away and I eventually got around to asking him if he would take me out to Abu Nuhas Reef. He invited me on board for a coffee and to look at the chart. It was quite surreal for me to be standing in the wheelhouse of a yacht in a port in the Gulf of Suez, desert sand filling the air, the harsh brown colours outside, negotiating a ride out to a reef. The coffee made by his wife was very welcome.

'It is a tricky passage, look,' he said, pointing at the chart.

'No problem for you, I'm sure,' I laughed.

'There is the fuel, and we would need special permission, it is all very difficult,' he said looking at me.

I realised what he was after. I must have been a bit slow on the uptake.

'No problem, I will pay. I would like to charter your yacht for the day to take me out.'

His eyes lit up, but mine popped when he told me the fee. I negotiated, and he finally agreed a charter rate all-in of $5,000, and I had to obtain the permission. I could have chartered a ship for that amount, but I was extremely pleased to have found a way to reach the *San Juan*.

I went ashore to find my agents still at the gate but with another group of Europeans. They turned out to be the Greek ship owners' representative John Goodis and his British consultant Harry Lambert.

'I have transport,' I announced once I had found out who they were.

Their faces lit up and the agents looked surprised.

'We are going out by yacht,' I said, pointing to the *Gabriella*. 'Just have to obtain permission.'

As might be expected it was a bureaucratic nightmare. I had a pass for myself from the immigration but I had to obtain them for the others, including the owner of the *Gabriella* and his wife and daughter. Then I needed these passes to be stamped by the military authorities so we could enter the military area. Who was going to check the pass on the reef I did not know or care. We needed customs permission as well, but they were helpful after a small honorarium. It took all afternoon but finally it was done. I had permission, I paid the charter fee, and we were ready to go. But it was too late to leave that day. The owner was not prepared to proceed at night, and I did not blame him. It was blowing a full gale.

Salveritas

We spent a very jolly evening on board the yacht. The owner's wife and daughter served us a very tasty dinner washed down with wine. I even managed to get a message to Singapore via another OSA supply boat, the *Lübeckertor*, who made contact with the *Salveritas*. I was well pleased with the day's efforts.

The next day – I remembered that it was my mother's seventieth birthday – we left just after 0700. The wind had gone down a little but it was still blowing hard and the air was filled with sand. It was very rough outside the port and the old *Gabriella* rolled and pitched her way for the 22-mile trip. No one felt like breakfast. I stayed in the wheelhouse with the owner, spray obscuring the windows at times.

Two hours after leaving I spoke with the captain of the *Salveritas* on the VHF. 'Pick up

The *San Juan*, aground among the wrecks she was threatening to join.

your anchor, Captain, and come round into the lee of the reef to pick us up,' I instructed.

'OK Cap,' he replied. 'The *San Juan* has moved during the night and is very close to the mast of another wreck on the reef,' he informed me. It sounded as though the casualty was actually on top of another wreck. No doubt I would find out soon enough.

The *Salveritas* steamed towards us and an hour later we met in the shelter of Abu Nuhas Reef. The Z-boat came alongside the *Gabriella* and took the three of us over to the tug. We waved goodbye to the yacht as they left to return to Hurghada, the wind and sea now behind them.

The *San Juan* was on the north side of the reef, the windward side, her bow high in the air, her stern low in the water. She was miles out of her draught. I could see the masts of not one but two wrecks close by her. It was rough and the waves were breaking around her stern; there was no proper lee on either side. It was a fine day, albeit hazy with sand in the air, and blowing hard. At this time of year the wind could blow for weeks like this, increasing to gale in the afternoons.

I conferred with Captain Gianan and read his report.

Three days ago he had taken the *Salveritas*, a twin-screw Kort nozzle tug, alongside the port side of the *San Juan*, slightly damaging his starboard bridge wing. The Lloyd's Open Form was signed that day between him and the master of the casualty. During the night the weather became worse and he pulled off, further damaging the tug. I could see it was going to be very difficult to go alongside. The starboard side was blocked by the mast of the wreck, which was almost touching her, leaving only the port side.

We discussed the situation and decided to have a go 69, that is the stern of the tug to the bow of the *San Juan*. This tug was very manoeuvrable, and the idea was to get myself and the owners' representative with his consultant on board the casualty as easily as possible. It was not a good decision, and almost caused complete disaster. I should have risked using the Z-boat straightaway.

We went in stern-first because of the rough seas. Had we gone in bow-first the seas would have been astern and coming aboard the towing deck, making it much more difficult to manoeuvre. With the bow heading into the seas, Captain Gianan manoeuvred towards the casualty. The *Salveritas* was pitching heavily and he was having difficulty keeping the bow up into the wind. It was essential to do this, because if the bow fell off to port it would hit the *San Juan* and cause damage, and if it fell off the other way he would have to pull off and out to avoid the tug being rolled onto the reef. It was a tricky and dangerous situation. The bow did fall off just as we were coming alongside, and the fenders were insufficient to prevent damage. I was standing next to the captain as she hit the *San Juan* a mighty thump, almost knocking us off our feet.

'Pull off, Captain. Go full ahead and away,' I said quietly.

The *Salveritas* leapt ahead, her bow plunging into a breaking wave, black smoke pouring out of the funnel. The wave came on board and swept over the wheelhouse, the windows totally obscured by water.

'No need for a wash-down,' I laughed.

Captain Gianan was not very amused, and even less so when I suggested he had another go.

'I will take responsibility for the damage,' I said. 'We must get on board.'

He tried again and the same thing happened, but even worse: a line we had not seen entangled itself round the port propeller and the engine stopped. It was a very tense moment with the bow falling away to starboard towards the reef. He increased to full-ahead power on the starboard engine in an attempt to stop the swing. It was very rough and at one point it was touch and go but as speed picked up the bow began to swing away from the reef.

'OK, take her round into the lee of the reef and anchor,' I instructed, my heart working overtime but my voice, I hoped, sounding calm and confident. It had nearly been curtains. If the tug had touched the reef she would have rolled over and there would have been much loss of life. The tug would have been lost. I was not very pleased with myself.

We limped round on one engine, rolling very heavily, and anchored. It was a relief to be in the lee of Abu Nuhas Reef, where it was quite calm, and the tug lay quietly. It was still blowing very hard, the air filled with sand, the visibility under two miles.

I was still no closer to getting on board the casualty, and now I had a crippled tug on my hands. However, the divers were soon over the side. They reported there were seven turns of a black ship's mooring line round the propeller shaft. It would take some time to clear. There was damage to the bulwarks aft and on the bridge wing.

The only way to get on board the casualty was in the small rubber-bottomed Z-boat. I was not looking forward to the attempt. It was rough. There was no proper lee on either side of the *San Juan*. Her stern was pointing in the direction of the wind and sea, which at times broke in a white mass. It was going to be a perilous trip.

The Z-boat was launched and the three of us climbed on board, with the best boat driver in charge. It was low tide and we decided not to risk crossing the reef against the wind – a damaged outboard engine or propeller would be a disaster. It was fine in the lee of it but once clear it was very rough indeed, with short steep seas and a seven- to nine-foot swell. We were all kept busy bailing and holding on as the little boat shipped seas heading into the weather. Once off the *San Juan* he headed in with the wind and sea astern. The best lee was on the starboard side, and to get there we had to cross the wreck with the mast alongside the *San Juan*. As we crossed it I saw the black mooring lines moving in the water, snake-like. It was obvious where the *Salveritas* had picked up the line round the shaft. One of them must have managed to float underneath the casualty.

I was exceedingly relieved to climb the pilot ladder rigged by the *San Juan* crew, who quickly heaved up our luggage. The other two followed me up the ladder, while the Z-boat, with its engine lifted, drifted back to the *Salveritas* across the reef.

I walked round the casualty. On the starboard side the plating was actually touching the mast of the wreck. She was in fact on top of it. There was considerable movement. The *San Juan* was pitching, the bow hard aground but the stern afloat and moving up and down. As a result the hull was grinding against the mast of the wreck.

'Send the pelican hook with the salvage crew,' I instructed the captain of the salvage tug on the walkie-talkie. 'We will get connected up and keep the *San Juan* off the mast of the wreck.'

'OK Cap.'

Early in the afternoon the chief officer and the salvage crew arrived. We secured the pelican hook, backing up the bitts with wire lashings. The occasional spray came on board from the waves pounding the stern, drenching us. The movement was quite marked and I wondered what damage the bottom of the ship had suffered. It was fine and sunny but quite cold in the wind, and made more so by our wet clothes.

I conferred with the captain and chief officer in the captain's cabin, putting paper on the settee to protect it from my wet trousers. I asked to see the stability information and found out it was not good. The GM was only 0.26 m, not allowing for any upthrust as a result of being aground. If I got it wrong she might capsize on refloating.

I went aft. Waves were breaking round the stern, hitting with a thump, spray coming on board. Everything was ready and I told the captain of the *Salveritas* over the radio to come in and make his connection. The salvage crew were standing by.

Just at that moment the chief officer of the *San Juan* approached me and said, 'The duct keel is flooding and the pump is not containing it.'

I followed him down into the engine room, leaving the *Salveritas* chief officer in charge. He showed me the sounding pipe, which was under pressure, the cap securely screwed down, and the manhole lid, which was leaking. The engineers were standing around looking at me.

'Keep pumping,' I told the chief engineer.

My heart was in my boots. A duct keel is an absolute curse because it runs all the way forward under the holds. Water might leak into the holds and progressively flood the ship. If this happened the ship would be lost and all our efforts would be for nothing. The surrounding wrecks, and the fact that we were on top of one, rather emphasised the point. There was nothing I could do so I returned aft.

The *Salveritas* was approaching stern-first, rolling and pitching, the aft deck often flooded, soaking the crew. When she was close to a heaving line was thrown from the *San Juan*, quickly grabbed by those on the tug and made fast to the messenger. The messenger was heaved on board the casualty and put round the capstan. With power it was easy to heave the forerunner on board, where it was connected to the pelican hook. The spray from an occasional breaking wave round the stern drenched us.

It was 1600 and it had been a busy and eventful day. I was exceedingly pleased the *Salveritas* was safely connected after the problems and the damage. It was a huge morale boost to everyone: something was happening. I made my way up to the bridge while the tow wire was streamed, and the salvage crew greased the fairlead and checked the lashings.

'All yours,' said the captain as I entered the wheelhouse, a bit crowded with a helmsman standing by, the owners' rep, the consultant, the officer of the watch and a few hangers-on. I pressed transmit on my radio,

'OK, Captain,' I said, 'we will make a refloating attempt. When you have secured your tow wire slowly increase to full power and tow on the port quarter.'

I walked out onto the port bridge wing in the late afternoon sun, the wind cold through my wet clothes. I watched the tug, rolling and pitching, and once the wire was secured I could see him increasing power as the white water round his stern built up. I watched the bearing of the wreck on the port bow and the ship's head from the wing repeater compass. The heading changed a few degrees to starboard from 102 to 105, which was encouraging, but the ship felt dead, there was no astern movement. I walked quickly through the wheelhouse, past the expectant faces, onto the starboard wing and looked over the side. Yes, as I thought, the hull was now just clear of the mast of the wreck, no longer touching it.

I went back to the port wing so I could see the tug, now towing at full power, the sea around her stern a mass of white water. The heading was now 112, a full ten-degree change, and the bearing of the wreck had changed slightly. But there was no further movement. I walked over to the wheelhouse door.

'Full astern,' I ordered.

The captain swung the telegraph and the ship came to life as the engine was started, the deck vibrating under my feet as power was built up. I let it run for a few minutes but there was no astern movement, I knew then she was hard aground.

'Stop,' I ordered. The vibration stopped and it was again quiet except for the sound of the wind.

'Reduce power and tow at slow speed fine on the port quarter,' I spoke into the radio. 'Don't let her drift down near the reef.'

'OK Cap.'

The *Salveritas* would be quite safe as long as a good watch was kept to make sure the current did not drift her onto the reef.

I went down to the cabin I had been given and changed into dry clothes. In the captain's cabin I had discussions with the senior people. It was obvious the casualty was hard aground and was in serious danger with the leaking and flooded duct keel, and I was worried about her stability.

The senior diver reported to me there had been no movement astern. The salvage foreman reported the holds were empty of water and the double bottoms were intact except for the forepeak and numbers one and two. There was no further damage to the hull.

The discussion continued on how to pump out the duct keel and what my plan was. I told the captain to transfer the fuel from the forward double-bottom tanks to the aft ones, both to increase the trim and to protect the reef if any more became breached. I mooted the idea of jettisoning cargo, but this was rejected. They wanted to wait for the coaster which was supposed to be on the way. How I was going to get her alongside in the prevailing weather, let alone keep her there, I did not know. If I could not manage a manoeuvrable tug I was certainly not going to be able to get a single-screw coaster alongside. However, I held my tongue. No point in depressing people.

I reworked the stability and found it to be even worse, with a GM of only 0.19 m – very small in the situation. But I was certain cargo would have to be offloaded one way or the other, and that would increase the stability. The meeting broke up when we went to the saloon for the evening meal. My salvage crew were supplied by Z-boat from the tug. They much preferred their own food, whatever the difficulties of obtaining it!

It turned out to be a busy and frustrating night, and I was hard pressed to keep up spirits. A lot went wrong.

At 2000 the valve room flooded. A little later the hold soundings revealed number three flooding, which would damage the cargo. The duct keel continued to defy our attempts to pump it out. An air pump was sent over from the *Salveritas*, even though Z-boat work was much more risky at night and the sea had not gone down. The valve room was pumped out and the leak in a pipe was patched. Number three hold continued to flood.

We worked all night and I was tired when I tried another refloating attempt on the morning of the 11th. It seemed I had been on board a lot longer than 24 hours. As expected, the attempt was unsuccessful – but it was good for morale to try.

The salvage crew prepared the equipment for blowing compressed air into number one and two double bottoms. The idea is to blow air into the tank from the air pipe and blow the water out of the hole from which it came. It is an excellent way of emptying a flooded tank but only works if the tank top and air pipes are air-tight, otherwise the air escapes and the water comes back in. The forepeak was opened up but the divers reported the damage was too great to repair. This was also prepared for blowing.

During the afternoon we rigged what were in effect ground-tackle wires to the wrecks, using the wrecks as anchors. It was strange to see the Filipino crew clambering around on the mainly submerged hulls, the spent waves swirling around them. The idea was to hold the casualty in place while the cargo was thrown over the side. I did not want any movement until I was ready, The wrecks were mute reminders of what would happen to the *San Juan* if we were not successful, or if she capsized on refloating.

The coaster had been delayed. I decided to force the issue, because even if the coaster arrived I would not be able to get her alongside until the weather moderated. At this time of year it could blow for weeks on end.

On the morning of the 12th I persuaded the owners' rep, consultant and captain to sign a letter with me agreeing to the jettison. It was a major step to jettison cargo. For the salvors it was throwing

Jettisoning cargo from the *San Juan*

value over the side and reducing the potential salved fund, while for the owners it created problems with the cargo owners and consignees. Once the letter was signed, jettison started immediately. The salvage crew worked numbers one and two holds.

The *San Juan* crew refused to help. This was a big problem. I coerced the owners' rep and consultant to help and I drove a winch, but I had too few men and discharge was slow. The sacks in the holds were stacked onto rope slings, which we hoisted out of the hold by derrick and placed on the gunwale. The wire holding the sling was slacked off and the bags were pushed into the sea. It was slow and hard work and at the end of the first day only 87 tons had been jettisoned. We were all exhausted.

On the 13th our rate improved a little and we managed 108 tons. The weather remained fine but it continued to blow. The waves swept the bags clear and they burst on the reef.

I was seriously annoyed that the crew would not help. I considered it their duty but they refused. Eventually I decided to offer a monetary inducement, and after much haggling a figure was agreed. On the 14th they started work, and work they did, jettisoning 137 tons. The weather remained the same although it blew harder and some of the waves reached almost up to deck level, sweeping along the side of the ship.

The next few days passed in a blur of hard physical labour, eat, sleep, and more work. Number three hold continued to flood up to sea level and there was nothing I could do about it. The deep tanks then flooded. That was solved by placing an electric submersible

pump from the *Salveritas* into the tank and pumping on a regular basis.

A week of hard labour saw 1,942 tons of barley jettisoned. The *Salveritas* continued to tow all this time and the casualty's bow was secured to the wrecks. The tides were rising.

In the early-morning darkness of 22 January all was ready. Number one and two double-bottom tanks and the forepeak were blown empty by compressed air. The deep tank was pumped dry. The engine-room pump was on the duct keel. I was on the bridge.

At 0530 I instructed the *Salveritas* to tow at full power. Once full power had been achieved the captain started to salvage yaw, throwing the tug from side to side and moving from the port quarter to astern and back again. I watched him like a hawk from the bridge wing so I could advise if necessary. I told the captain of the *San Juan* to put his engine full astern, and the deck was soon vibrating and going up and down as though straining to refloat. The heading changed but there was no movement astern.

Some time later I was beginning to despair. I worried that the main engine would overheat. It is not a good idea to run the engine on a grounded ship for too long astern. I was about to order the engine stopped when suddenly there was a tremendous bang forward of the bridge and a violent movement. I was almost thrown off my feet. Quite suddenly she slipped into deep water.

I immediately told the *Salveritas* to reduce power. The salvage crew on the forecastle were all ready and let go the wires leading to the wrecks. It was a huge relief for me, and the men on the bridge cheered, although I was concentrating on watching the tug. She towed the *San Juan* stern-first into the lee of the reef. The casualty yawed violently but it did not matter at slow speed, and soon I was able to instruct the captain to let go the anchor. The sun was rising, shining on the wrecks, cheated of their new companion. The salvage crew aft slipped the tow wire from the pelican hook and the *Salveritas* recovered it and came alongside later. It was calm in the lee of the reef.

The divers sealed any holes they could find, especially in the duct keel. The damage to number one and two double bottoms was too great to patch, but as long as the air pressure was maintained in the tanks there was no problem.

The tow up the crowded Gulf of Suez was made without incident, but I remained on the bridge all the way. The weather was fine but it was still blowing.

'Is that a speed boat you are towing?' asked one passing ship over the VHF – a reference to the excessive trim of the casualty, more than 20 feet by the stern.

It took a week of negotiations to obtain my termination letter. My last sight of the *San Juan* was her bow sticking up in the air like a sinking ship, her stern far down in the water, her excessive trim emphasised by the normal ships anchored close by in the Suez waiting area, desert sand close by, dust in the air, the smell of Egypt – all a far cry from where it began for me, at Thorns Beach.

My agents arranged the recovery of my passport from Hurghada.

FROM *LLOYD'S WEEKLY CASUALTY REPORTS*, 1982

San Juan (Greek) – **Piraeus, Feb 4** – *San Juan:* Salvage services terminated 1100 GMT, Feb 2. Vessel anchored in Suez waiting area, lat 29 50 42 N, long 32 35 36 E. Forepeak, Nos 1 and 2 double bottoms open to the sea, tank tops tight. Duct keel partly sealed with controllable leakage to engine room. – Salvage Association's Surveyors.

Gay Fidelity
Ablaze and sinking in the Red Sea

FROM *LLOYD'S WEEKLY CASUALTY REPORTS*, 1982

Gay Fidelity **(Greek) – Port Said, Mar 9** – MV *Gay Fidelity*, Bremen for Dammam with 10,207 metric tons of barley, exited Suez pm, Mar 5, reported caught fire in Red Sea.

Suez, Mar 12 – Fire on the *Gay Fidelity* forced the entire crew to abandon ship, maritime agency officials said today. The crew abandoned ship apparently after failing to control the fire, which started in the engine room, they said. The *Nasaud* rescued the crew of the *Gay Fidelity* while on the way to the Suez Canal on the way to Romania. – United Press International.

I was phoned early in the morning in the Hyatt in Cairo, Egypt, almost a miracle in itself because the phones often did not work, especially the international ones.

'Go and join the *Salviva* in Suez and proceed south,' instructed Ismail. 'There is a ship on fire in the Red Sea.'

This was more than enough for me to shrug off Egyptian torpor. I was ready for some action.

Ismail passed the phone to David Hancox, the then Selco manager.

'*Salviva* has sent the message,' he informed me, 'and the captain says there is another cargo ship standing by.'

'OK,' I said. 'Telex Port Said Navigation and Shipping and instruct them to telephone Suez and tell Hassan to organise clearance. I shall be signed on to the *Salviva* so I can leave Egypt, so have a boat standing by.'

'Will do, and good luck,' he signed off. I arranged for a car, packed, paid the hotel bill, dispatched documents to Geneva, and departed within 45 minutes of the telephone call. I urged the driver on through the dense Cairo traffic, promising him a bonus if he got me to Suez within two hours. Despite a sand storm crossing the desert, he set me down at the agent's office within an hour and a half, thus earning his bonus.

Sayeed Hassan's brother, who ran the Suez office, had got his act together and had told the captain of the *Salviva* to remove the salvage equipment on his tow and prepare to depart.

I spoke with the master of the *Salviva*, Captain Loretto Gajardo, who had been second mate and then chief officer with me on the *Salvaliant*. He told me that they were still waiting for the water barge ordered two days before. Hassan said it was on the way. He took me in his car to immigration and I was cleared, although my passport was once again taken off me so that I was forced to return to Egypt. A launch was chartered and I was on board before noon, just three hours from receiving the telephone call. It must have been a record for Egypt!

'I have been calling for the pilot since 0130 this morning,' Captain Gajardo told me, 'but no luck so far.'

'*Granship, Granship, Granship*,' I called on the VHF, and Hassan answered.

'Go round to the harbour master and give him a present and ask him if we can sail without a pilot. We will pay the normal fee.' I instructed.

'OK.'

I was in a fever of impatience to be away. Another salvor might turn up or the fire might now be out of control. I was within an inch of sailing without permission, but I knew it would cause problems when we came back if I did so.

Salviva

Just after noon, the water barge turned up and I told the chief officer to get as much water on board as quickly as possible.

An hour later, Hassan called on the VHF.

'I am at the harbour master's office,' he said, 'and a pilot will be on board in fifteen minutes.'

The water man was given an honorarium and cast off. The anchor was heaved up and full speed was rung on the telegraph as the pilot stepped on board. It is not exactly difficult to take a tug out of the Suez Bay, and the channel for Newport Rock is well marked.

Fifteen minutes after boarding, the pilot departed off Newport Rock and *Salviva* headed south down the Gulf of Suez at full speed. The wind was southeast, so *Salviva* was heading into it, the barren, brown hills on either side of the Gulf visible in the haze. The Gulf of Suez is comparatively narrow and the traffic is very heavy, with many oil rigs and platforms to be avoided.

Full speed was maintained, the tug rushing through the night, the lights on the oil rigs bright under the clear sky. The wind went round to the northwest and increased, blowing the funnel fumes over the bridge. Shadwan Island, at the entrance to the Gulf, was passed early the next morning, Tuesday 9 March.

Salviva was fitted with telex over radio but it had broken down, so all communication with head office in Singapore was by wireless telegraphy, i.e. Morse code. I kept my messages as short as possible. From the messages received, I knew that the casualty was the *Gay Fidelity* and the cargo ship standing by was the *Ibn Sina*. The *Gay Fidelity* was a

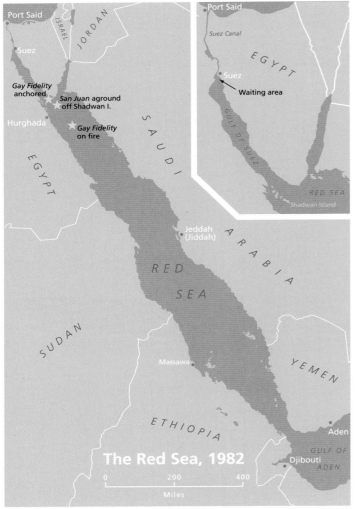

The Red Sea, 1982

five-hatch cargo ship, fully laden with a cargo of barley of about 10,000 tons deadweight, about 390 feet long. The *Ibn Sina* was slightly bigger and had a British captain. The two ships close together would make a good radar target.

It was a fine morning and the white horses on the waves glinted in the sunlight. Shortly after breakfast, I spoke with Captain Campbell of the *Ibn Sina* on the VHF.

'Our DR from last night's star sight is 27 06 N, 34 56 E. The fire appears to be out and I'm connected to the *Gay Fidelity*, but not towing,' he informed me.

'OK, we will be with you shortly,' I said.

Captain Gajardo plotted the position we had been given and found that we had apparently passed them. We altered course to the east-north-east from the southerly course we had been steering. This meant that the two ships had apparently been drifting in an east-north-easterly direction from the position I had been given yesterday, which was against the prevailing strong northwesterly wind and the southeast current. Something was wrong, I thought.

At 0930 I calculated that we were only ten miles from the casualty and we should have been seeing them on the radar, but there was no echo, and it would be easy to identify stationary targets.

'*Ibn Sina*,' I called on the VHF, 'please check your position because I cannot see you on my radar. I am sure of my position because we have satellite navigation on board.'

'27 35 N, 34 56 E,' came the reply.

'But that means you are drifting against the wind and current,' I pointed out.

'Sorry, 26 35 N. I will instruct my radio officer to send a signal on the radio direction finder frequency,' said the captain.

'Good idea,' I said, and turned on the DF.

The tug was rolling and pitching with the quartering sea and swell, much rougher in the Red Sea proper. Two hours later, the *Gay Fidelity* and *Ibn Sina* were in sight and we were up with them at noon. The wind was blowing from the northwest, force six, and it was fine and sunny. The *Ibn Sina* was hanging off the stern of the *Gay Fidelity*, attached by a bow line.

'The fire was in the engine room, which we had closed up, and the CO_2 was let off into it,' he told me over the VHF, 'but nobody has been in it. The accommodation is intact. All the crew was picked up by a Romanian ship from the lifeboats. The port anchor and cable have been lost and the starboard anchor has been let out to five shackles in the water. There are three people from my ship on the *Gay Fidelity* and my owners require two of my officers to be on board for the tow to Suez.'

A bit of a mess, I thought. The anchor was going to be a problem, and I did not know if the fire was out – though with luck the CO_2 would take care of it.

We circled the casualty, noting the empty port hawse pipe and the cable up-and-down from the starboard one. She was listing heavily to port and rolling, being beam-on to the sea and swell. A lifeboat from the *Ibn Sina* was alongside to port, opposite the number four hatch, which was abaft the accommodation. The *Ibn Sina* was hanging off the stern, severely restricting manoeuvring room for the *Salviva*, so it was going to be difficult to get alongside.

The *Salviva* carried two small Yokohama-type fenders, and these were launched in the lee of the *Ibn Sina*. The Z-boat took the salvage crew to the casualty for an inspection and the chief officer reported that number four hatch was on fire. Real problems, I thought, as the Z-boat took me over to the burning ship.

I asked *Ibn Sina*'s chief officer about the list, which made getting around the ship difficult with the rolling.

'The weather was fine, flat calm, yesterday,' he said, 'but it blew up at 0200 this morning. There was no list at first, then a small starboard list, then the port list, which increased steadily but has remained the same for some time now. It's much too dangerous and hot to go into the engine room and I don't know what has caused the list,' he told me.

The salvage chief officer had been sounding the bilges in numbers four and five holds and he told me they were 2.5 metres on the port side, which was a lot of water. The smoke from number four hatch was increasing. Water was clearly getting into the hold and, I thought, the engine room as well.

I took one of the salvage crew with me and entered the accommodation on the starboard side, which was the high side. We opened the engine-room door and were engulfed by hot air. We could hear water entering, which confirmed the engine room was flooding. We shut the door and went up to the bridge. The inclinometer showed the list to be eight degrees to port.

I sat down and appraised the situation. I had a burning and possibly sinking ship on my hands, but at least it was sunny, I thought. The casualty was rolling quite heavily about the eight-degree list. There was no point in the *Ibn Sina* remaining connected to the *Gay Fidelity*. She could not do anything, and was restricting the ability of the *Salviva* to manoeuvre. It was too rough for the *Salviva* to come alongside the listing casualty and pump: therefore I thought the *Salviva* should tow the *Gay Fidelity* to the nearest suitable beaching area. With the engine room and numbers four and five holds flooding, it was only a matter of time before she sank, fire or no fire. It was therefore imperative the *Salviva* was connected as soon as possible and the casualty towed towards the Gulf of Suez. If the weather moderated, then the *Salviva* could come alongside and pump.

I told the *Ibn Sina*'s chief officer what I intended to do and requested as many men as possible to assist in making the towing connection. In the middle of the afternoon ten more of the *Ibn Sina*'s crew arrived by lifeboat. We now had 22 men on the casualty, including the salvage crew and myself, which would be sufficient.

Salviva was rolling and pitching, shipping water on the after deck, making it very difficult for the crew. She came in, and we made fast with a mooring line taken up from her with a heaving line, but it parted with a bang. She came in a second time and we made fast with two mooring lines. The heavy wire forerunner was quickly heaved on board the casualty and the eye put over the forward bitts. I would not normally do this, because of the difficulty of letting her go in an emergency.

'OK Cap,' I said on the Selco frequency walkie-talkie, 'slack out your tow wire and just hold her. Don't tow yet. We still have to get rid of the *Ibn Sina*, which is connected astern.'

I told the *Ibn Sina*'s chief officer what I wished to do and he had relayed my request to disconnect his ship to her captain. We now awaited instructions from her owners in Liverpool, who no doubt wanted payment for their services. I had kept Selco informed via various short messages dictated to the radio officer aboard the *Salviva*.

At 1600 a message was received from Liverpool. An electrician and a junior engineer were to remain with the casualty, while the rest returned to their ship. She would then resume her voyage. This was done, and the line connecting the *Ibn Sina* let go. We were alone with our casualty.

I went down to the CO_2 room, which was at tweendeck level, with the salvage engineer. I knew that number four hold and the tweendeck were on fire from the smoke coming out of the ventilators. It was important to get it out. Putting CO_2 into this hold space would exclude oxygen, hence the fire would go out, I hoped.

The bridge valves had previously been opened, so it was merely a matter of opening the valves on the CO_2 bottles, which we did. We could hear the hiss of the gas escaping into the hold, and it could be clearly heard on deck as well. The ship was rolling, or wallowing in the swell. I wanted to see the engine room and we entered, using torches. The list and rolling made it extremely dangerous in there, with oily plates underfoot increasing the risk of slipping. It was essential to be ultra-careful to prevent injury.

It was still hot, but the fire was completely out. Sea water had entered and was three-quarters of the way up the generators, which ended any ideas I might have had of starting them. We saw that the door leading to the propeller shaft tunnel was under water. The engine room was covered in black soot and completely dark. It was eerie peering round with a flashlight, the only sound being that of water sloshing around. The ship was completely dead.

Coming out of the engine room, I went onto the fo'c'sle and instructed Captain Gajardo to start towing towards the Gulf of Suez. The salvage crew with me greased the wire forerunner and backed up the towing bitts with wire lashings around the next bitts.

We poured buckets of water down the smoking ventilators and plugged the scupper pipes in the galley, where smoke was coming out.

It was noticeable that the wind had dropped, and the sea fell rapidly as well. I decided it was possible to get the *Salviva* alongside. We would pump out the engine room and stop the leak. Although it would soon be dark, I thought it important to seize this opportunity to pump, and some of the equipment could be left on board during the tow.

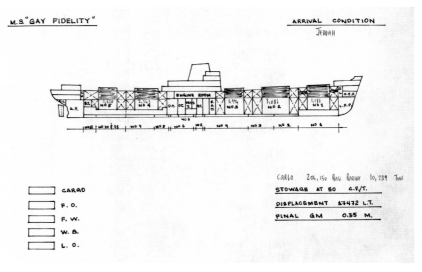

Sketch made at the time showing the *Gay Fidelity*'s arrival condition – the distribution of cargo in her holds and the locations of oil and water tanks, etc

'*Salviva*,' I called on the Selco radio. 'Captain, shorten the tow and we will disconnect you. You can then come alongside and pump out the engine room. Hopefully, we can find the leak.'

'OK Cap, I will give you a call when we have shortened.'

The salvage crew had sounded round the holds and gave me the result:

1830, list eight degrees to port

Port	Starboard
Number One blocked pipe	Number One blocked pipe
Number Two empty	Number Two empty
Number Three 0.1 m	Number Three 0.5 m
Forward Number Four 2.1 m	Forward Number Four 1.2 m
Aft Number Four 2.0 m	Aft Number Four blocked pipe
Number Five 2.5 m	Number Five 1.8 m
Engine room part flooded	

There was over six feet in the bilge of numbers four and five holds, which meant the bilges were full with approximately three feet of water in the bottom of the holds on the port side.

The salvage crew had prepared the fo'c'sle for slipping the tow. It was dark by the time the *Salviva* came alongside on the port side of the casualty. The Yokohama fenders kept the two vessels apart.

A busy night followed, loading pumps and equipment. Heavy electric pumps were manhandled with block and tackle into the engine room and pumping commenced. Electric lighting from the tug was rigged in the engine room. Fire hoses were rigged and number four hatch continuously sprayed to cool it. Number four ventilators were covered with blankets and water sprayed into the port one.

over the walkie-talkie with Captain Gajardo and suggested he look at the chart to find a suitable location in the lee of Shadwan Island, which is at the entrance to the Gulf of Suez. It was going to be a race against time.

I returned to the engine room and shut all the doors including that of the CO2 room. The idea was that if the flooding rose high enough, it would stop the water running into the tweendeck and so into the holds.

The ship was pitching into the head sea, and the only sound was the swishing of the water along the deck outside the accommodation on the port side as the waves came on board. I had a cold breakfast on the bridge, master of all I surveyed, a loaded, sinking, burning ship, devoid of any other human being. However, it was daylight and things always seem better in bright sunshine, even if it is blowing a gale. The white horses of the breaking waves were somehow cheerful under a cobalt-blue sky.

I spent the morning trying to close the steel door to the shaft tunnel. I was finally defeated by the rising water, unable to free it. I greased the tow wire on a regular basis. My clothes were oily and damp, but I could not do anything about it, not having brought a change from the tug.

At noon, Captain Gajardo told me we had run 23 miles at an average speed of 3.8 knots, which was not bad.

During the afternoon, the water continued to rise in the engine room. I was concerned at the hot bulkhead in the provision room. If it became too hot, it might set the paint alight and set fire to the whole accommodation. Smoke continued to come out of the ventilators and from the top of the hatch of number four hold. If the accommodation burned I could live in the fo'c'sle, but if she sank my only means of escape was the paint raft by number five hatch – or swimming.

Before it became dark, I found the emergency oil lamps were filled, so I could use them instead of my torch. My walkie-talkie battery was very low but I was still able to talk to Captain Gajardo. I had found a Straits of Gubal chart and saw there was an anchorage in the lee of Shadwan Island. I instructed him to tow towards that position and, if the *Gay Fidelity* was still afloat, we would anchor.

'It is deep water right up to the anchorage,' I said. The anchor, although hanging at a depth of 360 feet, would be clear. As we came into the anchorage it would drag along the bottom until it held.

'My battery is running out,' I said, 'so I won't be sending any more, but hopefully I will be able to receive you. Try and be there at 0800.'

'OK Cap.'

It was too rough to launch the Z-boat and bring me another battery.

I had a cold supper by the light of the oil lamps. I noticed that the list had decreased slightly to eleven degrees. The *Gay Fidelity* was yawing thirty to forty degrees each way, pitching and rolling. It was an odd feeling to be alone on the casualty and unable to talk with the tug. I felt cut off and thrown back very much on my own resources, but there was plenty to do, and I kept busy.

I made regular inspections during the night and made sure the tow wire was greased. She was shipping water on the port side alongside the accommodation.

The next morning Shadwan Island, high and barren, was in sight, but the anchorage was not reached until afternoon. The engine room was still flooding and the list had decreased to eight degrees to port. As the island was approached, the sea, but not the wind, went down. The Z-boat was launched and brought across a spare battery for the walkie-talkie. Good boat work was required in the gale-force conditions.

I discussed the situation with Captain Gajardo. He would remain connected to the *Gay Fidelity* in the rough conditions to prevent her from dragging after I had anchored.

I was on the fo'c'sle when the anchor started dragging on the bottom, the chain rattling against the hull. At 1450 the *Salviva* reported shallow water, so I released the brake and let the cable run out to eight shackles in the water. Shadwan Island Light was two and a half miles away, bearing northeast. Captain Gajardo anchored the *Salviva* and let out the tow wire. We were safely anchored in Egyptian waters. I had not tried to contact any authorities, and hoped for the best.

I made up a sounding line and discovered that the *Gay Fidelity* was anchored in 35 fathoms of water. I took a sounding in the engine room and found it to be almost 20 feet.

Just before dark, although it was still blowing a gale, I decided that the *Gay Fidelity* was not going to drag. I called up the *Salviva*.

'OK, she won't drag. Disconnect and come alongside. We need to get the engine room pumped out,' I told Captain Gajardo.

The salvage crew came over in the Z-boat to disconnect and I went back to the *Salviva* for a shower and shave and to change out of my oily clothes. I enjoyed my first hot meal for some days in the company of fellow human beings.

At 2000 the *Salviva* was alongside, using her Yokohama fenders. The salvage foreman split the men into watches and they pumped out the engine room, sealed the galley doors, removed all the dry provisions, flooded the floor (to keep the deck cool from the heat in the hold) and rigged the anchor light. I went to bed for a well-earned sleep.

The next week was spent at the anchorage, unmolested by any officialdom, preparing the casualty for the tow to Suez. The weather remained fine, sunny and warm during the day and cool at night. The tug lay quietly alongside in the sheltered waters although, at times, it blew quite fresh.

The main objective was to stop the leak and put out the fire. One of the divers was sick and the other could not dive alone, especially as there were sharks around. So if we could not stop the leak by plugging the intakes from the outside, we would have to do it internally. All the salvage crew was mustered in the engine room, after we had pumped it out. The list had increased again to twelve degrees to port, which was worrying. Every valve was shut and a wire marker put on it. Eventually we were able to discover which pipes were leaking and, when the divers were able to dive, these were plugged and the main leak was stopped. I slipped and fell in the engine room and hurt myself, but luckily not badly. It was a miracle that I was the only one.

The only way we could put out the fire was to starve it of oxygen. It was not possible to get into the hold, and if the hatch was opened it would only fuel the fire. So the whole of number four hatch and the surrounding deck was continually sprayed with water, using the tug's fire pump. The ventilators were re-sealed with wet blankets and kept damped down. The galley floor, which was on top of the tweendeck, was kept flooded. The entrance to the provision room was kept flooded and the bulkhead sprayed with water. Although it would take time, I felt sure that, if we persevered, the fire would eventually go out.

Raising anchor was a major problem. The various methods previously described were tried again, without success. It was imperative that it be lifted because the Gulf of Suez was not deep enough to leave it hanging. We could not drag it along the bottom, not least because the Gulf of Suez was full of underwater pipes and obstructions from the oil industry. A way had to be found.

The freezer room was a horror story: it was full of blackened, rotting, putrefying flesh. The smell was quite unbelievable and it required a strong stomach. It was emptied by the salvage crew, wearing breathing apparatus. Handling the slimy mess was quite awful. We were able to recharge the air bottles with the divers' air compressor.

The rudder was a problem, being jammed hard a-port. We tried to centre it in the steering flat, but the emergency system would not work. Eventually we disconnected the hydraulics and the divers attached wires to the rudder itself and, using snatch-blocks, the wire was led to the capstan of the *Salviva* and the rudder physically heaved amidships. The wires were secured on both sides of the poop to keep it so, and further lashings were put on in the steering flat. The two lifeboats were missing, taken by the abandoning crew. The davits were still swung out and these were wound in and secured. The cabins on the port side main deck had water in them, and these were dried out. I decided to remove the list, so various tanks on the starboard side were filled by hose through the air vents. This reduced the list from twelve degrees to six degrees to port.

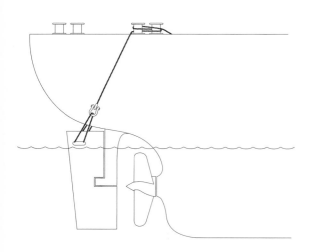

Lashing *Gay Fidelity's* rudder (not to scale)

Eventually, a complicated system was devised for the recovery of the anchor. The only power available was on the tug and the only equipment strong enough was the main towing winch. So, using snatch-blocks and wires, the system was as follows. The main tow wire was heaved through the fairleads on the forecastle back to number one hatch, where a wire forerunner passed through a block, which was made fast. The end of the forerunner was at the water's edge, where it was shackled onto a strop passed through the cable. The main tow wire was heaved up, lifting the cable to the roller fairlead. A special third wire was lowered to the men in the Z-boat, who shackled it onto the cable. This wire was heaved tight, using the capstan on the *Salviva*. When tight, it was stopped off and made fast. The main tow wire was slacked off and heaved forward on the forecastle using a recovery wire, lowering the strop to the water's edge. The cable was thus hanging in the bight. The strop was removed and re-secured to the cable, underneath the wire holding it. Meanwhile the main tow wire was connected to a wire with turns around the capstan drum and heaved up, the brake being loosened. The drum revolved and the bight of cable was stowed in the chain locker. It was an arduous, laborious and time-consuming process, but it worked. It took three and a half hours to lift one shackle, so it was going to take a long time.

On the final day at Shadwan Island, we had some luck lifting the anchor. We again tried the method of using turns around the windlass drum and heaving with the main tow wire. In four and a half hours the anchor was dragging and there were only one and a half shackles of cable in the water. Using the laborious method as the tug and casualty slowly drifted out of the lee of Shadwan Island, the cable was heaved up to approximately 56 feet of chain, plus the anchor, hanging in the water. The main towing winch of the *Salviva* was having problems being used for something it was not designed for. I checked the chart and saw that there was sufficient water in the Gulf of Suez to tow with this amount hanging, so we secured the cable.

The main towing wire was connected to the pelican hook, all services disconnected from the tug, navigation lights switched on, food put on board, and the tow to Suez started at 1930. I had three salvage crew members with me and put them in watches. The tow wire was greased every hour and the engine room inspected every two hours. The bulkhead to number four hold was checked to make sure there was no increase in the heat. It was a great deal less lonely having other human beings on board.

By 2200 we had passed Shadwan Island to port and were in the Gulf of Suez, making about three and a half knots. I remained on the bridge with the walkie-talkie to communicate with the tug and monitor the VHF, which had been rigged up with

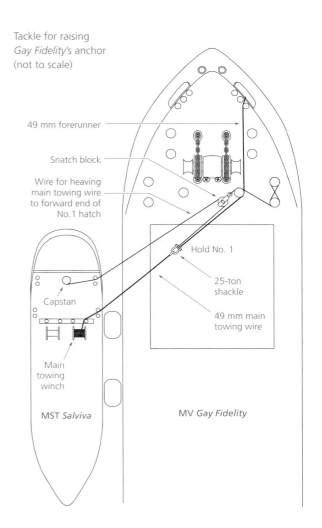

Tackle for raising *Gay Fidelity*'s anchor (not to scale)

49 mm forerunner

Snatch block

Wire for heaving main towing wire to forward end of No.1 hatch

Hold No. 1

25-ton shackle

49 mm main towing wire

Capstan

Main towing winch

MST *Salviva*

MV *Gay Fidelity*

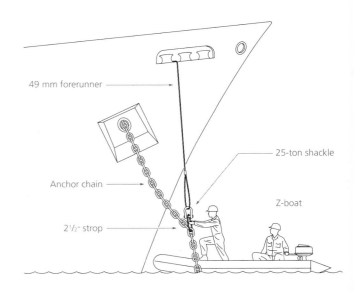

49 mm forerunner

25-ton shackle

Anchor chain

Z-boat

2½" strop

a battery on channel 16. The Gulf of Suez is very busy, and I did not want a collision. The *Gay Fidelity* yawed 80 degrees each way, which made the tug and tow a difficult target for south-bound ships though, of course, we kept to the starboard side of the Gulf. However, it was a tense time, especially at night. The towing diamond was hoisted at daybreak and the tow proceeded satisfactorily. Just before dusk, the Z-boat delivered a very welcome hot meal.

There was a problem with the port engines and they had to be shut down. The tow continued at reduced speed with the casualty yawing much less violently. Luckily the wind had dropped and it was a fine night. The next morning, the port engines were re-started and full speed regained. We wanted to try and anchor in daylight.

At 1100 I heard Al Minya, the Government agent, call the *Salviva* on channel 16 and identify themselves as the agent for the *Gay Fidelity*.

'Captain, call the pilot station when you pass Number One Buoy,' the voice instructed.

'OK,' the *Salviva* replied.

'*Salviva*,' I called on the Selco channel. 'Captain, take no notice of Al Minya. They probably don't realise the *Gay Fidelity* is under tow. Proceed to the waiting area and we will anchor.'

The waiting area was outside the jurisdiction of the Suez port and so no pilot was required. During the afternoon, the VLCC anchorage was passed and by tea time we were off the waiting area.

I took the draught of the casualty from the Z-boat: forward 28'01" aft 29'09". I went onto the bridge of the *Salviva* and looked at the chart with Loretto. We agreed on the anchorage position and I returned to the casualty.

A lot of businessmen turned up in their launches and came alongside the casualty. The salvage crew prevented them from boarding. An axe or crowbar is an effective deterrent! It was essential to keep them off for the ship was unmanned and if they got on board it would be impossible to get them off. I did not want the ship looted. The Schermuly rocket pistol proved an effective deterrent as well, and eventually they got the message and left us alone, for the moment.

At 1725 I let go the anchor in the waiting area and the salvage crew slipped the tow wire. The voyage was over, the average speed from Shadwan

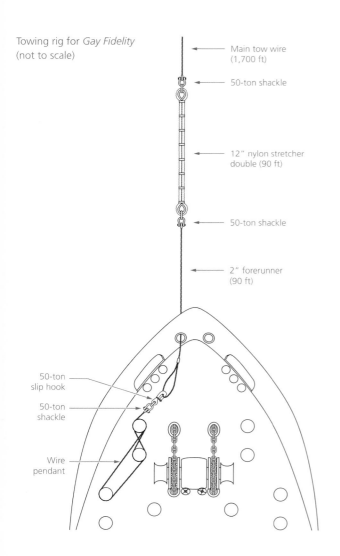

Towing rig for *Gay Fidelity* (not to scale)

Main tow wire (1,700 ft)

50-ton shackle

12" nylon stretcher double (90 ft)

50-ton shackle

2" forerunner (90 ft)

50-ton slip hook

50-ton shackle

Wire pendant

Niam,

        Please ring El Minia and tell them the Harbour Master
Captain Gamal is very angry that they did not tell him that the
"Gay Fidelity " was arriving. Also through them contact the Owners
Representative and the Surveyor Mr Proctor from Perfect Lambert and
ask them what they are doing. They said that they would be out today
to see the ship.If they are comming tomorrow please let me know.
        I am giving my passport to Mohamed so that you can get me
a shore leave pass or sign me off whichever is best. I need to come
ashore and also be able to visit the ship, at anytime.
        Please also tell the Owners Representative that he must bring
out some , say 20 padlocks so that we can lock up the "Gay Fidelity
because we are having difficulty keeping all the " Business " boat"
off.

        Regards

Letter to the Selco agent, giving a flavour of communications and concerns during salvage operations

The Master   MST "SALVIVA"
"GAY FIDELITY"   Waiting Area
On Board "SALVIVA"   Suez
Waiting Area
Suez

                                2nd April 1982
                                Time 1915 Local 1715 GMT

Dear Sir,

        I give notice on behalf of Selco Salvage Ltd that the
"Gay Fidelity" is safely at anchor in the safe anchorage of
the Waiting Area Suez and tender formal notice of Termination
from the LOF 80 signed in Suez on the 9th March 1982 by Captain
Anastasios Exacoustos for and on behalf of the Owners of the
"Gay Fidelity" her cargo freight bunkers and stores and Port
Said Shipping and Navigation Co. Ltd. as Agents for the Owners
of the "Ibn Sina" countersigned in London on behalf of Selco
Salvage Ltd.

                        Yours faithfully,

Acknowledged receipt
ANASTASIOS EXACOUSTOS   I. G. TEW
Master "Gay Fidelity"   Selco Salvage Master

Letter to the captain of the *Gay Fidelity*, giving notice of termination being about four knots. The *Gay Fidelity* was safely anchored. Now came the shore-side problems.

The captain of the *Gay Fidelity*, together with the owners' representative, a Greek lawyer and a surveyor, came on board and I showed them round the ship. They left shortly afterwards.

The Selco agents came on board and I arranged for the *Ibn Sina* men to be repatriated. The harbour master, whom I knew, came to call, seemed satisfied and departed. The salvage crew was put into watches to maintain a watch on the casualty and chase off the businessmen, who appeared at regular intervals.

During the next twelve days the divers placed seals on all the engine-room intakes. All the salvage equipment was hoisted back aboard the *Salviva*. Temperatures were taken every six hours in number four hold to prove that the fire was out.

I went ashore and took up residence in a hotel and chased up the agents for domestic matters concerning the tug. I then went to Cairo and commuted between there, Suez and Port Said.

Finally, on 3 April, I got verbal agreement that the fire was out and the ship was handed back to her owners, who had actually put a watchman on board. It had been a dramatic

Letter to the captain of *Salviva*, with a typical list of matters to keep an eye on

```
                      " GAY  FIDELITY "  SALVAGE.

To Captain Gajardo   Master "Salviva"           28th March 1982.
From Salvage Master.

        I am going ashore to confer with the " Gay Fidelity" people.
While I am away please;

1/ Make sure the bridge of the " Salviva " is manned at all times
   and the VHF s  are on channel 12 and 16 at all times.
2/ Maintain watches on the " Gay Fidelity " with twice daily inspections
   of the engine room and engine room and funnel bulkheads.
3/ Take the temperatures of No. 4 hold at 0800, 1200, 1600, 2000. The
   Second Officer knows what  is required.
4/ Take the draught and note the list every morning.
5/ Make sure the hold soundings and Nos 3 and 4 double bottoms are taken
   every day and all the tank soundings every other day.
6/ Take all necessary action to ensure no one especially from the
   " Business " boats goes onboard the " Gay Fidelity ". It is better
   that no boat is allowed alongside either the tug or the Gay Fidelity
   and no one has any right to come onboard either vessel without your
   permission.
7/ Don't forget that we are still  responsible for the " Gay Fidelity"
   and anytnihg that goes missing will be blamed on Selco and thus
   "Salviva".
8/ DO Not unseal Hatch No. 4 without instructions either from me or
   from Singapore.
9/ The " Gay Fidelity" is anchored to 5 shackles. If the wind becomes
   too strong for you to remain alongside and you think necessary,
   slack out the cable of the " Gay Fidelity " to 7 shackles in the
   water, leave at least two men onboard with the radio and anchor
   close by. Make sure the stern and forward anchor are lit and remain
   lit at night.
10/ Any problems call Granship and or Singapore.
11/ If you have any urgent messages for Singapore send via Portishead
    or Berne Radio if the R/O has difficulty getting through on the
    usual methods.


                 I.G. Tew
                            Salvage Master.
```

<u>LETTER OF TERMINATION</u>

THIS IS TO CERTIFY that the services rendered under the
LOF 80 signed in Suez on the 9th March 1982 by Captain
ANASTASIOS EXACOUSTOS for and on behalf of the Owners of
the "GAY FIDELITY" her cargo freight bunkers and stores
and Port Said Shipping and Navigation Co. Ltd. as Agents
for the Owners of the " IBN SINA " countersigned in London
on behalf of SELCO SALVAGE LTD. have been satisfactorily
today completed with the "GAY FIDELITY" safely afloat in
the safe anchorage of the waiting area Suez.

Date...15th.April.1982 Time..1500. Local...1300.....Gmt

SIGNED:

I. G. TEW

For and on behalf of
SELCO SALVAGE LTD.

ANASTASIOS EXACOUSTOS

For and on behalf of the
Owners of the " GAY FIDELITY "
her cargo Freight Bunkers
and Stores

The formal letter of termination that brought the operation to a close, signed by me and the Captain of the *Gay Fidelity*

salvage, bringing to mind the *Flying Enterprise*, which famously sank in January 1952 when under tow towards Falmouth by the tug *Turmoil*. But Captain Carlsen was not alone on his ship – unlike me, he had the mate of the tug as company. And we succeeded – the *Flying Enterprise* sank.

FROM *LLOYD'S WEEKLY CASUALTY REPORTS*, 1982

Gay Fidelity (Greek) – **Port Said, Mar 21** – MV *Gay Fidelity*, in tow of tug *Salviva*, arrived at Suez pilot station at 1700, local time, today. Owners' representative and solicitor, P & I representative and Italian hull underwriters' representative now attending at Suez.

Blue Express
Patched up in Trincomalee

FROM LLOYD'S WEEKLY CASUALTY REPORT, 1982

Blue Express **(Panamanian) – New York, June 11** – Following received from master of MV *Blue Express* H3JK (Kobe for Karachi): *Blue Express*, crew 27, loaded 5,700 tons steel bars, 110 cars and about 3,000 tons general cargo: At 0230, GMT, June 10. about lat 05 56 N, long 82 30 E, found No. 4 hold and steering-gear-room lot immersion. Steering gear out of order until now, 0140 GMT, June 11. Steering-gear-room immersed about 1 m, No. 4 hold 10.35 m, immersion slow. Please arrange emergency salvage assistance. – United States Coastguard.

Singapore, June 11 – *Blue Express* – M tug *Salveritas* departed her station at Colombo at 1220 GMT, June 10, and arrived at casualty at 0825 GMT, June 11. *Salveritas* connected at 0930 GMT, and proceeded towards Trincomalee.

Colombo, June 14 – Agents of *Blue Express* report vessel entered Trincomalee June 14 in tow of *Salveritas*.

A ship had been aground north of Mogadishu, Somalia, and I had been sent on spec to salve her. Unfortunately, Selco did not obtain the contract and I returned to Singapore from Dubai, where I had been 'stopped'.

The next day, Friday 11 June 1982, I went to the head office in Jurong. The manager told me that the *Salveritas* had sailed from Colombo to a ship in trouble off Sri Lanka. It was the beginning of the southwest monsoon, so it would be rough. I was handed the file and went through the telexes to bring myself up to speed. Never a dull moment in the world of salvage, I thought.

The *Salveritas* had been instructed to sail for the *Blue Express*, which was loaded with steel and general cargo for Colombo. Selco's agents in Sri Lanka would try to contact the managing director of Blue Ocean Lines who, it was believed, had flown into Colombo and was staying at the Oberoi. I knew the Oberoi Hotel well, having stayed there myself on more than one occasion. It had a huge, open atrium, the first I had seen. The idea was to get him to agree that our salvage services were to be given on the basis of a Lloyd's Open Form.

Colombo had sent the following:

To Selco Singapore

Top urgent

Foll. message received by local agents from MV *Blue Express*

Quote

Number four hold and steering gear room immersed – now rudder out of order. Request tug.

Position: 5 54 N, 82 26 E.

Unquote.

It sounded interesting, and she would certainly need assistance if she couldn't steer.

The second mate of the *Salveritas* had been ashore, and the captain rather foolishly sent the mate ashore to find him, thus delaying the sailing. Considering the Smit tug *Poolzee* was in port, this was very stupid because there was every chance that Smit might find out about the casualty and beat us to her. Luckily for the captain, the second mate was found and he sailed before the *Poolzee*. In salvage, being first is the most important thing – whoever reaches the casualty first normally wins the contract. There was then a further delay waiting for the mooring gang to let go the lines. 'Cut and go,' I would have told them!

There was then a series of messages between Singapore, Colombo and Taipei in Taiwan, trying to get an LOF signed, but the owners seemed reluctant to act. In Colombo, the owners' representative seemed unwilling to do anything.

I went out to the operations room and looked at the chart on the wall, where the position of the *Blue Express* had been plotted. It was to the east of Sri Lanka and she would be drifting away, further from safety, in the southwest monsoon. The ship was old, and leaking might start in number five hold and/or the engine room. The sooner she was brought into shelter, the better. The obvious place to head for was Trincomalee, not Colombo, which was her destination. She would be in the lee of Sri Lanka and Trincomalee was a safe harbour, in fact one of the finest natural harbours in the world.

During the day, telexes and messages were flying. The *Salveritas* had not made contact with the casualty yet, which was worrying because she had wireless telegraphy and should have been in contact by now, unless the *Blue Express* had lost all power.

A message from Taipei suggested that Selco would be awarded the contract and the LOF would be signed in Colombo, so we authorised the agents to sign on our behalf. It was all exciting stuff! A little later we had confirmation that it had been awarded to Selco, and that the ship was loaded with 5,670 tons of steel bar, 1,500 tons of cement and some general cargo. Thus, apart from the ship itself, there was some value in the cargo, and if we could salve her there would be a decent bonus, always a good spur to make our best endeavours.

At about noon, a message from the *Salveritas* reported contact with the casualty by wireless telegraphy, which, of course, means Morse code.

AA Direct contact with casualty on 500 khz W/T.

BB Present position 5 56 N, 82 30 E. According to casualty, the condition is about to abandon ship and they are awaiting of agent reply message.

CC ETA there at 1100 hrs local today.

Regards: Master.

It sounded serious, and I hoped that she did not sink before the *Salveritas* reached her with pumps and the salvage crew.

It was agreed I should proceed to Colombo immediately and make my way to Trincomalee, where I would try to obtain permission from the harbour master to bring the *Blue Express* into port. I went over to the communications barge moored in the creek and spoke to the *Salveritas* by telex over radio.

The master told me he was in contact with the *Blue Express* and they had not abandoned ship. There was sea water in number four hold and it was very deep. The master of the *Blue Express* had agreed that salvage would be performed on Lloyd's Open Form. The sea was rough, with a strong southwest wind. I told him I was flying to Sri Lanka and to telex us as soon as he had more information.

This was good news. The casualty was still afloat and the *Salveritas* would shortly be with her. It's always better for the LOF to be agreed master to master – it prevents lawyers from making problems.

I arrived in Colombo that night and had a meeting with the agent's shipping manager at the Oberoi Lanka. He told me that the owners' representative was staying in the hotel but was not travelling to Trincomalee and would be quite happy if the ship sank. He was not making any arrangements for the ship to enter port, nor did he want to see me. I told the manager to tell the rep to proceed to Trincomalee and assist in obtaining permission to bring the casualty into port. After the manager left, I went to the communication room in the hotel and made my number with the operator. This was a courtesy I always followed, and it assured me of good communications. He would call me immediately, should any telex arrive, thus making sure there was no delay.

In the middle of the night I received a telex informing me that Selco had agreed a Lloyd's Open Form with another ship in distress and wanted the *Salveritas*. This complicated the situation a little, and I replied that I would need more personnel to be flown to Sri Lanka to take over after the casualty had been delivered to Trincomalee. I would hire additional salvage equipment here.

At 0630 on Saturday morning, I was telephoned by Mr K, the owner of Selco. He told me that the tow wire on the *Salveritas* had broken and asked what they should do about the new casualty. I told him the *Blue Express* had to be delivered first, and presumably the master of the *Salveritas* had been told to reconnect with the spare tow wire. I was not too

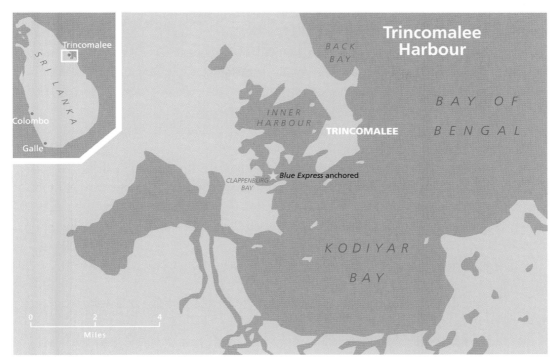

Map labels:
SRI LANKA
Trincomalee
Colombo
Galle

Trincomalee Harbour
BACK BAY
INNER HARBOUR
TRINCOMALEE
BAY OF BENGAL
Blue Express anchored
CLAPPENBURG BAY
KODIYAR BAY

0   2   4
Miles

sure what he had done wrong, because the tow wire should not have broken, however rough it was. I suspected he had not let out enough wire.

After breakfast I had a meeting with the owners' representative, a man from Taiwan named Mr Lim. He told me the owners were not interested in continuing the voyage: the ship was old and he had been told there was oil in number four hold leaking from number seven fuel tank. This was bad news, because Trincomalee was a tourist area, though at present there were few due to civil unrest in the area. The threat of pollution would make my negotiations with the harbour master very difficult.

Mr Lim told me there was no mortgage on the vessel but that she was insured for $1.8 million. I suggested it would be a good idea if he came with me to Trincomalee to attend to his crew and help me obtain permission to move the casualty into port. He said he had no intention of coming and was going back to Taipei, where he had more important things to do. I told him it was a bad show and it was his duty, but he was adamant. No doubt the arbitrator would take this into account when he made his award, assuming of course that we were successful.

The car journey across Sri Lanka was interesting scenically, a lot of it heavy jungle, but the road was terrible and it was the hottest and most uncomfortable car journey I have ever made. The car was not air-conditioned.

It was late afternoon when I met the manager of the sub-agents in Trincomalee. I was not impressed, although I am sure he was doing his best. No ships had come to Trincomalee for years due to the Tamil insurgency. He was only a clerk, so I had to instruct him as we went along. I looked at the chart he had provided of one of the finest natural harbours in the world to decide where to place the *Blue Express*, and to prepare myself for the meeting with the harbour master.

Because of the insurgency, Trincomalee had been in decline for years. There was no direct international communication at all. Everything went through Colombo, which, of course, included telex. The telephone system was erratic, to say the least, and depended on the goodwill of the operators.

The agent did not have a car, so I kept the car that had brought me from Colombo, along with its driver.

The harbour master's house was in the naval base and had a magnificent view over the harbour, surrounded by rich green vegetation. Captain Prince was the deputy harbour master, and his boss was Captain Hendrikus, the master attendant at Colombo, whom I knew very well. We had met five years earlier over the salvage of the barge *Pastee 1802* outside Colombo.

I gave him a resumé of the situation, sitting on the sofa in his drawing room.

'Will the ship sink?' asked Captain Prince.

'No,' I replied, 'she's been afloat for some days since the damage and under tow. If she was going to sink, she would have sunk by now.'

'Will she hazard the port?' he asked.

Considering the port was empty, except for a few laid-up ships, there was not much to hazard except, of course, the environment.

'Given the information I have at the moment, the answer is no,' I replied.

'I will have to consult with Captain Hendrikus in Colombo.'

'Tell Captain Hendrikus that I'm in charge of the salvage and I will not bring her into the port if the information proves to be wrong. Remind him that I saved the *Orient Welfare* from sinking and blocking her berth in Colombo. And remind him of the trouble we had over the barge *Pastee* just before the riots in 1977. I will not do anything to jeopardise the port, and I will keep you fully informed at all times.'

Captain Prince telephoned Captain Hendrikus through the naval exchange and I listened to the conversation. Captain Hendrikus wanted to leave the casualty at Round Island, which was outside the harbour, whereas Captain Prince seemed willing to let me bring her inside. It was important to get the ship out of the swell. There was no way permission would be granted to take her to Colombo.

The harbour was under naval control. I asked Captain Prince if I could have permission to use the Z-boat on board the *Salveritas*. He said I could only use her around the tug and ship, and to come ashore only in grave emergency. Normally, I would have to use the local launches. In the absence of the owners' representative, I guaranteed payment for port dues, light dues, pilotage, tugs and any other port expenses I might incur. It was a measure of my own and Selco's reputation that my verbal assurance was sufficient. I was not asked to put anything in writing.

He also agreed I could bring the ship into Trincomalee provided I personally guaranteed that she would not sink, which I did. I said I would tow her out to sea if necessary

Blue Express in a perilous condition in the Bay of Bengal, yawing wildly as she is towed by *Salveritas* towards Trincomalee

to prevent her sinking in the harbour. I also guaranteed to divulge all information to him and hide nothing. He said he would hold me personally responsible for the safety of the ship.

We shook hands on our agreement, and I momentarily wondered if I had moved back in time to when a gentleman's word was his bond. I had assumed an onerous responsibility, but that is all part of the salvage game. I thought it reasonable to assume that if the casualty remained afloat in rough weather, she would remain afloat when it was calm.

I checked in at the Club Oceanic and immediately investigated what communications were available – and the answer was almost none. However, there was a telephone operator on duty 24 hours a day, so I went to see him. I told him why I was in Trincomalee and that, if I received good service, he and his colleagues would be rewarded. In the event, I did receive good service from the operators.

I spoke to the wives of the senior agency people in Colombo, their husbands being out, to try and get a message through to Singapore. Eventually, the operator in Trincomalee got through via Colombo and I dictated a message to the operations room at Selco outlining my agreement with the authorities. In turn, they relayed a message from the *Salveritas*, giving her ETA as tomorrow evening and saying that the tunnel and steering room doors were shut and there was no more flooding. This was good news. The tug had obviously reconnected.

On Sunday, the *Salveritas* had towed the casualty through rough weather into the lee of the Sri Lankan coast and managed to anchor. They had got their pumps and a salvage crew on board. They pumped out the steering gear, thus lifting the stern, but could not lower the water level in number four hold. The damage must therefore be extensive. The salvage crew remained on board while the *Salveritas* resumed the tow to Trincomalee.

On Monday morning, 14 June, I was telephoned by Singapore and told that the *Salveritas*, with *Blue Express* in tow, had arrived off Trincomalee. I was not too impressed with the agent, who had earlier told me that the radio station had said she had not arrived. I set him to work finding pumps and establishing the cost of discharging cargo. This was not going to be easy because no general cargo had been worked in Trincomalee for twenty years. I left the agent's office on the south side of the harbour, facing the Bay of Bengal, and proceeded to the more hilly and jungle-covered north. Captain Prince's office was situated in the naval base, so I had to go through naval security.

He had spoken to the *Salveritas* on the radio and had given permission for the convoy to proceed inshore of Round Island, where the pilot would board. He was quite happy with the report he had received from Captain Gianan and agreed that I could go with him in the pilot launch. I spoke with the *Salveritas* from the naval radio station, where the operators were all smart in their white uniforms. The situation was well in hand and there was no pollution, although the water level had not gone down in number four hold despite the pumping.

In the early afternoon I met Captain Prince at the boat house where the pilot launch was kept, and we set out. We agreed that Captain Prince would pilot the tug and I would go on board the *Blue Express*. He had not piloted a tug towing a ship before, and I would tell him if I did not like anything he was doing.

When the convoy came in sight I could see that the *Blue Express* was well down by the stern with smoke coming from her funnel. I called up the *Salveritas* on Captain Prince's portable VHF and spoke with Captain Gianan. I suggested to him that he tell the master of the casualty not to use the engine without our permission. I did not want any vibration to dislodge the patch on the bulkhead of number five hold. The sea was calm and there was little swell in the sheltered waters. It was hot and sticky.

The pilot boat went alongside the *Blue Express* first. I boarded her and was met by the chief officer of the *Salveritas*, who was leading the salvage party. He showed me the oil-covered water in number four hold, and then I proceeded to the bridge.

The Taiwanese master spoke good English. There was an anchor party at the bow and the second officer was making fast the tug *Vasasha* aft (this was a harbour tug). I was in continuous communication with the *Salveritas* and directed operations.

Clappenburg Bay, on the west side of Trincomalee and outside the harbour proper, was entered, with Clappenburg Island on one side and French Point on the other. In the middle of the bay, I instructed the master to let go the port anchor when the *Vasasha* had succeeded in taking the way off the ship, and told the *Salveritas* to let go her anchor. Once she was anchored, they could disconnect the tow and come alongside the *Blue Express*. The divers should be sent immediately across to inspect the damage. I was very conscious that the ship had been brought in on my say-so and that I was responsible.

Ahead of the *Blue Express* were a run-down jetty and a mosque among the coconut trees. It was completely calm in the bay, and there was no swell: perfect conditions to salve a ship and cargo.

The pilot boat picked me up and took me across to the tug, where I conferred with Captain Prince and read all the telexes. I could not release the tug until the divers reported, which they did at 1600.

Their report was a shock. The hole on the port side, by the flooded number four hold, was 27 feet long, 14 feet high, and there were no frames in way of the hold. This was far worse than I had anticipated, and I was not sure that I would have given my word, had I known. However, we were in a sheltered anchorage and the sooner I got on with making sure she did not sink, the better things would be. I instructed Captain Gianan to set a watch in the engine room and number five hold and report immediately if any sign of leakage occurred. I told Captain Prince what we had found. He was as shocked as I was, but agreed to inspect the casualty with me.

We inspected the bulkhead at the forward end of number five hold by clambering over

Salveritas brings *Blue Express* into Clappenburg Bay, Trincomalee

the cargo. It was exceedingly hot in the hold. The bulkhead was not in the best condition, but it was propped up by cargo and there was no sign of bulging or leakage. We discussed the situation and I persuaded him to let the *Blue Express* stay. I decided to pump out the steering flat, which would lift the stern and reduce the water pressure on the bulkhead. If the bulkhead collapsed, number five hold would flood and the ship would certainly sink. The ship was in a critical situation. I had to make sure that, when we lifted the stern, no oil leaked from the surface of number four hold and caused pollution.

I informed Selco Singapore of the situation by telex over radio and said there was no way the *Salveritas* could leave until another tug relieved her.

I went ashore with Captain Prince in the pilot boat and he telephoned Colombo from his house. Captain Hendrikus was not pleased. He said if there was any further trouble with the ship, we should beach her. I telephoned Mr Maralande at the agency in Colombo and told him to find an oil boom and send it across the island as quickly as possible together with any dispersant he could find. He should also ask Colombo Dry Dock if they could make a plate to patch the hole with.

Darkness was falling, and it was peaceful outside the house, with tropical sounds, when I called on the radio.

'Captain, number five hold is flooding,' said the excited voice of the captain of the *Salveritas*. 'The bulkhead between four and five is leaking.'

My heart sank and I felt sick, for this was the worst possible news. I would have to tell Captain Prince.

'Start the pump in number five hold,' I ordered. 'Make preparations to reconnect the casualty and I'll be out as soon as possible.'

I left the peaceful scene outside and returned inside the house, where I told Captain Prince what had occurred. He went as white as a sheet.

'Oh my God,' he exclaimed, 'you will have to beach her.'

'You had better put the port tugs on standby in case that becomes necessary,' I said, 'but let's get out first and make an inspection.'

After alerting the port tugs, Captain Prince telephoned Colombo and spoke to Captain Hendrikus. I could imagine the other end of the conversation from watching Captain Prince's face. Captain Hendrikus had a very deep voice and a strong personality to match it.

'Captain Hendrikus has instructed me to beach the *Blue Express* in Back Bay,' he told me as he put the telephone receiver down.

We drove down the hill to the pilot boat through the calm, tropical night in Captain Prince's car. I was hot and extremely worried.

'Where is Back Bay?' I asked.

'Near your hotel,' he replied.

'But that would be a complete disaster,' I said, filled with dread. 'It's outside the harbour and there is a swell running. We won't be able to patch her, there will be pollution, and she might break her back. We can't possibly do that. We must find a better place.'

'I cannot possibly disobey Captain Hendrikus,' he said sharply.

I kept silent. There was no point in antagonising him, I thought.

In the launch, I said 'If we beach, it must be inside the harbour, free of any swell.'

'Captain Hendrikus ordered her to be beached in Back Bay and I cannot change that. If we don't beach there, you will have to tow her out to sea.'

'Then she will founder,' I retorted.

He did not reply.

The *Salveritas* was alongside the *Blue Express*. As we boarded from the pilot launch, the chief officer reported to me that the divers had patched the leak in the bulkhead.

What a relief. Captain Prince looked a bit more cheerful as well.

It was dark, but the deck lights of the *Salveritas* and *Blue Express* were on, illuminating both ships. We made our way over to the *Blue Express* and into number five hold. Cargo lights had been rigged, so there was sufficient light to clamber over the general cargo towards the divers, who were standing on top of the cargo on the starboard side.

The hole had been stopped with a wooden plug. The first attempt had merely made the hole bigger in the rather rotten bulkhead. A bigger plug held; this had been sealed with epoxy and was not leaking. The bulkhead was not bulging in any way and the bottom portion was held up by cargo.

'It doesn't look so bad,' I said.

'You will still have to beach her in Back Bay,' replied Captain Prince.

'Let's go on deck where it's cooler,' I said.

'It seems very odd to me that a hole should suddenly appear in the bulkhead in the calm conditions now prevailing,' I remarked to the chief officer of the *Salveritas*, who had accompanied us in the hold. 'Were any of the *Blue Express* crew in the hold when the leak started?'

'Yes.'

'Do you think this was done deliberately?' I asked.

'Don't know,' he replied.

'Keep a salvage crew on permanent watch with a radio,' I said.

We returned to the bridge on *Salveritas*, where the captain was sitting. I told him about number five and the watchmen I required there, and in the engine room. I asked him to rig a pelican hook on the bow of the *Blue Express* so that, if necessary, a quick connection could be made.

'More importantly,' I added, 'we can slip it in an emergency or when beaching.'

Captain Prince had so far not actually ordered me to tow the casualty out to what, in my mind, would be her certain death. In my most charming English manner, I set about persuading him to let me leave her in Clappenburg Bay. It was cool in the air-conditioned accommodation and the captain had the messman bring refreshments.

I laid out the charts of Trincomalee and suggested other more suitable areas for beaching. Captain Prince was adamant: Back Bay or out to sea. However, now the leak had stopped and the stern flat was being pumped, the stern would lift a little.

I went on board the *Blue Express* and told the master we were going to beach his ship. The *Salveritas* would tow her to the beaching area, assisted by the port tug. The *Salveritas* would be slipped before she ran aground herself while the port tug would remain alongside. He did not seem particularly interested.

Having made all the arrangements to beach, I went to work on Captain Prince. I knew he did not have any experience in towing, let alone beaching (I had never beached a ship myself, but I was not going to tell him that), so I emphasised the difficulties and dangers of a night-time beaching. Eventually I persuaded him to return ashore to telephone Captain Hendrikus and delay beaching until daylight.

We went over and inspected the bulkhead. There was no change. The *Blue Express* was quite stable. All the soundings remained the same and the steering flat was emptying. We returned ashore in the pilot launch.

It was late when we reached Captain Hendrikus in Colombo. Captain Prince gave his report on the present, now stable situation and handed the telephone to me.

'Don't worry, Captain Hendrikus,' I said, 'I won't let the *Blue Express* sink in Clappenburg Bay. She is stable at the moment. I would like your permission to leave her there overnight.'

'You must give me your word that you won't let her sink,' he said in his deep voice.

'You have my word, Captain Hendrikus,' I said formally.

'You may leave her there overnight,' he consented.

'If all is in order in the morning, perhaps she could stay?' I asked tentatively.

'Ring in the morning.'

Mrs Prince had prepared supper and I was invited to join them. It was a very welcome and enjoyable meal, with a view over the darkened, empty harbour.

After supper, I returned in the pilot boat to the *Salveritas*. I was informed that another crack, 22 feet long, had been found in way of number four tweendeck. I made a full inspection of the *Blue Express*, which was hot work after the curry, and I found all in order. I wrote out my report, to be sent by telex over radio to Singapore.

Discharging the deck cargo of buses into barges alongside

A close watch was kept overnight on the bulkhead and in the engine room. At 0430 on Tuesday I was called by Captain Prince on the VHF and was able to assure him that all was in order. The ship was stabilised. I told him I had a plan to alleviate the pressure on the bulkheads and I hoped to commence discharge soon.

The agent boarded at 0615, and I gave him instructions to obtain barges and stevedores. Colombo Dock would be invited on board to quote for supplying the steel patch and an oil boom. Now that I had permission to stay and the ship was stabilised, the more exciting part of the salvage was over. A new phase started, consisting of long, hard work beset by the difficulty of operating in a type of war zone with bureaucratic controls. This could only have been done by a company like Selco, which had the personnel and the resources. It turned out we needed the shipyard support in Singapore as well.

The barges and stevedores I had ordered did not arrive until the evening. The barges arrived first, but discharge could not start until the stevedores arrived almost five hours later. I was in a fever to start the discharge: the more cargo I could get off, the safer the ship would become. I started with the deck cargo in way of numbers four and five hatch, and then the number five tweendeck.

The divers plugged the 22-foot-long crack in way of number four tweendeck and we used air pumps to skim the oil off the surface of the water in the hold and pump it into the sound tanks. The steering flat was pumped dry.

It became clear that Colombo Dock were not able to fabricate a suitable steel patch, or did not want to. Thus we were thrown back on our own resources. The diving work required the assistance of Selco's expert shore divers. It was decided to fabricate the steel patch in one piece at the Selco shipyard in Singapore. A Selco tug would then tow a Selco barge with the patch on board, together with a suitable crane to lift it. It seemed slightly crazy to have to bring a steel patch 1,450 miles by barge to a country which had a perfectly good shipyard. Politics creates odd situations.

At the end of each shift, the port authorities removed the barges we were loading, whether they were full or not. This was another crazy situation, because the barges always arrived some hours into the shift and thus cargo work was slow. I managed to get this rectified two days later after consulting with the officials concerned and talking to the agents in Colombo.

As the days passed, the situation slowly improved on board. I was confident we would eventually be successful. There was no more talk of beaching or towing out to sea. I kept Captain Prince informed on a daily basis. I had been acutely aware of the responsibility I had undertaken by giving my guarantee on behalf of Selco and, of course, myself.

The afterpeak was pumped dry to lift the stern. The divers arrived from Singapore and we discussed the best method of securing number four and containing the oil in the hold. If the stern was lifted much more, the oil would escape into the sea. I could not allow that to happen. We decided to utilise steel angle bars from the cargo and fit them onto the broken frames, then, using plywood from the cargo, fit a temporary patch until the steel patch arrived from Singapore.

All the deck cargo was discharged, and this made it much easier to get around the ship. It was hot and sticky, being the southwest monsoon, and sometimes the cargo operations were halted by rain.

I had many meetings ashore with port officials, stevedores, customs and others. Everyone wanted to be involved. The Colombo cargo was to be transported overland to Colombo but, of course, customs dues had to be paid first. There was an argument as to whether customs dues should be paid on the trans-shipment cargo. There was disagreement about the payment of dues on damaged cargo. I spent hours in discussions to keep the whole operation running night and day.

Hot work was performed in number four tweendeck to fit the temporary frames. I was acutely aware of the fire risk in the oily atmosphere. I had a fire hose permanently running in the tweendeck. I had the aft peak ballasted after a little pollution occurred from number four. The draught had been decreased sufficiently for it to occur. The pollution was contained by the oil boom we had brought overland from Colombo and rigged. Oil skimmed from number four hold was pumped to the settling tank, allowed to settle, and then the oil was transferred to a double-bottom.

On the 22nd, some eight days after our arrival, the temporary plywood patch was fitted.

It was a relief not to worry about pollution – but even so I kept the oil boom in place. The afterpeak was pumped out. The forepeak was filled with fresh water from the port water barge. However, the stevedores were working so slowly that the cost of discharge was beginning to exceed the value of the cargo. I therefore stopped work and cancelled all the gangs, which put a fox among the poultry. All concerned quickly came to their senses and cargo work resumed the next day.

The tweendeck had pulled away from the hull in way of number four hold, and I had a cement box made to secure it. The shaft tunnel, which had filled with water, was pumped out, as was number five hold.

By the 25th, all the Colombo cargo had been discharged and cargo work ceased. The divers sealed the rudder trunking to prevent leakage into the steering flat. We had now to wait for the *Salvalour*, towing Barge number AN2801 from Singapore, loaded with the steel patch, crane and, I hoped, lots of additional equipment. She was delayed by bad weather in the Bay of Bengal.

Fitting a sealing patch in No. 4 tweendeck

This, however, presented a problem. The customs men wanted dues paid on all the equipment on the barge, because it would enter the port. I argued that, technically, Clappenburg Bay was outside the commercial port, that no equipment was to be landed, and thus that no dues should be paid. This was no small matter. During the unsuccessful salvage of the barge *Pastee*, the agents had had to put up a bond for the value of any equipment we took ashore, including spanners, and they had to pay duty on anything not brought back on board. Eventually, with Captain Prince's help, it was agreed that duty would only be paid on anything brought ashore. This was no problem because I did not intend to bring anything ashore.

Many people wanted to come on board, or so it seemed: surveyors for the ship and cargo, average adjusters, lawyers and so on. I had to be constantly on my guard because, if the wrong person came on board, I might be creating a situation where our salvage efforts would be criticised. Equally, the owners would blame us if we let on board someone who might criticise them. Keeping it all straight involved numerous telex messages to and from Singapore. Communications with Singapore were via the telex over radio on board *Salveritas*, which was a complete boon. Communications between Trincomalee and Colombo were bad enough, let alone trying to contact to the outside world.

It was a big relief when the *Salvalour* arrived early on the morning of 30 June, her master's unmistakable voice booming over the radio. Captain Pedro Ragasia was a Filipino equivalent of Peter Lankester, large, strong, confident and knowledgeable.

'What have you done to the barge?' I asked upon boarding his tug.

'The weather was rough,' smiled Pedro.

The barge was down by the head and had a four-degree list to starboard. I sent the divers down and they reported that number two starboard tank was open to the sea: a bottom plate had been torn away and was hanging down from the hull. The crane and all the equipment were safe. Repairs to the barge would have to be left until after the patch was fitted to the *Blue Express*. We rigged the Selco oil boom from the barge and sent the other one ashore for overland transport back to Colombo.

Selco's diving superintendent and the crane driver had arrived by air from Singapore. The divers began shaping the steel patch from the barge to fit the hole in the *Blue Express*. They cut holes in the patch for the bolts that would hold it to the hull. Rubber packing was glued to the patch. Two Dunlop fenders and rubber tractor tyres were placed on the side of the barge, and she was towed alongside the *Blue Express* and expertly berthed by Pedro. The fenders kept the barge well clear of the hull, so the divers could work in safety.

There was still oil on the surface of the water in number four, despite all the skimming. We now pumped the skimmed oil into one of the tanks on board the barge.

Once the barge was in position, the *Salvalour* went alongside the casualty with the *Salveritas*. The divers removed the plywood patch with chain blocks. The crane lifted the steel patch and lowered it into the water over the hole, again with chain blocks. The patch weighed some tons, and it was tricky work. The divers worked underwater, cutting holes in the hull to marry up with the ones on the patch. Any pollution was treated with oil dispersant brought from Singapore on the barge.

Salvalour

The crucial problem was solved by ballasting and increasing the water bottom in the hold. By late afternoon on 3 July the divers had fitted the patch and secured it with 109 bolts, all tightened by one diver inside the hull and one outside. They were then all epoxied. When all was ready, the afterpeak was again pumped out. Number four hold was emptied with salvage pumps, with the oily water being transferred to the barge. When the oil had settled, the clean water was pumped over the side into the sea, the oil remaining on the barge. Thus there was no pollution.

The pumping took a long time. It was difficult and dangerous clambering over the oily

239

Salveritas, a barge, *Blue Express* and *Salvalour* in Clappenburg Bay, surrounded by an oil boom

cargo to position the pumps, and safety lines were rigged. By late afternoon on the 6th, the entire inside of the patch was clear of the water and visible. I inspected all the bolt holes and declared the patch tight. The divers had done a magnificent job.

The next day, the Salvage Association surveyor from Singapore inspected the patch with me and agreed it was tight. The *Blue Express* was thus salved and in a safe anchorage. The master signed the termination certificate.

Two years later, the salvage was arbitrated. I was told that the arbitrator had acknowledged the risk I had taken in giving a verbal guarantee. If the *Blue Express* had sunk in Trincomalee, the liability to Selco would have been huge. He praised the skill and resourcefulness of Selco in fitting a steel patch transported from Singapore. His award of over half the salved fund reflected this. A satisfactory outcome for all concerned, I thought.

Wind Enterprise
Aground in the Persian Gulf

FROM *LLOYD'S WEEKLY CASUALTY REPORTS*, 1983

Wind Enterprise **(Norwegian) – London, Aug 15** – Steam tanker *Wind Enterprise*, fully loaded, reported aground off the coast Qatar.

Bahrain, Aug 16 – Following received from Lloyd's Agents Doha: *Wind Enterprise* ... vessel aground at Shah Allum, lat 26 25' 06" N, long 52 29' 24" E at 2305, Aug 14.

I was in the Fujairah Hilton, a grand name for a modest hotel, finalising the completion of a successful operation. We had salved the loaded cargo ship *Cotton Trader*, aground after a fire on the coast of Oman, and towed her to Fujairah. The air conditioning worked well, which was very welcome after the heat outside, and I enjoyed a swim in the pool. The hotel was on the beach, the Arabian Sea lapping the shore. It was very pleasant, like a mini holiday after my exertions.

I was returning to the hotel after my morning swim in the Arabian Sea, my feet covered in sand, when the hotel operator thrust a telex into my hand.

'Ring Singapore urgent,' It said.

Fujairah was four hours behind Singapore so I telephoned the office at once, it being almost noon there.

'*Wind Enterprise* aground off Bahrain, fully loaded, 350,000 tons of crude. She is big. We have told *Salvalour* to proceed her location,' Alan Bond told me. 'Join her either at Dubai or Bahrain. No contract yet. Keep me informed.' He hung up.

I absorbed the information, and the enormity of the situation hit me. Three hundred and fifty thousand tons of crude oil, the ship must be enormous, an ultra-large crude oil carrier. She was much bigger than the *Showa Maru*. Eight years earlier, Captain Hancox had kept me on board the casualty as his assistant for the salvage, and had taught me much about tanker salvage. I had thought her big, and you needed a bicycle to get around the ship – but she was under 250,000 tons. This one must be well over 1,000 feet long and draw well over 60 feet, utterly dwarfing the little *Cotton Trader*.

'No good day-dreaming,' I told myself. 'Get your act together and do something.'

I returned to my room, showered the salt water off my skin and the sand off my feet, and got dressed. After a quick breakfast I got a taxi to Gulf Agencies, our agents in the United Arab Emirates. I conferred with the manager and agreed I would charter a crew boat from Dubai and rendezvous with the *Salvalour* inside the Persian Gulf.

I talked to Alan Bond in Singapore. He would arrange with Gray Mackenzie in Bahrain for ship-to-ship transfer hoses, fenders and extra tugs. We had agreed she would have to be lightened. I suggested getting John Carter from Marine Safety Services in London to be our safety officer.

'OK,' said Alan, 'I will fix. You get out to the tanker. We still have no contract, and the sooner you are on board the better. No doubt everyone else will be after the LOF.'

I went into the radio room and spoke to the *Salveritas* on the VHF. She also had been with me on the *Cotton Trader* salvage and was with her now. The *Salvalour* was still in VHF range so I spoke direct with Pedro Ragasia, her captain, a tough, burly Filipino.

'ETA off Dubai 0100 tomorrow,' he said in his deep gravely voice.

'OK. I will meet you off Port Rashid in a crew boat,' I said. 'Proceed at full speed.'

The drive through the mountains to Dubai was spectacular. Dry, harsh, barren, dark, almost lunar, then the contrast of the desert on the Dubai side, and the modern tarmacadamed road all the way. I appreciated the air-conditioned Mercedes taxi, because it was hot outside.

At Dubai Gulf Agencies I arranged the charter of the crew boat for that night and retired to the Dubai Hilton, a much more impressive hotel, to await events. I enjoyed the pool.

'Lloyd's Open Form has been agreed,' said Alan Bond on the telephone midnight time Singapore. 'You sign with the master when you get on board. We're negotiating the charter of a tanker and will keep you informed. The master reports he is five feet out of his draught but no pollution or leakage. Yet. I have arranged with Gray Mac Bahrain for hoses etc, and additional tugs. You let me know what you want.'

I was elated, but in some ways fearful. This was a salvage, and salvage was my business, but tankers were not my favourite ships. And this ship was huge. There was no room for error with a fully laden tanker and a third of a million tons of crude oil. I thought about the *Showa Maru*, and the calm and meticulous way Captain Hancox had gone about it. That was the trick, meticulous planning. This was no 'smash and grab' connect up and pull. This was a real planner's dream, lighten and lift off gently to ensure no further damage to the bottom, no pollution.

The first and most essential thing was to have the right people around me, and the most important was the 'tanker safety man'. I rang Marine Safety Services in London, it being late afternoon there. My luck was in. John Carter, the man I wanted, was available and would be on the next flight out. I felt a lot more confident knowing John was on the way.

I joined the *Salvalour* shortly after midnight off Port Rashid, and Captain Ragasia set course for the *Wind Enterprise* at full speed. He had plotted the position on the chart, which was half a mile southwest of the racon beacon on Shah Allum shoal, some fifty miles off the coast of Iran. It gave me food for thought.

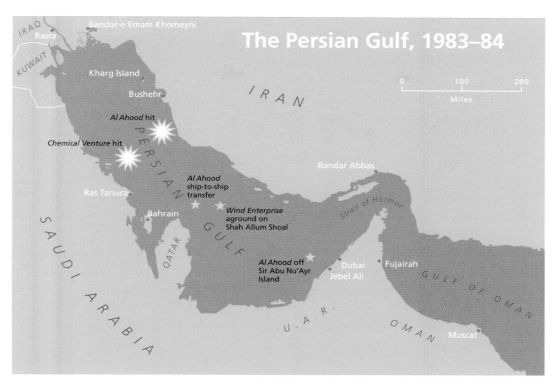

The Persian Gulf, 1983–84

I knew the sovereignty of the shoal was in dispute. The Iranians claimed it. I wondered if the Iranian authorities knew about the *Wind Enterprise* and, if they did, whether they would interfere. They were busy with their war against Iraq. On the other hand, if the Iraqis knew they might attack. I was thinking of the attack on the ship the *Salveritas* had been attending in Iranian waters less than two months ago when seven of her crew were killed by an Iraqi rocket (including my messman from the *Salvanguard*). I decided the less the radio was used the better – keep quiet, and get the ship out of the waters as soon as possible, I thought. An attack on the loaded *Wind Enterprise* was too awful to contemplate and I rigorously thrust it from my mind. The night was fine and clear, and the *Salvalour* thundered through the Gulf at her best speed.

At noon on Tuesday 16 August we were 5½ cables off the casualty. She looked even bigger in the flesh than in my imagination, a huge red-brown monolith stationary in a calm sea, the water surface glinting in the harsh midday sunlight. I swallowed hard as I studied her through the powerful binoculars.

I heard the VHF chatter and walked back into the wheelhouse. Doha Radio were talking to the master of the *Wind Enterprise* – so much for my idea of radio silence.

'We grounded at 10 knots heading 126.5 true at 2305 GMT on 14th August (0305 15th local time) with a draught of 71' 11" forward, 74' 11" aft. There is no pollution and we are registered in Norway. The tug *Salvalour* is on the way and my owners are chartering a lightening tanker.'

'OK. If you need assistance let us know,' Doha Radio replied.

I had studied the chart, and it appeared the casualty was aground in 20 metres on the southwest extremity of the reef. I watched the echo sounder as Pedro took the tug slowly round the *Wind Enterprise*. She was huge, vast, filled with crude oil, a dangerous cargo and a terrible pollutant if I breached one of her tanks. The *Showa Maru* was quite small in comparison; this was going to be a major operation. I hoped we were not going to be interfered with by the Iranians or attacked by the Iraqis.

The circumnavigation completed and the immensity of the task under control in my mind, I went over to the casualty in the Z-boat. Pedro had anchored the tug about 3 cables astern. I climbed up the pilot ladder on the starboard side, the sweat pouring off me in the heat of the noonday sun. I was met at the top by the chief officer.

'Welcome aboard,' he said, shaking my hand once I was standing on the hot deck. It was huge, all the same colour, and seemed to stretch for ever in all directions, reflecting the heat of the sun, the smell of crude lingering in the hot still air. I told the *Salvalour* chief officer and party who had followed me up the ladder to check out the stern of the ship with a view to making a towing connection. I followed my welcomer to the bridge. It was a long climb.

The captain introduced himself and took me down to the cool air-conditioned conference room. 'We are fully laden, all nine centre tanks full, and the wing tanks. Number five port and starboard are the permanent ballast tanks,' he informed me. 'She was upright before grounding but now has a one-and-a-half-degree list to starboard. The owners suggest we ballast number five starboard ballast tank to relieve the pressure on the port side caused by the reef. What do you think?' he asked.

'Don't do anything until the divers report. They are – or will be shortly – making a diving survey,' I instructed him.

'What is the weight of your anchors?' I asked.

'Twenty-seven tons.'

'Too heavy,' I laughed. 'That idea out of the window. We can't run them with my tug. It would have been good to have held the bow while we discharged cargo.'

'The crew have inspected the empty wing tanks and the forepeak and cannot find any damage.' He said.

'That is excellent news. Let's keep it like that.'

My spirits were rising all the time. I felt very much in charge of the situation and quite confident I could refloat her. It would be a matter of careful planning and good execution. I produced my Lloyd's Open Form, and at 1315 the captain signed on behalf of the owners, cargo, and freight and I signed on behalf of the contractors. I had committed Selco to salve what, at the time, was the largest loaded tanker ever to be aground. It was an awesome responsibility, yet challenging, and I felt excited and exhilarated – although I hope I just showed quiet confidence.

We discussed the situation further. Everything – engines, steering gear, all other systems – was working and in good order. The inert gas system was operational and the ullages were all inerted.

'Now we have signed LOF, Captain, nothing should be done without first clearing it with me,' I instructed.

'All right, Captain,' he replied. 'I will have a cabin made ready for you.'

The *Wind Enterprise* had been built seven years earlier, in 1976, and was 1,190 feet long with a beam of 197 feet and a loaded draught of 73 feet 4 inches, and she could carry about 350,000 tons of cargo. Her gross tonnage was 178,573 tons and her loaded speed was 15.5 knots, burning 195 tons of fuel per day. She was longer and deeper draught than the *QE2*. The engine was a steam turbine producing 40,000 shaft horse power, and the astern power was 13,000. The propeller, four-bladed, weighed 69 tons and I believe at the time was the largest on any vessel in the world. Total bunkers on board was 6,055, which included 270 tons of diesel. There was plenty of fresh water, 538 tons.

We discussed the refloating plan. The ship was 3 feet 5 inches out of her draught, and was hogged (or bent like a ruler, the middle up and the ends down) six feet. With a tons-per-inch immersion of 492 it would require 28,772 tons of cargo to be discharged. The capacity of the ballast tanks was 28,590 and that of the forepeak 10,900 tons. This meant we would be able to ballast her down while discharging to hold her firmly aground on the reef while the lightening tanker was alongside and the offloading took place.

'We should limit the use of the radios to the absolute minimum,' I said. 'No point advertising our presence to the Iranians and Iraqis.'

'I agree.'

'I am going back to my tug. I will return when the divers have completed their survey,' I said.

It was very hot on deck in the mid-afternoon sun after the air conditioning.

'OK Pedro,' I said once on board the tug. 'Connect up and you will be the ground tackle. Your chief officer thinks the centre lead is the best, and I agree; there are bitts forward of it to connect the pelican hook.'

'OK Cap.'

Singapore were sending more personnel to assist me, all of whom I knew to be good salvors, and John Carter was on the way from London. I sent a message to Singapore setting out my basic salvage plan:

AA Singapore arranging lightening tanker.

BB Required 4 Yokohama fenders.

CC 2 berthing tugs needed.

DD Minimum sized ship-to-ship transfer hoses 16 inches or bigger.

EE Transfer cargo using ship's pumps hull intact everything working.

FF Ballast while discharging cargo. Refloat by pumping out ballast.

GG *Salvalour* to be connected as ground tackle.

HH Singapore to send *Salveritas* to assist.

We would have to offload about 30,000 tons to refloat the ship. The divers reported that she was aground from number one tank to the accommodation on the port side and to number six tank on the starboard side. The propeller and rudder were clear of the bottom by seven feet, which was good news. Indents on the bulbous bow had been noted, so another internal inspection was required. If I just lifted the ship clear of the reef by lightening cargo then there would be no damage to the bottom. I wanted the *Salveritas* as another ground tackle and to assist the *Salvalour* when refloating.

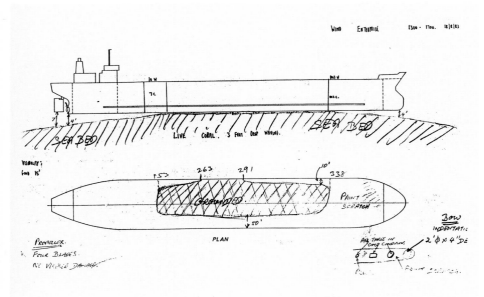

Diver's sketch of the grounded Wind Enterprise.

Captain Ragasia made a neat and efficient connection, manoeuvring close under the stern of the casualty so that a heaving line could be thrown. The messenger was quickly heaved on board the casualty by the crew, supervised by the *Salvalour* chief officer. The forerunner was heaved on board and connected to the pelican hook, which had been secured to the bitts. Pedro then streamed 1,800 feet of tow wire and anchored. The tow wire was heaved tight so that the *Salvalour* was working as a ground tackle to hold the *Wind Enterprise* steady on the reef. The 90-foot double nylon stretcher, 12 inches in circumference, was connected between the forerunner and the tow wire, thus incorporating a good spring into the towage connection.

Once anchored at 1715, the second officer and two ABs took the Z-boat away to complete the sounding plan around the casualty. They then painted white marks at one-foot intervals on the racon beacon to act as a tide gauge. This and the draught were to be read every hour, so in 24 hours' time I would have an accurate timetable of high and low water for the reef area. I would know the best time to refloat.

I sent a telex to the *Salveritas* telling the captain to fit spark arrestors on his funnel, and if he did not have any to make them. The *Salvalour* had fitted hers before making the connection.

In the evening I returned to the *Wind Enterprise* and gave the captain a sketch of the diving survey and sounding plan. This showed him exactly how his vessel was aground. I told him the arrangements in hand and retired to my cabin to write up my notes. Later I checked on the Selco man standing by the pelican hook with a suitable hammer close by. There was to be a 24-hour watch in case it became necessary to slip the *Salvalour* at any time. It was a fine calm night so I retired to bed.

```
M'01860'


♣
SALVERITAS9+?
SALVALOUR 9VCR


.TOR
TO    SALVERITAS
FM    SALVALOUR
DTG   161100Z  AUG 83


FOR CAPT GARINGALAO

                ''WIND ENTERPRISE''


1) I HVE ASKED FOR YOU TO PROCEED AND ASSIST ME.

2) PLSE HAVE SPARK ARRESTORS READY FOR YOUR FUNNEL.

3) IF NONE ONBOARD MAKE SOME.


REGARDS   TEW


♣
SALVERITAS9+?
SALVALOUR 9VCR

HW PSE+?
RGR FINE QSL AT 1438Z
```

Telex to the resourceful Captain Garingalao of *Salveritas*

I was up early the next morning. The weather was still fine. At apparent low tide, 0700, the *Wind Enterprise* was hogged ten feet, an increase of four feet.

After breakfast I joined the party to inspect the forepeak. We found that five longitudinals had been set up (pushed in) over a distance of about 5 feet as a result of the grounding. One was close to the ballast valve. The tank was huge and it was a 90-foot climb down. It was a hard and sweaty climb back up in the heat and confines of the tank.

Various telex messages were brought over to me by Z-boat. Selco had chartered the 80,000 ton *Talia*, which was at Fujairah. The additional personnel had arrived in Bahrain and were checking equipment. The Iranians knew about the grounding and Selco through their agents in Tehran and London expected to obtain permission for the salvage. The classification society Det Norske Veritas were making calculations as to the best way to discharge the cargo.

The captain now told me that an Iranian tug had turned up two nights earlier, but no one had come on board. I hoped that it did not come again, and sent a telex informing Singapore.

At 1400, apparent high water, the hog had reduced back to six feet. I now had a pretty good idea of the times of high and low water. The hourly observations of the tide gauge and draught continued.

Later in the afternoon the ballast system was tested and found to be working satisfactorily. I did not want to ballast and then find we could not pump it out.

In the evening more telexes told me the *Salveritas* was on the way. The Iranians had given permission and the *Talia* had left Fujairah. The tugs and equipment and personnel had left Bahrain. It was all beginning to happen.

On Thursday 18 August I was on the bridge early in the morning. The weather was still set fair and all was in order, the *Salvalour* tow wire tight. The heading of the casualty remained the same, no movement.

In the still air the unmistakable sound of a helicopter made me look up. A frisson of fear, that sinking feeling in the pit of my stomach, struck me until I saw it and realised that it was coming from the opposite direction from Iran. It landed on the foredeck and various owners' and underwriters' personnel climbed out and were taken to the conference room. I felt rather left out of it, especially as my own people had not yet arrived.

When the *Gray Amazon*, towing three Yokohama fenders, hove in sight just before noon, I went over to her in the Z-boat. Captain Carter greeted me like a long-lost friend, and I was more than glad to see him. A few Selco salvage personnel were with him, and the transfer hoses for the ship-to-ship transfer. I briefed them on the plan.

During the afternoon I held a big meeting with all interested parties, owners' representatives, surveyors, underwriters' representative and key ship's personnel. I introduced Captain Carter to them, emphasising that his word was law as far as safety was concerned. I was acutely aware that as long as the LOF was in force I was responsible for what happened on the ship. If anything went wrong I would be blamed – so I was determined that nothing would go wrong. I outlined the salvage plan and said that Captain Carter in conjunction with the chief officer would work out the discharging sequence, aiming to induce a trim of 5 foot 6 inches, to conform with the sea bed, and to minimise stress and bending moments. We distributed the Selco checklist and filled it in as far as could be done at that time. I told the meeting that the radios should be used as little as possible so as not to upset the Iranians, and issued code names for the tugs and key personnel:

From a telex showing my anxieties over the risks of air attack

```
TOR
TO      SALVENGER
FM      WIND ENTERPRISE     VIA SALVALOUR
DTG     180730Z  AUG 83

IMMEDIATE AB

              ''WIND ENTERPRISE'' . ''IRANIAN TUGS''

1)  I AM SURE YOU HAVE THE BEST POLITICAL ADVISE AVAILABLE AND
    HAVE TALKED TO NORWEGIAN AMBASSADOR.

2)  HOWEVER AS I SEE IT

    AA  SHAH ALLUM SHOAL IS IN DISPUTED WATERS WHICH IRAN MAY OR
        MAY NOT HAVE A VALID CLAIM. IT IS OUTSIDE ''PROHIBITED
        AREA''

    BB  IF IRANIAN TUGS ARE USED WLD THIS NOT BE AN INVITATION
        TO IRAQ FOR AN ATTACK BY AEROPLANES.

    CC  THE GROUNDING HAS BEEN ON BAHREIN NEWS.

3)  CONCLUSION.

    AA  WORLD WIDE BLACKOUT ON NEWS.

    BB  IF IT IS THOUGHT FEASIBLE GET IRAQ AGREE LEAVE US ALONE

    CC  THUS NOT USE IRANIAN TUGS.
```

Wind Enterprise: Whisky Echo

Salvalour: Pedro

Salveritas: Edgar

Gray Amazon: Spike

Gray Hercules: Silas

Captain Tew: Mike 6

Captain Carter: Mike 7

Craig Southerwood: Mike 8

Talia: Peter

There were no objections and the meeting broke up in amicable agreement. A good start to a major salvage.

During the afternoon the equipment from the *Gray Amazon* was loaded onto the *Wind Enterprise*. Strict safety procedures were in place: no smoking anywhere on the tug, no galley fire, spark arrestors on the funnel. Once landed on deck the transfer hoses were connected together and the equipment prepared. Captain Carter made his calculations with the aid of the ship's loadicator. A gauge was rigged on the foredeck so the hog and sag could be watched visually. The *Salvalour* prepared wire pendants for the Yokohama fenders to make fast to the *Talia* when she arrived. The divers with Than Divet, the Selco diving supervisor from Singapore, made a further survey. The hourly tidal observations were maintained. Everyone was busy, all with a sense of purpose.

At 1900 the *Salveritas* arrived and I told the captain to anchor off. Her crew brought over their pelican hook and connected it to the starboard bitts on the stern of the *Wind Enterprise*.

Early the next day, Friday 19 August, another fine clear night, I was on the bridge when the *Talia* arrived. I instructed the captain to anchor off a mile south of the casualty, and at 0340 she anchored. Half an hour later the *Gray Hercules* arrived with Craig Southerwood, who would supervise all the deck work, and a load of anti-pollution equipment and firefighting foam. I told the captain to go alongside the anchored *Salvalour*. My fleet was building up nicely!

Just as it was becoming light the *Salveritas* weighed anchor and manoeuvred close under the stern of the casualty and made her towing connection. She then streamed enough tow wire so that she could anchor opposite the *Salvalour*. I now had two powerful ground tackles out to hold the ship steady on the reef, important for bringing the *Talia* alongside.

The two Gray Mac tugs towed the Yokohama fenders over to the *Talia* and secured them on her port side. Captain Carter led a party to take the ullages of all the tanks to confirm the quantity of cargo on board. It was essential for accurate figures to be maintained to prevent disputes in the future after the conclusion of the salvage, such as how much cargo was 'lost'.

Once the ullaging party was over I boarded the *Gray Hercules* with John Carter and went over to the *Talia* for inspection and the safety meeting. The *Talia* did not have an inert gas system, but all but two wing tanks were gas-free. We decided these two wing tanks should be ballasted to reduce the risk of explosion in the unlikely event of them being damaged during berthing. The rest of the safety checks and meeting went well, and ballasting of the two tanks was started straightaway. It was going to delay berthing but I had to take every precaution to prevent anything going wrong.

Work continued on the *Wind Enterprise*, with the salvage crew preparing for the discharge, supervised by Craig Southerwood. I remained on the *Talia*.

It was early evening before the ballasting was completed and the tanks were safe. I was keen to berth as soon as possible and before dark. The longer we were there with my fleet the more likely we were to attract unwelcome attention. I was to act as pilot, so I spent the time familiarising myself with the ship. The *Talia* was much bigger than the first ship I had piloted, the twin-screw *Uranus*, during the *Sarah C Getty* salvage nine years earlier.

At 1745 I told the captain to weigh anchor. When it was housed I performed various manoeuvres with the ship to get the 'feel' of her. She manoeuvred quite well, being in ballast, and the sea was smooth with no wind. It was becoming quite hazy. I like piloting and manoeuvring ships and tugs, but on this occasion I was very cautious. I could not afford to let anything to go wrong.

An hour later I was shaping course to go alongside the *Wind Enterprise*, which still looked huge even from the height of the *Talia* bridge. I called in the two Gray Mac tugs to assist. The current, about half a knot, was setting onto the casualty so I had to allow for this. The *Gray Hercules* made fast forward and the *Gray Amazon* aft, so they could either push or pull. Twelve Selco salvage crew were on the deck of the *Wind Enterprise* to take the lines. At 1945 the first headline was run and made fast and the *Talia* was all fast three-quarters of an hour later, the three Yokohama fenders keeping her well clear. Deballasting was started immediately. I felt quite pleased with my berthing – it had all gone very smoothly and well.

The Gray Mac tugs were let go and I sent them to anchor, designating the *Gray Amazon* to be the *Talia* fire-watch tug. I returned to the *Wind Enterprise* by climbing down the pilot ladder onto the aft fender, walking across the fender, and then climbing the pilot ladder onto her deck. The Selco salvage crew were busy connecting up the ship-to-ship transfer hoses.

Early on the morning of Saturday the 20th all was ready. The *Talia* tanks had been inspected and a dry certificate issued. The tugs and all personnel were placed on standby. Captain Carter was stationed in the *Talia* control room and I was in the one on the *Wind Enterprise*. I had radio communication with all key personnel on deck, with the tugs, and with Captain Carter. The tension mounted in me as at 0240 I gave the order to start the discharge. The cargo pumps were started slowly and the transfer hoses checked for leaks. All was in order, and the rate was increased to 4,000 tons per hour, Captain Carter's discharge sequence being followed. Ballasting of number five wing tanks was started.

At 0515, 10,000 tons of ballast had been loaded and 16,000 tons of cargo offloaded. There had been no movement in the casualty, and the list remained at one and a half degrees to starboard. By 0700 we had loaded 15,000 tons of ballast and discharged 18,000 tons of crude, all in the correct sequence. All was well on deck and still there had not been any movement in the casualty. The *Talia* remained quietly alongside in the still conditions. The lines were tended and adjusted as she sank lower in the water.

All was completed by early afternoon, and I felt relieved and elated that it had all gone so well. I was not intending to refloat until the morning high tide, giving plenty of time to deballast. A total of 40,375 tons of oil had been offloaded and 25,000 tons of ballast taken on board – so the casualty had been lightened by half the amount required to float her at high tide.

I was approached by the owners' representative and captain, who insisted I make a refloating attempt that afternoon at high tide.

'It is not according to the agreed salvage plan,' I pointed out. 'I am not at all happy and would much rather wait until all the ballast is out. The salvage has gone well and I don't think rushing the refloating is a good idea at all. We don't want anything to go wrong now.'

'We think you should make the attempt and request you do so.'

I reluctantly agreed, and everything became rushed, increasing the danger of an accident. The hoses were disconnected and landed on the deck of the *Wind Enterprise*. Captain Carter piloted the *Talia* and took her away with the Yokohama fenders, assisted by the Gray Mac tugs, in his usual efficient way. I ordered the captains of the *Salvalour* and *Salveritas* to weigh anchor and start slow towing, heading 300, the reciprocal direction to the heading of the casualty. The Gray Mac tugs returned, and I positioned them on either bow. Deballasting started as soon as the *Talia* was clear, but that was not until half an hour before high water.

All personnel were on standby. The Selco salvage crew were aft with hammers, ready to slip the salvage tugs. The *Salvalour* second officer was standing by the racon tide gauge with a Z-boat. The other Z-boat was reading the draughts. They indicated that the ship was now sagging just over a foot, which was good news and what was required in the floating condition. The list was almost out of her, indicating she was close to floating, but it was not close enough, and the ballast was not being pumped out fast enough.

By 1700 the tide was falling on the tide gauge, albeit slowly. I told the two salvage captains to increase to full power, but it was no use, and at 1815 I stopped the attempt. I wished I had been firmer – but there was no movement and so no damage. I kept the two tugs towing at slow speed in case anything happened during the night before the next high tide at 0430. All personnel were stood down except the two on pelican-hook watch. The deballasting continued with a couple of interruptions due to mechanical faults and internal transfer of cargo to keep the correct trim. At 2330 there were 11,626 tons of ballast still to discharge.

Sunday 21 August, everything was calm and still on the bridge just after midnight, the lights of the two salvage tugs towing astern, the Gray Mac tugs and *Talia* anchored to the south. It was still four hours before high tide, but the ship had now been lightened enough to refloat at high water.

Just before 0100 the bow started to move and the heading increased from 121 to 142 degrees. I called up the *Salvalour* and *Salveritas* captains and told them to increase power and turn in tandem to port to stop the casualty's swing. I watched them like a hawk, ready to warn if they got too close together. I told the two Gray Mac tugs to weigh anchor and stand by, one on the port bow and one on the starboard bow, ready to push. The salvage crew were called and stood by on deck and forward. The engine room was warned and the engine, already warmed through, was ready. Once the swing had stopped I told the two tugs to tow at full power on the reciprocal heading of 300.

At 0100 the *Wind Enterprise* slowly started to move astern, the only visible evidence of movement being the changing bearing of the racon beacon. I told the Z-boat to keep clear once the refloating draught was taken.

As soon as I was certain she was afloat I told the two salvage tugs to stop towing. It was going to take ahead power to stop the astern movement. I did not want to anchor with much way on her: she was a huge ship and would take a lot of stopping. I had to be very careful. I used the two Gray Mac tugs to push as necessary to keep the correct heading and prevent a swing starting. Once a yaw started it would be very difficult to stop. The great ship moved slowly northwards clear of the shoal and beacon.

At 0240 the racon was 3.1 miles away, and I instructed the captain to put his engine on dead slow ahead and walk back the port anchor. It was too heavy and too deep to drop it. I told the salvage crew to slip the *Salvalour* and *Salveritas*, and the tugs recovered their towing gear and moved out of the way. The two Gray Mac tugs were told to go and anchor. Shortly afterwards the anchor was on the sea bed, the cable let out to eight shackles, and the mammoth ship was brought up three and a half miles from the beacon. I felt immensely relieved and elated. I had done it. However, it was most important to maintain the utmost vigilance; it would be so easy for things to go wrong in the euphoria of refloating.

Now the ship was afloat and apparently undamaged the captain wanted to get rid of me and take his ship back under his command. But we still had to reload the cargo. I was still responsible until the LOF was terminated.

I wanted to clear the area as soon as possible, but a diving survey had to be made first, and we had to wait for daylight before they could start. While the diving survey took place Captain Carter and interested parties went over to the *Talia* to check how much cargo had been loaded. The diving survey was most satisfactory, no real damage, and I was able to get my fleet under way. While the anchor was being weighed there was a most unwelcome visit from an Iranian vessel, who wanted to know why we had not kept the Iranian navy headquarters informed.

I replied that they had been kept informed by my head office in Singapore and they should check. The boat steamed round the casualty and sped off back towards Iran. This merely emphasised my desire to clear the area soonest.

As soon as the anchor was aweigh I navigated the *Wind Enterprise* clear of the shoal and set course for my rendezvous point thirty miles off Dubai. With a ship drawing 75 feet under my command, I studied the chart with more than usual care. I informed my fleet of the position and the Gray Mac tugs escorted the *Talia* on watch for the Yokohama fenders while the salvage tugs escorted the casualty.

The passage to the reloading position was uneventful, the *Salvalour* and *Salveritas* giving me their sat nav positions at regular intervals. The weather continued fine, the mammoth ship gliding through the night with no vibration from her steam turbines.

The new position was reached the next morning, Monday 22 August. The anchor was walked back and the ship brought up at 0700. The *Salvalour* was again connected aft to hold the casualty steady while I berthed the *Talia*. All the safety procedures were followed, extra vigilance being required in the more relaxed atmosphere.

I was on tenterhooks lest anything might go wrong at this late stage, but all went well and the back-loading was completed satisfactorily. I again piloted the *Talia* when she unberthed. A helicopter brought out the Norwegian Ambassador for an enquiry, and I felt even more excluded! All the equipment was loaded onto the Gray Mac tugs and the pelican hooks were taken back to their respective tugs – all very necessary work but a complete anticlimax for me. I was in a hurry now to have the termination letter signed and to end my responsibility.

My fleet dispersed, the Gray Mac tugs to Bahrain with the equipment and personnel, the *Talia* off hire to an unknown destination, and the *Salveritas* back to Fujairah and the *Cotton Trader*.

At 1700 the termination letter was signed on the bridge of the *Wind Enterprise*, with mutual congratulations. I went to Sharjah with the *Salvalour* well satisfied with mine and Selco's world first, the largest loaded ship at that time to be successfully salved. The Selco people had performed in an exemplary way. My ego received a further boost when my name and picture appeared in the local paper – and even more so when a full-page article was published in *Lloyd's List*.

From the
Khaleej Times
(Dubai),
26 August 1983

Giant refloated unhurt in record rescue operation

By Staff Reporter

THE biggest tanker to be refloated anywhere in the world has left the waters off the coast of Dubai for Europe setting at rest fears of an oil slick in the area.

Captain Ian G. Tew, salvage master of Singapore's Selco group, who supervised the one-week salvage operation near Shah Alam Shoal in the Gulf said in Dubai yesterday that an underwater survey had shown that although some damage had been caused in the front of the vessel, there was nothing that needed urgent repairs. "Therefore it was decided that Wind Enterprise should proceed to its destination."

Giving details of how the Very Large Crude Carrier (VLCC) was refloated with the help of four salvage tugs, one tanker and nearly 90 men, he said it was "almost a miracle" that the 357,000-ton tanker could be refloated without making a hole.

"The operation is a new world record. The biggest tanker to be salvaged before this was the 237,000-ton Showa Maru in 1975. But in that case, a hole had to be made and the damage was extensive."

Captain Tew said a day after

CAPTAIN IAN TEW

Wind Enterprise ran aground on hard coral, the Selco group went into action. A lightning tanker was chartered from Fujeirah and fenders and other equipment were obtained from Bahrain.

Two of Selco's tugs, which were off Fujeirah along with two others from Bahrain, were taken along to the Shah Alam Shoal. Talia, the chartered tanker was brought alongside the VLCC and 41,000 tons of oil was transferred into it.

After the tanker moved off, all the four tugs were used to refloat the VLCC which was embedded in

hard coral.

"If we had made a hole, oil would have spilled and we would all have been surrounded by it. The air was still and that made the danger of a fire very real. A fire would have destroyed everything."

Once Wind Enterprise was refloated, all the vessels were anchored about 30 miles off the coast of Dubai. The oil was once again transferred to the VLCC which sailed off after an underwater survey established that the damage caused by the accident did not need immediate action.

Earlier, the vessel had loaded part of its cargo in Dubai and was proceeding to Europe.

Captain Tew said it was fortuitous that another empty tanker, salvage tugs, fenders and other equipment were readily available in this area itself.

But what is more important was that the VLCC could be refloated without making a hole. Everyone is surprised that this could be done. A hole in a tanker of this size could have created the spectre of another oil slick, he added.

Although the Selco group which is active in marine salvage and ocean towing is based in Singapore, it has substantial interests in the Middle East. Last year, the group salvaged a 100,000-ton tanker in the Suez Canal.

Al Ahood
War zone

FROM *LLOYD'S WEEKLY CASUALTY REPORTS*, 1984

Iraq–Iran Dispute

London, May 8 – It is understood that m tank *Al Ahood* has been hit by a missile in lat 28 07 N, long 51 06 E, and on fire. One crew member lost. At the moment vessel is off Iranian borders. Believed crew has abandoned vessel. Incident is believed to have happened last night. Vessel had just loaded at Kharg Island.

Oslo, May 8 – *Al Ahood* ... the crew of the vessel was taken off by a Greek vessel and landed at Kharg Island early this morning.

Kuwait, May 9 – Shipping sources in the Gulf said *Al Ahood* was ablaze from stem to stern and was likely to be a complete write-off. Selco Salvage was taking charge of the salvage operation and two tugs were on their way to the vessel – Reuter.

Despite what politicians tell us, terrorism is not new. It is over forty-five years since, as a fresh-faced teenage cadet, I was blown up and violently entered the adult world. The *Dara* was on the Persian Gulf mail run, Bombay to Basra. We had put to sea from the open anchorage off Dubai, due to bad weather. The bomb went off early in the morning and 238 people perished. The *Dara* subsequently sank, and she still lies beneath the waters of the Persian Gulf. It was the worst peacetime disaster involving a British ship since the *Titanic*.

The terrorists who planted a bomb on the *Dara* were Muslim, and the majority of those who died were Muslim too. And when, as a salvor, I became embroiled in a war, it was again Muslim killing Muslim, the Iran–Iraq war.

I had been to Iran before the war started in September 1980, soon after the revolution which toppled the Shah. It was a hairy time to be in Bandar Abbas, with the young, bearded Revolutionary Guards being driven around in open-topped lorries brandishing rifles and shouting revolutionary slogans. As one of the very few westerners in the country at the time (I had come in on the *Salveritas*), my life was completely in the hands of our agent. I got to know Mohammed very well and he proved a valuable asset to Selco and a good friend to me.

The danger of working in Iranian waters had been tragically brought home to me when seven salvors from the *Salveritas* were killed, including my messman from the *Salvanguard*. They were working in the engine room of the *Iran Enghelab* when she was struck by an Iraqi missile in 1983. The *Salveritas* escaped across the Persian Gulf to the United Arab Emirates.

Since then I had watched the war expand from my safe haven in Singapore. The land war, which had been raging for three and a half years, with more than half a million dead, now took on a new and ominous dimension for us.

At the beginning of 1984, the commander of Iraqi naval forces warned that their air force would attack any ships approaching the Iranian oil terminal at Kharg Island. At the end of January, Iraqi aeroplanes attacked a convoy bound for the Iranian port of Bandar Khomeini, right at the head of the Gulf (formerly Bandar Shahpur, where I had towed the barges with *Salvaliant* eight years earlier). In the middle of February, Iran started an offensive in the central combat centre, with many dead. At the end of the month a Baghdad report suggested that Iraq was planning to blockade Iranian ports and attack strategic targets at sea.

On 27 March, the motor tanker *Filikoni* (85,123 tons deadweight) was hit by an Iraqi missile launched from the air. On the same day, the motor tug *Heyang Ilho* was hit, and sank with loss of life. In the middle of April, the Iranian Nowruz oilfield was attacked from the air and three production platforms were set on fire. A few days later, the Iraqis hit the motor tanker *Rover Star* (50,975 tons deadweight). On 25 April, the first of the loaded supertankers, the *Safina al Arab* (357,100 tons) was set on fire by Iraqi missiles. The tanker war had started with a vengeance.

This is my story of the *Al Ahood* salvage, the pinnacle of my physical salvage days. Never in the annals of salvage had commercial salvage been performed in a declared war zone. I was to change that.

The Iraqi objective in attacking the tankers was to hurt the Iranian economy, dependent on oil exports, by starving it of oil. Our mission, as neutral salvors, was to salve such ships and, more importantly, their cargoes, to keep the oil flowing in the interests of the world economy. Without the salvors, insurance rates would have risen so high that no ships would have entered the Gulf, and the oil flow would have ceased.

The *Al Ahood* was hit in the declared war zone south of Kharg Island, where all vessels were targets, including tugs and supply boats. The time-honoured practice of the sea was ignored and broken. There is an internationally recognised duty to assist all those in distress at sea, and it is public policy to encourage the salvage of property. In this place, the Iraqis not only caused the distress, usually by missile, but then sometimes even attacked the salvors trying to salve the ship and cargo, as had happened to the *Salveritas*.

The *Al Ahood* (916 feet long, with a gross tonnage of 58,277 and deadweight of 117,710 tons) was hit by two missiles on 8 May 1984. The first hit the engine room and caused damage. The second pierced the starboard side just above the waterline and entered the fuel-oil settling tank, where it exploded, starting a fire. This in turn ruptured the adjacent cargo tank loaded with crude oil, which caught fire. The bulkhead to the engine room was fractured and crude leaked into the flooding engine room, setting it on fire. The crude burned on the surface of the water, fuelled from the cargo tank. The accommodation caught fire and the whole thing became a giant furnace.

When I received the telephone call that changed my life, taking me out of my safe haven in Singapore, I had none of these details. All I knew was that she had been hit, abandoned by her crew, and was on fire. She was eighty miles south of Kharg and eleven miles off the Iranian coast, inside the declared war zone. Smit's were in the Gulf, and I expected them to obtain the contract. However, I set the process in motion, talked to our agent Mohammed in Tehran and Gray Mackenzie in Bahrain.

In the evening there was a small oyster-eating party hosted by the Salvage Association principal surveyor, Keith Townley. Alan Bond and his wife were there as well. It was a typical Singapore night, hot and sultry. The evening was going well, New Zealand oysters washed down with a Chardonnay. The telephone went and I was told it was for me. It was Alan Scofield from our salvage brokers Samuel Stewart in London.

'*Al Ahood*,' said Alan. 'Smit's say she's unsalvable and have turned down the Lloyd's Open Form.'

I was electrified. My brain raced. War zone, loaded tanker, burning.

'Is she still afloat?' I asked.

'As far as we know. The Iranians are supposed to be in attendance,' he said.

'So, she is afloat and has not exploded,' I mused. 'Do we know where she was hit?'

'Aft, as far as I know,' said Alan.

'Must be a chance, unless the Iraqis hit her again,' I said.

There was silence, then –

'The owners are prepared to offer you the Lloyd's form,' he said.

My brain raced even faster. If we salved her when Smit's said it could not be done, Selco would gain tremendous prestige – it would be a world-beater.

'OK,' I said, 'tell the owners we accept the LOF.'

'It's dependent upon you obtaining permission from the Iranians,' he pointed out.

That meant they wanted money.

'We can fix that,' I said.

'OK, I'll get back to the owners,' he said.

'Right, we'll start mobilising now, tugs out of Bahrain,' I said, switching into operational mode, and then hung up.

I wandered over to the group round the oysters. They knew about the *Al Ahood*, but expected Smit's to do it, as I had done.

'Samuel Stewart report that Smit's say *Al Ahood* is unsalvable and have refused the LOF.'

Keith and Alan looked surprised.

'I've accepted the LOF for Selco,' I said, throwing in the bombshell.

'You've done what?' exclaimed Alan.

'She is still afloat and I've accepted the LOF,' I reiterated.

'Well,' said Alan, recovering from his surprise, 'if you have accepted the LOF, you can go and do it and prove Smit's wrong.'

That wiped the smile off my face. Little did I dream that the name *Al Ahood* would reverberate around the world. She became synonymous with the start of the tanker war and featured in countless newspapers in many countries, on the front cover of *The Economist*, *Time* and *Newsweek*. I appeared on TV in the slot after Reagan on his visit to the UK. In the most famous picture of all, a figure clad in a white boiler suit stands on her deck, facing the wall of flame that was her accommodation. It was posted in the Room at Lloyd's of London, and the same picture was the centrepiece in *Lloyd's Log* and in some of the newspapers. The figure is that of a brave Filipino, Captain Juanito Ventura, who volunteered to lead a team from Singapore to help me. I took the photo – but I am getting ahead of myself.

The first thing was to mobilise the tugs from Bahrain. This was done by telephone, the ground work having been completed during the day. The next thing was to get permission from the Iranians. Getting through to Tehran by phone was not always easy, but the telex usually worked. I called Ismail, head of Selco operations, and told him to talk to Tehran. He had met and got on well with Mohammed. The simple thing was to charter whatever vessels the Iranians had on location. That would solve the money problem and bring the Iranian vessels under our wing.

Although nothing was confirmed in writing with either the owners or the Iranians when I left Singapore for Bahrain, I knew it was only a matter of time. It was all agreed verbally. Telex confirmation of the LOF was duly received after I arrived in Bahrain.

How different Bahrain was from Singapore. The smell and dry dusty heat and, for me, tension, especially as the plane took two shots at landing. I was about to go into a war zone and salve the unsalvable. I had been under open arrest in Ethiopia, threatened with bombing, shot at while passing Perim Island in the *Salvanguard*, fought fires on burning tankers, been for a swim in the Gulf, but a war zone was a first. We simply did not know if or when the Iraqis would attack again.

It was early Thursday morning, 10 May, when I was briefed at the Gray Mac office in Bahrain. Two tugs were on site, the *Jiddah 1* (firefighting) assisted by the *Gray Atlas*. The stern of the *Al Ahood* was submerged to the funnel deck and the accommodation was ablaze, engulfed in fire. She might sink. It was not encouraging, and the sooner I got out there, the better. I had to stop the situation deteriorating any further, otherwise I would have to beach her. What a target she would make for the Iraqis – a burning tanker beached on Iranian soil. It would be irresistible, and would be equally irresistible with the fire out and a lightening tanker alongside. I had to keep her afloat and tow her out of Iranian waters.

The *Al Khalij* was alongside the quay and all ready to leave. I stepped on board and, using the radio, spoke with the senior Iranian official on site at the *Al Ahood*. He told me the fires were almost out. That told me a lot about his knowledge of ship fires. A fire is either out or it is not, there is no in-between. You cannot have a half-pregnant woman – she is or she isn't – and so it is with fires.

We were delayed leaving the berth because of documentary details for the Salvage Association surveyor, which, I'm afraid to say, annoyed me intensely. A surveyor is merely an observer, an important observer maybe, but the risk was mine, or rather Selco's. In my mind, however, Selco's risk was my risk. With a case of this magnitude, if the salvage went wrong, it could bring down the company.

Al Ahood burning in the dusk, well down by the stern

Eventually, after two hours waiting, we sailed at 0500. There was nothing I could do during the trip out of Bahrain and across the Gulf. It was a fine day and the visibility was very good. I spoke with the captains of *Jiddah 1* and *Gray Atlas* and told them to use their initials rather than their names on the radio. I wanted to keep security as tight as possible. There was no point in telling the world what we were doing and inviting a further attack.

I saw the plume of black smoke, which announced the position of the *Al Ahood*, thirty miles away. My heart sank. It was quite obvious that the Iranians, who had departed, were wrong. The *Al Ahood* was massively on fire.

It was becoming dark as we approached the burning tanker, the Iranian mountains dark against the sky, a spectacular backdrop to the flames and smoke. The *Al Ahood* was well down by the stern, which was under water. Flames were shooting out and up from the starboard side of the accommodation, the side into which the missile had ploughed. It was a truly awe-inspiring sight, and I wondered if I had bitten off more than I could chew. Was this to be the financial pyre of Selco, as the *Tojo Maru* had almost been that of Wijsmuller; and in the Gulf too.

I vigorously thrust such negative thoughts aside, and thought only of success. If the ship had remained afloat for so long then I surmised she should remain afloat for longer. It was only the after part of the tanker that was in trouble; the whole of the fore part was intact, loaded with crude oil. It was a vast, floating bomb, my negative side protested. If it had not gone up by now, why should it go up at all, I thought, especially if we cool it and keep the flames blowing aft, not forward.

Right, I thought, to action, exude confidence, make everyone think there can only be one outcome, success. Forget about the Iraqis, the Iranians, war zones and missiles and concentrate only on the salvage.

Firefighting

The *Gray Atlas* was connected to the bow of the burning tanker, but she was not moving. The tug was only small, but big enough to keep the head of the casualty into the wind. I instructed the master to do so. The *Jiddah 1* was on the port side of the tanker, and I instructed him to fight the fire from the other side.

The *Al Khalij* went alongside the *Al Ahood* on the port side, so I could board the tanker. It was dark now, but the flames illuminated the decks, painting them orange, so I could see what was around me. I felt I was walking on a bomb or a mine, and tiptoed to start with, until I realised I was being ridiculous. I put my booted foot firmly on the deck and it did not explode. I felt particularly alone, the roar of the flames burning the accommodation loud in my ears. The intense heat was making me sweat and turning my face red. My survey confirmed what I had seen from a distance: forward of the pump room, nothing was wrong; aft was a different matter. We had to contain the fire to the accommodation and stop it moving forward. It was imperative not to let the flames blow forward, for if they did, there was a very real risk that my floating bomb would become a reality. We must fight the fire with all the firefighting kit we could muster. Back on the *Al Khalij*, I sent a message to Singapore via Bahrain. It was short and to the point:

'Send salvage team.'

The ship was being held into the wind, and the *Al Khalij* was pumping water from her powerful masthead fire monitor onto the flames, which were apparently contained. It had been a long day, and I decided to have a catnap. What a mistake I made.

'The pump room's on fire,' said a worried voice, as a hand shook my shoulder. I leapt up and saw flames shooting out of the pump room. It was the last sleep of any sort I was to have for six days and nights.

Jesus, I thought, she's going to explode if we don't get the fire out.

'Put it out with foam,' I instructed the captain.

I knew we did not have enough foam to put out the fire in the accommodation, but we had to stop the flames moving forward, which had just happened with the pump room catching fire. If we did not deal with the pump-room fire, I felt all was lost.

The foam-tank valves were opened and white foam jetted out, directed into the pump room. The fire was soon out, and I instructed the captain to shut off the foam and redirect the monitor towards the accommodation. I remained on the bridge and directed the *Gray Atlas* as required to keep the casualty's head into the wind. When the tidal stream turned

Fire reaches the pump room

it became more difficult, and leaking crude, instead of streaming aft and away from the casualty, now streamed forward, surrounding the *Al Khalij* and *Jiddah 1*. Crude oil has a distinctive smell and it invaded everywhere. I hate the smell, which is a constant reminder of danger. Every now and then I directed the monitor onto the water around the tug to clear it of crude. The *Jiddah 1* was standing off, but still fighting the flames.

There was a sudden flare-up in the early hours of the morning. The flames leapt high above the accommodation, the port funnel glowed red, the metal almost melting. It was an awesome sight and with my two small firefighting tugs I felt totally inadequate.

The leaking oil on the surface of the water ignited, surrounding the *Al Khalij* and *Jiddah 1* with flames. The monitor was used to push the burning oil clear of the tug. Hand-held hoses were rigged to do the same thing, so I could keep the tug alongside as far as possible. I kept the crew busy and encouraged from the bridge. If I appeared unafraid and treated the fighting of a raging fire on a loaded tanker in a war zone, at times surrounded with burning oil on the surface of the sea, as all part of a day's work, I hoped they would do the same.

The *Jiddah 1* reported he had to pull off. I instructed him to use his monitor to disperse the flames on the water. It was a tense moment, but the monitor did the trick and we were able to go back alongside. We were all ready at a moment's notice to pull off again.

I could not understand why the *Al Ahood* did not move. The *Gray Atlas* had been towing for many hours and we should have been making two or three knots. Something was holding her. I thought maybe there were metal plates hanging down and anchoring her to the sea bed. The *Gray Atlas* could change her heading with no problem but we could not make any headway.

The *Jiddah 1* reported that his monitor had broken down and that he only had hoses with which to fight the fire.

'OK, Captain,' I said, 'you take over the tow from the *Gray Atlas*.'

The changeover of towing tug was successfully achieved and the *Gray Atlas* continued the firefighting in place of *Jiddah 1*. It was now daylight on Friday morning, the Muslim Sabbath.

The entire aft end of the ship was a mass of roaring flames being fed by crude oil leaking into the engine room. There had been nothing left to burn in the accommodation for days.

All I could do, until reinforcements arrived, was to contain the fire, which we did, and stopped it moving forward. The problem was the pump room, which was on fire again, and I had no more foam left. However, continuous firefighting with the monitors from the *Al Khalij* kept it confined to the pump room. The pump room must be full of water, I surmised, with burning crude floating on the surface.

I went on board the *Al Ahood* for an inspection. The foredeck forward of the pump room was intact and no problem, as before. I inspected the towing connection and found all in order.

I then entered the forecastle. It was eerie inside, dark, and I could hear the jet-like roar of the fire. I stood still in the middle, a little uneasily. Then I felt something, and I froze in horror. I knew that a crew member was missing. We had been alongside for more than twelve hours, and surely anything alive would have appeared by now. I again felt something on my leg, and I think I must have screamed. I leapt aside, away from what in my mind was some unimaginable horror. I don't think I have ever been so instantly or utterly terrified. 'Miaow,' screeched the cat, startled.

I laughed, the tension draining. Frightened by a cat, I thought! I remained in the forecastle until I managed to coax the animal to come back to me, picked her up, and took her back to the *Gray Atlas*. The missing crewman, or his remains, was never found.

Firefighting continued all day and the next night. I remained on the bridge of the *Al Khalij*, directing the *Jiddah 1* as necessary to keep the *Al Ahood* heading into the wind.

In my message to Singapore on Friday afternoon, I asked for more firefighting tugs and foam to be sent. Early on Saturday morning, the *Gray Search* arrived with welcome drums of foam, which were loaded onto the *Gray Atlas*. She then started firefighting under my direction.

An Iranian gunboat caused me concern, but she steamed around the casualty and promptly left. I was extremely thankful: a naval vessel on site seemed to me an invitation to the Iraqis to attack again. Later in the morning, the *Gray Search* sailed for Bahrain, her firefighting monitor having broken down.

Early in the afternoon, I was most concerned to see flames forward of the main fire, apart from the pump room. They were like giant Bunsen burners, leaping from pipe fitting to pipe fitting. The fire monitor put them out, much to my relief. More oil was streaming astern, some of it on fire; the sea was burning. The pump room continued to burn, the flames leaping out of the blown-off roof.

The tension was increased when the unmistakable 'thump-thump' of whirling helicopter rotors was heard above the noise of the flames. A military helicopter appeared and circled the burning tanker. It was a relief when it disappeared back to Iran.

I was in radio contact with Captain Mathieson in Bahrain. We discussed the possibility of blowing a hole in the side of the *Al Ahood* in way of the pump room in an attempt to put out the fire in it. However, I felt the pump room must be flooded, considering how much water we had been directing into it, and the burning oil was floating on the surface of the water. Therefore I suggested this operation be put on hold for the moment but that we keep the divers and explosives on standby. My message, telexed by Captain Mathieson to Singapore, dramatically highlighted the position:

1. The accommodation is totally gutted, but flames appear on the bridge and from the port funnel.

2. Pump room on fire with flames ballooning from all entries. Water has been continuously poured into pump room using entries including roof, which part blown off.

3. Port and starboard side of accommodation surface of water fiercely ablaze with flames leaping to bridge height and last night port funnel was red hot.

4. Flames appear to be fuelled from gas and bunkers or crude on surface of water.

5. Surface of sea to port and astern on fire; when areas break away and drift clear, fire goes out.

6. The five tons of foam from *Al Khalij* failed to make any impact.

7. Gas fires from deck fittings forward of pump room.

8. Entire aft end of vessel surrounded by black smoke.

I continued to direct the *Jiddah 1* to keep the *Al Ahood* head to wind, occasionally having to use one of the firefighting tugs to push on the bow to assist. It was absolutely crucial the flames blew astern, not ahead. When it was calm, the flames and smoke were vertical but I had to remain alert for when the wind set in to make sure the *Al Ahood* was bow into it.

The *Gray Fend* arrived that night (Saturday 2100), and what a huge and welcome relief it was for me to see Juanito Ventura and his team of five from Singapore. Juanito had volunteered to join me when others refused, and I was exceedingly grateful. His calm competence in the face of adversity and danger was an inspiration to all. I now had my own people with me, and with Juanito's tanker experience I felt sure of final success – although, looking at the burning hulk, accommodation gutted, flames glowing red through the burst portholes and shooting up above the bridge, I wondered.

Inferno aft, in the
early hours

Captain Ventura immediately set to work, rigging more hand-held fire hoses.

I spoke with Captain Mathieson in Bahrain and he told me there was no more foam available in the whole of the Gulf. The only stock was owned and held by Smit's, who would not sell it to us. It was Smit's, of course, who had turned down the Lloyd's Open Form and said the ship was unsalvable. Now, however, they said they were prepared for us to use their stock, provided they joined in on our LOF as co-salvors – partners, in other words. I thought about this. The *Salvanguard*, my old, first Selco supertug, was *en route* from Djibouti, but it would be days before she arrived. It would take much too long to mobilise more tugs from Singapore. I knew Smit's had tugs and equipment in the Gulf, and it made sense to bring them in. This was no ordinary salvage. It was of world importance that I succeed. I thus told Captain Mathieson that I agreed Smit's should join us as co-salvors. He had better tell Singapore immediately, and tell Smit's to get their skates on *tout de suite*. It was a relief, once I had made the decision, to know that I was doing everything possible in my attempt to salve the *Al Ahood*.

Juanito had been busy, and hand-held fire hoses had been lashed in strategic positions pouring water at the pump room and cooling the foredeck, with more directed at the accommodation. He had failed to locate the emergency fire pump on the casualty, which was a blow. He had put a Selco man on *Al Khalij*, and another on *Gray Atlas*, to assist and

264

activate the crews. Things were beginning to happen. We thought the fire pump must be in the steering flat, which was under water.

Early on Sunday morning, I was startled to see an unlit vessel appear out of the darkness. I could see from the light of the flames that it was a supply vessel. It turned out to be an Iranian and they were looking for another casualty. It sounded as though there might have been another hit, which heightened the tension we were all under. I asked if they had any foam on board that we could use, but there was none. The *Betram* soon departed back into the darkness.

Just before 0400, the *Rajawali* arrived on the scene, having been chartered by Selco. This was a modern supply vessel, with two powerful fire monitors and, even more importantly, foam. I consulted with Juanito, and we decided to have a go at getting the fire out with the foam. More hoses were rigged, which could also deliver foam. I transferred myself and my headquarters to the *Rajawali*.

Two hours after her arrival, we commenced the foam attack together with the *Gray Atlas*. The pump-room fire was soon out, and I moved the *Rajawali* aft to put out the accommodation fire. Foam was pouring out of both monitors but the porthole openings were not big enough to allow enough foam inside to put it out. It was a great

Captain Ventura with his Selco salvage crew heaving hoses on board the burning *Al Ahood*

disappointment, and my heart sank further when the pump room fire re-ignited.

Two Iranian supply boats had turned up and were indiscriminately spraying water at the *Al Ahood* from their fire monitors. It had broken the foam seal. I was in a quandary. In normal circumstances, I would have chased the Iranians away. But they were at war and I did not know whether they had weapons on board. We were in their territorial waters and their presence increased the risk of a further Iraqi attack. Another missile, with all the tugs alongside, would be catastrophic. I thought of the seven dead from the *Salveritas*. The Iranians took no notice of my request to keep clear, or to direct their monitors to my instructions.

Fighting the fire with foam and portable monitors

Just before 0800, I heard the welcome sound of a Dutch voice on the VHF. It was the *Drado*, the Smit specialised firefighting tug, and she had twelve tons of foam on board. I told him to put out the pump-room fire with his foam. Juanito reported from the *Gray Atlas* that there was a crack in the aft port wing tank and that it was leaking oil. This was serious: it might indicate that the *Al Ahood* was breaking up.

The Selco and Smit men were working well together. We had a vital common interest: get the fire out.

The fire in the pump room was put out but re-ignited a couple of hours later when the Iranian monitors disturbed the foam seal again. It was most disheartening. I was still having to continuously direct the *Jiddah 1* and occasionally use another tug to keep the *Al Ahood* head to wind.

At noon we had run out of foam and the fire was as bad as ever. All our efforts were now directed at keeping the foredeck cool as well as the deck in front of the accommodation. The Iranians pulled off, but did not leave.

In the early evening, the *Gray Range* was on site with senior Smit personnel on board. I had arranged for a meeting to be held on the Iranian supply vessel *Beata*, and we all went over on the *Gray Atlas*.

Aad van Wijngen was head of Smit's firefighting team and a world fire expert, and Gerd Koffeman was Smit's tanker expert. Luckily they knew the senior Iranian official from Kharg Island, so we had a productive meeting. Smit's would lead the firefighting effort, although I retained overall command of the salvage. The Iranians would obey Smit's instructions. We would cool the steelwork, while awaiting the arrival of more foam, and keep the fire from spreading.

This was done, and Smit's message to headquarters indicated we were pumping 59,000 litres per minute of water over the *Al Ahood* from five vessels, with two tugs holding the casualty head to wind at my direction. Late in the evening, the two Iranian vessels silently withdrew. Singapore was most concerned with the crack, which was increasing in size and length.

The *Jiddah 1* continued to tow the *Al Ahood*, keeping the bow into the wind under my direction. Other tugs were used as necessary to assist. When the more powerful *Gray Hercules* arrived from Ras Tanura in Saudi Arabia, she took over the tow.

The early hours of the morning, the graveyard watch, were the worst for me. It was the fourth night without sleep, and 96 hours is a long time to stay awake. But I did not feel tired in the accepted sense. The stimulus of the salvage, the roar of the flames, the surreal sight of the slowly collapsing accommodation, the portholes glowing red with the fire behind, the tension of being in the war zone half-waiting for a second attack, continually directing the tugs, answering and deciding on the many varied questions I was asked, the responsibility of command – all combined to keep me alert. It was an incredibly intense form of living, which I had never experienced before and have never experienced since.

When crude oil burns, the lighter products of the oil burn first, leaving an increasingly heavy crust. The temperature of the crust may be over 300 °C and it slowly sinks into the lighter oil underneath and a new surface forms, replenishing the fire from the lighter components. Sometimes, however, the dense, hot crust sinks so low it hits a water level, which of course results in instant steam.

Such a boil-over occurred in the early hours of Monday morning. We heard a deep rumbling from the engine room of the *Al Ahood* and then a bang. Our first reaction was that it was a missile, as flames shot high above the bridge and funnel, the flames more intense and shooting out of the sides of the slowly collapsing accommodation. The men on deck ran for their lives.

Preparations continued for a sustained foam attack, while the cooling went on.

The *Gray Hercules* could not move the *Al Ahood* but only turn her in azimuth like the less powerful *Jiddah 1*. The draught aft was about 75 feet and the depth of water was about 100 feet. The *Al Ahood* was therefore afloat and should move. I had discarded the metal-plate idea and came to the conclusion that there must be a stern anchor, and somehow it had been let go and was holding the ship.

In the afternoon, the *Gray Search* returned with more foam. When it was unloaded to the *Drado*, she supplied bunkers to the *Gray Hercules* and *Gray Atlas*. Later on, the *Sandra L* arrived with more supplies of foam for the *Rajawali*. In the evening, the *El Alat 8* arrived with Robin Russell from Marine Safety Services to advise me on tanker safety matters in particular and tanker practice in general. Hans Walenkamp, the Smit senior salvage superintendent, arrived on the same vessel.

Cooling *Al Ahood's* heat-twisted superstructure aft, while smoke still billows from the accommodation

I held a meeting on the *Rajawali* with all the senior personnel. There was no more foam in the whole of the Persian Gulf. We had the lot; the last load was on the way out. There was no point in making a foam attack until there was sufficient foam to get the fire out once and for all. We had enough monitor capacity, including portable fire pumps, to keep the fire from spreading and cool the surrounding steel. However, water alone would not put the fire out. We decided to keep the *Al Ahood* angled to the wind, so the flames were blown to the port side, and cool the starboard side, thus reducing the area of flames and hot steel. The accommodation was beginning to look like some way-out modern painting or sculpture, with the port funnel bending outwards and the accommodation block leaning to port. The tugs were now well practised at keeping burning, floating oil away from themselves. All personnel were tired but in good spirits, determined to succeed and working well together. Captain Ventura and I had taken over operational control of the *Rajawali*, which I had made my headquarters and control centre.

The *Rhino* arrived just before dawn on Tuesday morning with the last load of foam. When it was unloaded, she supplied fresh water and bunkers to the tugs as required. The cooling continued at all times and I was constantly monitoring and, when necessary, giving instructions to keep the *Al Ahood* in position relative to the wind.

Just after noon I felt that curling flicker of fear when I heard the frantic voice of the *Gray Hercules'* master exclaim 'Towing connection broken, anchors dropped!'

The *Al Ahood's* head began to drop off. I instructed the *Gray Atlas* and *Jiddah 1* to push on the bow. Meanwhile, Juanito and his men on board the casualty went forward to the fo'c'sle to reconnect the *Gray Hercules*. I told Hans to send some of his men to help. I rushed across to the casualty and up to the fo'c'sle.

The wire lashings holding the anchor had broken, and somehow one shackle of cable had run out. The anchor had hit and pierced the bulbous bow, flooding it. The *Gray Hercules* was quickly reconnected and the *Al Ahood*'s position maintained. My heartbeat slowed to a more normal level.

Aad van Wijngen, the Smit fire expert, in fact one of the world's leading experts on ship fires, had not been idle. He had been studying the fire, trying to determine where the seat of the fire was and how to reach it, and so formulate and plan the foam attack. We would only have one chance with the foam on site, although Selco had chartered a jumbo jet to fly a further load out from Europe. The accommodation was slowly collapsing, the metal melting in the heat. We would have to get inside the accommodation. He had been stockpiling drums of foam and equipment on the deck of the *Al Ahood*, in addition to the full foam tanks on the *Drado* and *Rajawali*.

We made an inspection of the *Al Ahood* from the deck of the *Drado*. The starboard-side cooling of the accommodation seemed to have worked, and the flames were more concentrated on the port side. The cooling of the decks forward of the accommodation had worked, and the crack was no larger. We noticed the draught forward had increased due to the holing and flooding of the bulbous bow, and the draught aft had decreased. All in all, we felt confident that we could put the fire out. It would all depend on the skill and courage of the men to get to the seat of the fire before the foam ran out. The monitors could only do so much; it needed hand-held, close-quarters work with foam to finish it off. I decided the attack should be made the next day, Wednesday morning.

A full briefing meeting was held that evening so everyone knew what they were expected to do. Cooling continued at all times, and I was constantly monitoring the situation and instructing the tugs as required to keep the *Al Ahood* in position.

Hans Walenkamp was one of the world's leading salvors and I handed over operational control to him at midnight. It was the first proper sleep I had had in six days, but the tension did not leave me. When I felt a hand on my shoulder at 0430, I was instantly awake. There were deep indents in my hands where my fingers had dug in as I clenched my fists in my sleep. On the bridge of the *Rajawali*, all was in order. The roar of the flames had not diminished but we had got used to it by now. The monitors were still pouring tons of cooling water onto the casualty. The brooding blackness of the Iranian mountains seemed stark against the slowly lightening sky.

At 1125 on Wednesday 16 May, the foam attack started. I monitored and controlled the operation from the bridge of the *Rajawali*, where I had a good view. The Smit men, wearing full fire protective clothing, which was very hot inside, attacked the pump-room fire with hand-held foam monitors. One *Rajawali* monitor was directed into the pump room and one into the starboard side of the accommodation. The crew was constantly refilling the foam tank so there was no break in the attack. The hand-held fire hoses and monitors were using foam from the drums stored on the deck of the casualty. The *Drado* was on the port side with one monitor directed into the pump room and the other into the accommodation. The *Gray Range*, Smit's headquarters tug, directed her monitors into the accommodation.

Foam was everywhere and it stank, being made from organic waste, hoof and horn, but it worked. As soon as the fire in the pump room was out, the attack moved to the accommodation. The foam coating was maintained in the pump room to prevent it re-igniting. The firefighters entered the accommodation so they could reach the seat of the fire in the engine room, which the monitors could not reach. The Selco men sealed the cracks on deck to stop the leaking crude. Gradually the flames inside the ship died down. The outside of the accommodation, long stripped of paint, burned off days ago, was white with the foam coating. I continued to hold the *Al Ahood* in position.

Two hours later I was able to send a message to Singapore that the fire was out. What a relief it was. There was something strange, almost eerie, and it was some time before I realised what it was. The roar, the noise of the burning, was gone. Silence. We had lived with the noise for six days.

My message continued: 'Require divers ASAP. Largest tug available to tow. Divers to bring explosives to blow off whatever holding ship.'

I felt light-headed walking around the *Al Ahood*. We had done it. We had put out the fire, and we had done what was thought impossible. The accommodation was a modern sculptor's dream: the metal had melted and reformed itself into the weirdest shapes. Although it was still intact, it was lopsided, tilting over to port, highlighted by the port funnel, which leaned out at a considerable angle.

The fire is finally out

My light-headedness did not last for long. We were still in the war zone, and the priority now was to get out as soon as possible. I was still not sure what was holding the *Al Ahood*. Two surveyors had come out for a look-see and had left the general arrangement plan back in Bahrain. I told them that was not very helpful! They did not know whether the ship had a stern anchor.

I had enough tug power on site to tow the *QE2* so I decided to tow, dragging along whatever was holding her. I knew it was imperative to get out of the war zone. To hang around seemed to me an invitation to the Iraqis to attack again. I knew there had been attacks on other tankers in the last few days, although I did not have the full details. The risk now to my people, with all the tugs alongside, was enormous. If there was another attack, some of us would be killed, and I wanted to minimise that risk.

Fire damage aft

I later learned that on Sunday the 13th, while we were firefighting, three ships were attacked: the *Umm Casbah* (80,000 tons deadweight), the *Tabriz* (69,498 tons), and the *Esperanza* (61,928 tons). On Monday the 14th, the *Bahrah* was attacked. All were hit, and two were badly damaged.

Three hours after the fire was out, the tow southwards out of the war zone started. I controlled the operation from the *Rajawali*. The *Gray Hercules* towed ahead, with the *Rajawali* and the *Gray Atlas* secured on the starboard side and the *Jiddah 1*, *Drado* and *Gray Range* on the port. I instructed all the tugs to keep radio silence and use the VHF to the absolute minimum. My hand-held radio didn't have much range so I used that, rather than the main set.

It was a long and difficult tow. I did not leave the bridge of the *Rajawali*. There was no apparent rhyme or reason why the tow veered off course, but she did and I had to constantly bring her back, increasing or decreasing the speed of the tugs alongside. I shut my mind as to what was dragging along the sea bed (it turned out that it was indeed a stern anchor). I had one object: to get out of the war zone. Although we had achieved the supposedly impossible and put out the crude-oil fire, I was not out of the woods yet. I had to bring the ship to a safe place in a safe condition, and, until I had done that, Selco was still on risk. If there was a missile attack or we made a mistake and the ship blew up or sank, then all would be lost and Selco would not receive a penny. The outlay so far in tugs and foam and chartering a jumbo jet was huge. I had to succeed now. Thus, the longer the salvage went on the more the tension increased for me, and every little setback assumed a much greater importance than it normally would. There was no longer the stimulus of the fire. Not that I talked to anybody about this, of course – and I hope I was my normal, cheerful, optimistic self to everybody!

We were only making about one knot in spite of having 17,000 brake horse power towing and I rearranged the tugs, bringing the *Jiddah 1* over to starboard. Aad reported, by walking along the deck of the *Al Ahood* and leaning over the rail, that all was in order and that we could stop cooling.

The next day, Thursday 17 May, was fine. Juanito and his men were sealing cracks and building a breakwater to stop the water washing away the seals. Don't forget that the whole of the after part of the *Al Ahood* was still under water, the draught aft being almost 80 feet. They removed the part of the pump room roof which had been blown off and was on the gangway.

Now that cooling was not required, I decided that *Drado*, which was a comparatively small firefighting tug, but powerful, should tow on a separate connection alongside the *Gray Hercules*. I would have a tug on either bow, which might stabilise the *Al Ahood* and make it easier to keep her on course. This was done, and I moved the *Gray Atlas* over to the starboard side.

Juanito and Robin Russell ullaged the tanks to find out how much cargo was still on board and how much had been lost. They found 45 feet of crude oil in the pump room – no wonder it burned so well!

In the evening, twelve miles off Ras Tanura light (in Saudi Arabia) the *El Alat 8* came alongside with the Selco divers and equipment. It was a bit of luck that she found us. The captain did not know we had started towing and chanced upon us, a measure of how successful our radio silence had been. In fact no one knew I had moved the *Al*

Ullaging and sampling cargo – Robin Russell, Martin Eve and surveyors

Ahood until I told them. Our average speed since midnight on Wednesday was four knots, which was not too bad considering we were dragging a fifteen-ton anchor along the bottom. The difficult tow continued without serious incident and the next day, Friday, the Muslim Sabbath, I was glad to be out of the war zone. At noon, the convoy arrived at the anchorage off Bahrain I had decided upon.

Then the *Salvanguard* arrived, and at last I had a Selco tug with me. What a relief to have my own people, tug and equipment. The crews of the chartered tugs had done very well indeed but they were not salvors like

Robin Russell with
Captain Juanito
Ventura

Selco crews. The Smit personnel had worked magnificently with Juanito and his small team. Now, however, I had one of the Selco supertugs, full of equipment and a large, keen, eager crew as well. Captain Martin Eve was a live wire and a tanker man to boot so, along with Juanito, we had a strong team. And I had my communications system, for *Salvanguard* had telex over radio. I could communicate with the world without anybody hearing, unlike radio. Again, it was chance that the *Salvanguard* found us: I happened to hear Martin's voice on the VHF.

Martin came over in his Z-boat and we discussed how to get rid of the stern anchor. Once the plans were made, Martin and the Selco divers went back to the *Salvanguard* and he brought the tug to the stern of the casualty and anchored. Meanwhile, I held the *Al Ahood* in position with small tugs. It proved more difficult than we thought. Eventually the divers secured a wire and, with the help of the *Jiddah 1* holding the *Salvanguard*, the stern anchor cable of the *Al Ahood* was heaved out of the water and cut by the *Salvanguard* welder. It was dark by the time the *Al Ahood* was anchored with her bow anchor. That proved dramatic because the brake did not work and the cable ran out to the bitter end, which is extremely alarming if you happen to be standing on the fo'c'sle being showered with rust from the runaway cable. Luckily, the connection in the chain locker held. We wire-lashed the cable. Unfortunately, the *Salvanguard* lost her starboard anchor during the operation. However, I was relieved to have the *Al Ahood* safely anchored.

Now for the next part of the salvage, the cargo discharge into another tanker. Not so easy because, of course, nothing worked. Either it had been destroyed by fire or, in the case of the pump room, it was under 45 feet of crude oil. All the pumping and inert gas equipment had to be flown in from Singapore and Rotterdam. The fire was extinguished, we were out of the war zone, but we were not out of danger yet.

The tanker war was in full swing. On the 15th, while we were towing out of Iranian waters, Iraq denied attacking two Kuwaiti tankers, indicating that it was Iran. If this was the case, the areas of attack had extended. On the 16th, the Iranians issued a statement, 'If route to Kharg Island made unsafe, all other routes in the Gulf will be made unsafe.' And on the same day, the *Yanbu Pride*, 214,992 tons, was attacked in Saudi waters. Insurance rates at Lloyd's shot up by ten times. Also on the 16th, the *NBC Asil*, 34,996 tons, was hit. On the 17th, Japanese ship owners ordered all their tankers to leave the Gulf immediately. The *MIB Fidelity* was hit and sank on the 18th.

It appeared to me that nowhere was absolutely safe in the Gulf. If the Iranians were attacking shipping outside the war zone, I could not assume that pilots would be able to distinguish friend from foe, and the *Al Ahood* might easily be attacked by the Iranians as well as the Iraqis.

Apart from the danger of an attack, it was now a long, hard slog, and I had to be ever-alert for safety reasons. I had tugs alongside and personnel working on a heavily damaged, loaded tanker and there was always the risk of explosion. Much preparation work was done prior to the lightening operation, best summed up in my situation reports.

Saturday 19 May:

1. Vessels remaining will be *Salvanguard, Gray Hercules, Drado, Gray Range.*

2. *Jiddah 1* dismissed after supplying fresh water to *Drado* and *Gray Hercules.*

3. *Gray Atlas* dismissed after supplying bunkers to *Gray Hercules*.

4. Diving survey:

   AA Forepeak hole at 21 feet draught, 3 feet by 4 feet being patched with steel plate: expect complete 20th pm.

   BB Hole on starboard quarter (caused by missile) into engine room at normal waterline so large and mushroomed, or flower-shaped, that major operation to patch. It will come out of the water when cargo discharged, so intend to leave well alone.

5. Leakage of crude reduced to a trickle by dams and cement and problem will solve itself once stern lifted clear of water.

6. Towing connection with pelican hook made for *Salvanguard* in case of emergency.

7. Vessel anchored in position 26 38.5 N, 51 45.4 E in 27 metres of water to 12 shackles. Brake would not hold on port anchor, thus ran out to bitter end, which holding.

8. *Drado* as designated fire tug supplying salt water to ship's deck fire monitors.

9. Foam being transferred from *Rajawali* foam tank to *Gray Hercules* and, after topping up *Salvanguard* with fresh water, expect to depart tomorrow am.

10. Have ordered cargo transfer equipment from Gray Mac except fenders, which will order when tanker nominated.

11. Suggest you find 20,000 ton tanker for initial transfer.

I could not get a large tanker alongside at first, due to the stern of the *Al Ahood* being under water. We could do it once the stern was lifted, but initially we would have to run a shuttle service with the 20,000 tonner. All the cargo would have to be pumped using gas-safe, portable hydraulic pumps lowered into the cargo tanks, a slow and laborious process. Being close to Bahrain, Gray Mac were able to keep us well supplied with fresh food, mail, newspapers and magazines on a daily basis.

Hans and Aad flew home to Rotterdam while Gerd Koffeman remained in charge of the Smit input. We got to know each other well.

On Sunday I urgently requested that *Gray Range* should bring out an inert gas generator. If the cargo tanks were inerted it would minimise the risk of explosion – though we could not inert the engine room, which remained gas-filled and highly dangerous. A large number of people (surveyors, lawyers and so on, all with different agendas) wanted to come on board, but I insisted that the owners should submit a list of authorised people.

Later in the day, after seven shore people had visited the ship, I asked Captain Mathieson to make sure the *Gray Hercules* was fully supplied with food. She was my designated shore-personnel tug.

I was sorry to see the *Rajawali* go. She had been my headquarters and 'home' all through the intensity of the past week, and Juanito and I had got to know the tug and crew very well.

There was a considerable delay finding a lightening tanker, but there was plenty to do for the vessels remaining on site.

1. Vessels

   AA *Salvanguard*, Selco salvage team and divers, rigged for emergency towing and firefighting.

   BB *Gray Hercules*, standby firefighting, berthing, accommodation for surveyors and other non-salvage personnel.

   CC *Drado*, firefighting.

   DD *Gray Range*, firefighting, base vessel for Smit's prime movers [engines], personnel, inert gas generator.

2. Ullage taken daily: no change indicates tanks intact.

3. Commenced inerting *Al Ahood*.

4. Once inerted must keep inerted.

5. Already, the inevitable criticisms of:

   AA Why was fire was not extinguished sooner?

   BB Why did I tow with the stern anchor down?

   CC Why did we not release or cut the stern anchor sooner?

   DD Etc, etc.

6. Thus consider you should dispatch soonest:

   AA Lawyer on our behalf for initial evidence now.

   BB Fire experts on our behalf.

On Monday:

1. All surveyors and fire experts departed.

2. Pumping equipment arrived and loaded.

3. Rough weather this afternoon washed away part of dams and leakage increased. Will be repaired when sea moderates.

4. American warship inspected us this evening.

5. Ship's cat, which survived fire and abandonment, fell into oily sea but was rescued and has taken up residence on board *Salvanguard*.

That night, the weather became rough again, with seas sweeping across the after deck of the *Al Ahood* in front of the accommodation and putting at risk all our crack sealing. The tugs alongside had to move to the lee side as they were rolling and pitching.

This delay, after the intense excitement of the fire, war zone and tow, was very wearing

Lightening tanker *Kourion* approaching *Al Ahood* with Yokohama fenders alongside

on me. I wanted to get on and finish the salvage, both for personal reasons and to secure Selco's financial position. But there was a lot to do, and I kept everyone busy.

I wanted to transfer cargo internally to lift the stern of the *Al Ahood* and alleviate the hogging, but had to find out from the owners if I was allowed to do this. There was a fear that some of the cargo had been 'cracked' by the fire. I told Gray Mac to send out small Yokohama fenders for the *Gray Range*. She had the Smit portable inert gas generator on board and had to stay alongside, bad weather or no.

Tuesday 22 May was my forty-first birthday, and Singapore informed me: 'Shell asking US$50,000 a day, minimum five days, for *Aulica*, which is extortion. Now trying to firm up *Kourion*, 34,760 tons deadweight, length overall 655 feet, beam 86 feet. I realise she is a bit big but can be available 23rd/24th. Any objections?'

I replied with one word:

'No.'

It made a huge difference having direct telex communication via the *Salvanguard* with Singapore. My evening message summed up the situation:

1. Number five centre is common with pump room and engine room. Thus not possible to pump out water until stern lifted. Number five wings tight as are all other tanks, and low water. [Thus most of the valuable cargo was in good condition.]

2. Weather moderated and leaks resealed as possible and epoxied, new dams built and leakage much reduced.

3. Now everything ready for ship-to-ship transfer.

4. If position we anchored is a problem, thus Shell extortion, nothing to stop us towing outside Gulf, say off Fujairah. Have lots of horsepower and estimate speed of up to six knots. Would have to slip anchor as windlass damaged but no problem with starboard anchor.

On Wednesday evening, my message summed up the day's activities, but not my mounting tension:

1. Have received letter from cargo underwriters' surveyor Canepa requesting us not to mix cargo number five across, thus unable transfer cargo and will have to keep separated on lightening tankers.

2. In view of further bad weather have decided imperative lift stern and ballasting of cofferdam between forepeak and number one cargo tanks by *Salvanguard* and *Drado*. Will assist berthing larger tanker. Stress checked.

3. The Yokohama fenders in view larger tanker arrived in tow of *Gray Search*. Press and TV circled vessel this afternoon (and US warship and helicopter).

Later that night, I received the very welcome news that Singapore had concluded the charter of the *Kourion*, and that she should be on location the next day.

Thursday the 24th, however, did not go according to plan. The tension building up in me was shattered and drained in a flurry of extreme action, danger and activity. The day started normally, and improved when I spoke to the *Kourion* on VHF. She was expected to be on location that night. In the late afternoon I was in the radio room of the *Salvanguard* when I heard a shout from the second officer, who was on the bridge.

'Quick, Captain, distress!' he shouted.

I rushed up to the bridge with the radio officer, my heart racing. We heard a garbled message and decided between us that the position given was some 87 miles northwest of our anchored position, but in the war zone.

FROM *LLOYD'S WEEKLY CASUALTY REPORTS*, 1984

Iraq–Iran Dispute

Bahrain, May 24 – Following received from Bahrain Radio: At 1400, GMT, Mayday broadcast from *Chemical Venture* in lat 27 31 N, long 50 20 E. Vessels proceeding to distress position.

Following received from Bahrain Radio at 1629, UTC: Following received from Dammam Radio: Following received from diving support vessel *Pacific Teak* and Royal Saudi Navy: Present position of ship in distress (*Chemical Venture*) lat 27 31 N, long 49 58 E. One lifeboat and helicopter visible. Vessel seems to be in ballast. All crew picked up by Royal Saudi Navy ship. Suspect at present fire still on board ship's accommodation and bridge of ship still on fire. – Lloyd's Agents.

A distress is a distress, war zone or no, and I knew I had to respond. The psychological barrier to entering it had already been broken, so I had no hesitation in entering again. I decided to take the *Salvanguard* myself.

Of course, it would happen just as our lightening tanker was arriving. However, Martin Eve and Juanito Ventura were experienced tanker men and had taken part in ship-to-ship (STS) operations before, and I had no hesitation in leaving them in charge of the *Al Ahood* salvage with Robin Russell as the safety expert.

I took five Smit firefighting personnel, along with two of the divers from Selco Singapore to supplement the two on board *Salvanguard*. Within the hour, *Salvanguard* departed at full speed with all four engines at maximum power, lifting our Shibata fenders as we left. Singapore was informed and agreed with my plan. I sent a further message (how fantastic telex over radio was – fast, secure and secret) suggesting that the offloading of the *Al Ahood* would be more safely done if the *Monemvasia* (the large tanker Selco was chartering) remained outside Gulf and the *Kourion* ran a shuttle service.

The *Salvanguard* raced north in answer to the distress. We had obtained an updated position for the casualty, the *Chemical Venture*, which put her in Saudi waters. She had been hit by a missile, which had penetrated her wheelhouse. The fire was reported to be spreading fast.

It confirmed my worst fears. My *Al Ahood* salvage was at real risk of being attacked again, and not necessarily by Iraq. This was almost certainly an Iranian hit, and there was no way the pilots would be able to tell friend from foe. What if she was attacked when we had a lightening tanker alongside? The result would be catastrophic for us, with many killed or injured.

Salvanguard alongside Chemical Venture

However, I thrust such thoughts aside and concentrated on navigating safely as the tug rushed through the dark night. The weather was fine with the wind ahead, but not much of it.

Early on Friday morning, 25 May, we found the *Chemical Venture* connected to the ITC tug *Solano*. The accommodation was on fire and we could not see anyone fighting it. The ship appeared to be deserted. She was high out of the water, so must have been in ballast. This could make her a floating bomb if she was not gas-free.

I closed on the casualty and we trained our four searchlights on the burning accommodation. Great plumes of smoke were billowing almost vertically upwards into the night sky from the upper part. Flames could be seen through some of the portholes.

Some of the world's most experienced firefighters were with me, and I discussed the situation with the senior Smit officer. He emphasised that we should try to minimise

The missile hole
in the front of
Chemical Venture's
superstructure

water damage and that the best way to fight the fire was with hand-held hoses. Once the Shibata fenders had been launched, I therefore put the *Salvanguard* alongside the *Chemical Venture*, port side to her starboard side, as far aft as I dared. My agile crew climbed aboard to take the mooring lines. Strict safety rules were enforced, including no smoking and no galley cooking. I still did not know whether I had put my tug alongside a floating bomb. (It later turned out that she had been carrying a cargo of naphtha, which, of course, is highly explosive.)

At 0315, the Smit firefighters and *Salvanguard* crew entered the accommodation with hoses from the tug and put out the fires, cabin by cabin. The searchlights gave them enough light to work by, along with their hand-held torches. The mainmast fire monitors were trained on the outside of the accommodation to cool it.

The *Solano* started towing, and I used the *Salvanguard*'s engines as necessary to keep her close alongside, both for the hoses and for ease of access by my firefighters. The firefighters, wearing breathing apparatus, had their air bottles replenished by the divers, so there was no interruption. The port generator of the casualty was still running in the unmanned engine room and my chief engineer stopped it after checking that the engine room was safe to enter. The CO2 firefighting agent had not been used.

An hour and a half later, just before daylight, the fires were out. The turning gear had been engaged to lock the engine, so that the propeller would not turn. The *Solano* increased speed. The rudder was centralised and locked. As far as I was concerned, the sooner we were south and clear of the area the better, and I used my engines to good effect, having put a towing spring out. The speed increased to over seven knots. We were fearful of another attack at dawn, and also of the possibility of being detained by the Saudi authorities.

Fire damage in a cabin

The tow continued apace, and it was easier for the firefighters to inspect the accommodation in daylight. It remained calm, so the *Salvanguard* could stay alongside with no problem. The speed was a satisfactory eight knots.

Late in the afternoon, near the *Al Ahood* anchorage, two Selco personnel, who were remaining on the *Chemical Venture*, let go the *Salvanguard*'s lines. I steamed back to the *Al Ahood*. The *Chemical Venture* was eventually towed to Japan for repairs.

ITC tug *Solano* towing *Chemical Venture*

It had been an exciting and dangerous twenty-four hours, and it increased my concern for the *Al Ahood*. Nowhere in the Gulf seemed really safe, especially north of Bahrain. With both sides attacking merchant ships, it seemed to me only a matter of time before another tug was hit. However, there was no point in worrying about it: much better to get on with the salvage as quickly as possible.

Kourion alongside *Al Ahood*'s starboard side, with *Salvanguard* and *Gray Range* on her port side

Martin and Juanito had been busy. The *Kourion* was alongside the *Al Ahood*, her bow to the stern, and the transfer of cargo was in progress, which was all very satisfactory. I was pleased.

Early on Saturday morning, the situation changed. Singapore told me they were having extreme difficulty arranging for a tanker to proceed to my present location on any sort of reasonable terms. They told me to prepare to move the *Al Ahood* out of the Gulf, to Fujairah or Oman, and asked if the pumping rate could be increased.

On Sunday evening, the position was as follows:

1. 20,027 tons transferred to *Kourion*.

2. Draught forward 55'8", aft 49'0" (by the head).

3. Pumping out void space with *Salvanguard* electric pump to improve trim for towing.

4. Missile hole almost clear of water.

5. Rough weather last night and now may require transfer stopped because *Gray Range* cannot remain alongside [she had the inerting system].

It became very rough indeed and the transfer was stopped. Acting as pilot, Martin unberthed the *Kourion* and took her to anchor. I could have done without this particular excitement, because the delay and rough weather all added to the risk.

On Monday morning we aborted the re-berthing attempt because of continuing bad weather and a poor forecast. I sent the following letter to all parties on site:

Far too much information about this salvage and future plans is being given by VHF telephone conversations and radio telephony.

I would remind all parties that this salvage is being carried out on LOF 80, thus the risk and responsibility is with Selco, with Smit's as subcontractors. The salvage is complicated by the war now being fought in the Gulf area.

In future, there are to be no VHF telephone calls, and no positions are to be given over the radio. Messages from the various concerned parties to their principals are to be passed to the *Salvanguard* and they will be forwarded by telex.

It is in your own interest and for your own safety that we maintain some sort of security, and Selco will be responsible via myself for maintaining such security.

If you have any complaints, you should forward them to me in writing.

There were no complaints.

In the evening, the harbour master at Fujairah confirmed that we could perform ship-to-ship transfer outside his port. My report to Selco contained:

1.   Commenced pumping engine room.

2.   Divers completed patch at bottom of hole (thus engine room watertight and could be pumped out).

3.   *Kourion* re-berthed in conventional manner, i.e. bow-to-bow, it being considered open engine room and pump room reasonably safe and further light water sprayed on top oil. Resumed cargo transfer.

4   It would appear all bunkers burned or lost.

5.   What do you think of STS for *Al Ahood* in middle of Gulf of Oman drifting? We would be in international waters and if no one informed, no problems.

The missile hole in *Al Ahood*'s engine room

On Tuesday 29 May I heard that the major Swedish tanker operators Salen had withdrawn all their tankers from the Gulf. I expected the *Kourion* to complete today, and told Singapore. They told me to anchor *Kourion* close by as they were expecting to firm up the charter of a tanker which would work in the Gulf. *Kourion* was un-berthed successfully during the morning and anchored off. Over the past four days, 26,423.26 long tons of cargo had been loaded, about a quarter of the total.

It became very rough, and I was

glad the *Kourion* was clear. All the tugs, except *Salvanguard*, had to pull off. Pumping and patching of the engine room continued, as well as de-ballasting the cofferdam forward and the forepeak. That night it became so rough that I had to pull off the *Salvanguard*. It all added to the tension, and I sent the following:

1. All operations ceased. Blowing full gale, rough sea. All tugs at anchor. Will revert when weather moderates.

2. One Yokohama fender broke adrift from *Kourion* but recovered by *Gray Hercules*.

Salvana

The *Salvanguard* was rolling and pitching uncomfortably and I got fed up with it, so when she started to drag I picked up the anchor and made fast to the stern of the *Al Ahood*, which gave us a good lee.

There was no work on Wednesday, it being too rough.

On Thursday, work resumed and we were able to berth the tugs alongside the casualty. The tension of the prolonged salvage was increased even more by a report of two more attacks on tankers. Preparations continued for the tow to Fujairah.

1. Continuous pumping forepeak and engine room.

2. Divers sealed all but two intakes: will complete tomorrow.

3. Draught 48'6" forward, 42'0" aft.

4. Using large compressor loaded on deck of *Al Ahood*, shortening cable to seven shackles on deck.

5. I could commence tow tomorrow evening, which consider best thing to do, and get out of Gulf. *Kourion* could sail same time with fenders, escorted by one tug, and wait in new location.

In the event, the tow out of the Gulf was aborted. The *Galerie*, 137,325 tons deadweight, LOA 961 feet, beam 144 feet, was chartered, and the owners agreed she could work in the Gulf. I sent the master the following message:

Please anchor one mile off position 26 38 N, 51 46 E, where you will find two ships anchored with four tugs in attendance. Our working frequency is channel 70.

The number of shore personnel arriving to look at the *Al Ahood* was becoming a problem.

1. I see no reason why more surveyors should come out and, as I understand it, Caleb Brett and the Salvage Association act for all parties.

2. More surveyors cause delay, upset our personnel with stupid questions, and hinder, not advance the salvage.

3   With *Galerie* daily rate, every hour's delay is expensive. They expect free food, free accommodation and free transfer.

4   Please telex who, if anyone, should be allowed on board.

Selco agreed that anyone coming out had to have written authorisation.

In addition to two of its own tugs, the *Salvanguard* and the soon-to-arrive *Salvana*, Selco now had two tankers on charter, one loaded with cargo from the *Al Ahood*, various Gray Mac tugs, Smit's *Drado*, *Gray Range*, and over 100 personnel. It was a major operation in progress.

I boarded the *Galerie* on Saturday morning and, acting as pilot, anchored her. Martin piloted the *Kourion* alongside, her Yokohama fenders being in place. Tugs were used as necessary, the *Gray Hercules* towing astern of the *Galerie* to keep her steady. The *Kourion* was berthed before noon and, two and a half hours later, cargo transfer from the *Kourion* to the *Galerie* started.

On Sunday morning, all the tension that was building up in me exploded once again in a fever of activity. The *Buyuk Hun*, 153,274 tons deadweight, had been hit by a suspected Exocet missile. I again assumed command of the *Salvanguard* and headed north at full speed, but returned a few hours later. Our services were declined. However, it made me more determined to see the *Al Ahood* salvage through safely.

Breathing apparatus was needed for inspecting the tank

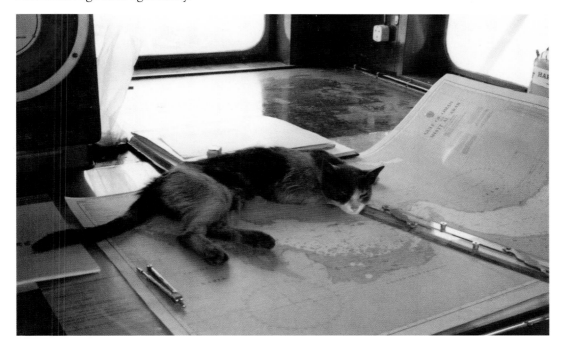

The ship's cat from *Al Ahood* plots a new course

Two captains humping hoses – Martin Eve and Juanito Ventura

At 2130, transfer of the cargo from *Kourion* to *Galerie* was completed, and in my message to Singapore I said:

> Two more Italian surveyors turned up, presumably with permission, but not mine. Now have entourage of five surveyors plus our own people for ullaging, dipping etc, which is ludicrous and time-consuming.

Just before midnight, the *Kourion* was un-berthed and went to anchor. It was much more dangerous to berth and un-berth at night but speed was required, not only for financial reasons but to complete the salvage as soon as possible, bearing in mind the constant danger of missile attacks.

My salvage problems now became further complicated by the problems of dealing with commercial tankers, when the master of the *Galerie* refused to supply inert gas. On Monday 4 June:

1. 0950 local, *Galerie* secured port side to starboard side *Al Ahood* (Martin piloting).

2. 1120 local, first line cargo transfer hose connected. IG system rigged from *Galerie* but master refused to deliver. Unable to start pumping.

3. 1335 local, second line connected. Master still refused supply IG, you appraised by radio telcon. Commence re-rig to portable IG.

4. 1425 local, commenced pumping after master finally agreed to supply IG and system re-rigged back to *Galerie*.

5. Unable pump engine room as master refuses allow pump into slop tank. I telephoned Troodos in London, who promised all cooperation, but at this time still unable pump.

6. Rate only 498 tons per hour.

7. *Salvana* anchored close by and crew incorporated into salvage teams for mooring, rigging hoses, pumping etc.

After one more frustrating day, my Tuesday evening report to Singapore summed up the situation as follows:

1. Pumping (with portable pumps in the tanks) continues on a 24-hour basis at an overall rate to date of 570 tons per hour: total 14,645 metric tonnes.

2. Trying improve.

3. Other pumps arriving tomorrow.

4. As no doubt you know, still have no agreement to pump engine room to slop tanks. If no agreement soon, must discuss what to do.

5. Inert gas rate from *Galerie* pathetic and oxygen content too high. Perhaps you can use this as lever. We now obtaining extra hose so can use portable inert gas generator as well.

Problems continued apace, and in the early morning of Wednesday 6 June the weather deteriorated once again. More lines were put out to secure the *Galerie* as the wind increased to a full gale. The *Salvanguard* was connected aft, but all other tugs were anchored off. It continued very rough all day. We kept pumping, managing to supply fuel for the prime movers, hoping that we would be able to keep the tankers alongside. In the afternoon two mooring lines parted, but we managed to replace them. By the end of the day we had discharged a total of 27,738 metric tones to the *Galerie*, leaving an estimated 53,890 still on board the *Al Ahood*. The *Salvana* was sent at top speed to Dubai, to pick up additional pumping equipment.

With all this going on, there was another distress call. This time it was south of our location, from the bulk carrier *Dashaki*. I again departed with the *Salvanguard* and her telex, leaving Martin and Juanito in charge. It was very rough and *Salvanguard* was shipping water overall as she steamed at full speed.

I came up with the *Dashaki* on Thursday morning and went alongside in the rough conditions, which was difficult.

Robin Russell

She was deserted, and after inspecting the ship I took her in tow with her engine room flooded. After conferring with Martin over the radio I sent the following message to Singapore:

1. All appears in order.

2. More lines put out. *Gray Range* back alongside.

3. Continuous pumping.

4. Total discharged 35,607 metric tonnes, remaining 46,021 tonnes.

And in the evening:

1. Weather moderated early a.m. and tug units recalled alongside.

2. Five forward mooring lines parted: all replaced.

3. New mooring lines ordered from ashore.

On Friday I brought the *Salvanguard* back to the *Al Ahood*, having handed the *Dashaki* over to the *Salvana*.

That evening I spent a long time dealing with possible problems and pointing out various reasons why there might be disputes. I proposed to solve all the problems, as far as Selco was concerned, by issuing a 'total cargo delivered' letter. All we were interested in was the quantity of cargo salved. I also intended to hold the surveyors liable for any delays over and above three hours after completion of cargo. One of the serious problems was what to do with the contents of the engine room, and this alone generated pages of telexes.

Just after midday on Sunday 10 June, I sent the following message:

1. I set time of un-berthing/sailing *Galerie* at 0700 local. Hopefully free-flow system will empty tanks but am not going to delay by humping pumps about to strip, taking about eight hours per tank. Have so informed surveyors.

2. After sailing *Galerie* intend tidying up *Al Ahood*, about three days' work, purge tanks and vessel ready and safe to be delivered to owners.

3. If owners want delivery outside Gulf, we will tow there.

4. Intend demobilise surveyor hotel tug *Gray Hercules* on sailing *Galerie*.

5. On completion cargo, demobilise all hired pumps.

Approaching the end of this prolonged salvage, the tension for me increased the closer it came. We were still at risk for everything with the loaded *Galerie* alongside. The men had all worked magnificently, hampered by the appalling bad weather. The war had spread and nowhere in the Gulf was really safe.

Not long after I had sent my message, a loud bang was heard. I'm ashamed to say I dropped to the deck, fearing it was a missile attack, and waited for the explosion and the demise of my salvage. It was indeed a missile attack, but not on us. The *Kazimah*, 294,739 tons deadweight, had been hit south of our location, quite near by. I heard the distress on the VHF and immediately sailed the *Salvanguard* in a state of controlled, fevered excitement. It could have been us, I kept thinking.

However, our services were not required; the crew managed to get the fire out themselves. I reported a new problem to Singapore:

1. Barring problems should complete by my deadline.

2. In view *Kazimah* incident, which appears to have extended the war zone south of this location, *Galerie* is being instructed to sail towards Dubai, once un-berthed, with surveyors if they have not finished.

3. A loud bang was heard just before *Kazimah* mayday, which has brought home the fact that there is a war and the belligerents are not abiding by normal, civilised behaviour, attacking neutral ships outside the war exclusion zone and, in this case, outside Iranian waters, in international waters well south of previous attacks.

4. I thus wonder whether *Al Ahood* should remain here, perhaps at the least towed to off Dubai, if not outside the Gulf altogether.

Galerie alongside *Al Ahood* on a calm evening

On Monday the 11th, Singapore was informed:

1. You will be pleased to know *Galerie* un-berthed and sailed for destination at 0900 local with instructions to keep close as navigable to Qatar coast and thence United Arab Emirates at maximum speed.

2. Cargo loaded 106,717.527 long tons.

However, it was not the end of the salvage. Almost a week of really bad weather delayed everything. The salvage crew were marooned on the *Al Ahood*, having to sleep in the fo'c'sle. We supplied food over the stern from the *Salvanguard*. They continued to skim oil from the engine room into number five port wing, using breathing apparatus to place and move the pump, a most unpleasant and dangerous task with everything covered with slimy, slippery, oily sludge. I reported gales on four days and strong winds on the other two.

It was still rough on Saturday, and with gale-force winds and the forecast bad, there was no prospect of moving that day, or maybe even the next. However, the *Gray Hercules* finally managed to take off some salvage crew who were due to fly to Singapore.

On Sunday 17 June I sent the following to Gray Mac:

1. No surveyors to be transported out in any of your boats without my authority. No surveyors to come out until further notice.

2. Intend towing to Sir Abu Nu'ayr Island to complete work. This confidential and must not be divulged yet.

I was thoroughly fed up with the bad weather and wanted some shelter. I wanted the move to be secret so as not to invite an attack.

Just after noon, the anchor of the *Al Ahood* had been lifted off the bottom: we had weighed it using the large compressor. I left it hanging because the anchor itself was too heavy for the compressor.

The *Salvanguard* was connected, and towed from ahead, the casualty presenting no problem to my powerful tug, now being used for its proper purpose! The *Drado* and *Gray Hercules* escorted the tow, and our speed was seven knots.

On Monday 18 June I reported:

1. 2000 local, anchored *Al Ahood* in lee Sir Abu Nu'ayr Island, position 25 13 N, 54 15 E.

2. All pumping etc completed.

3. Inerting complete tonight.

4. Vessel ready for re-delivery.

My part was now over, and I went ashore to Dubai. The *Al Ahood* was moved to the Jebel Ali anchorage, where she remained for another month before re-delivery was finally made.

Over a hundred men had been involved in our fight to save the *Al Ahood* and her cargo, including British, Dutch, Filipinos, Singaporeans, Norwegians and Iranians. Twenty-six

tugs and other vessels, including two tankers and a huge quantity of foam and equipment, even a jumbo jet, had been involved. It had lasted a total of seventy days (including the thirty which were spent waiting for re-delivery) and fourteen other vessels had been attacked during this time.

It is always the first time that is most difficult, the breaking of any barrier or taboo, and so it was with the *Al Ahood*. It was the first time commercial salvage had been performed in an active war zone. The second time is always easier. One first, and it was mine.

It was not just the perception of danger, even though that is sometimes more real than the reality of being attacked. The *Salveritas* and *Heyang Ilho* were the reality. They had been hit, and it was against that background that I had to overcome the perception, and thus the fear, and project an aura of normality. Even when we had escaped – and it was an escape, for I had neither asked permission nor told anyone we were leaving the war zone – the war followed us. The *Buyuk Hun* and *Kazimah* hits fed the perception, and were also dramatic reminders of the real danger.

There was a real, not just perceived, risk of the *Al Ahood* blowing up, from a second attack, or from the huge fire, or from a salvor's mistake, especially during the ship-to-ship transfer, when other tankers and large numbers of people were involved. I felt an enormous responsibility to all those taking part, and it is a tribute to them that we were successful.

Little did I dream, when I first joined the *Salvaliant*, covered in dust during her refit in the sticky heat of Singapore, that in ten short action-packed years I would be at the pinnacle of my salvage career, standing on the deck of a casualty whose name had reverberated around the world in the dry heat of a war-torn Persian Gulf, being photographed and interviewed for the evening television news.

For me it was not just living on the edge, it was almost over the edge, hanging on to reality by a hairsbreadth. It was the intensity of living, the feeling of being so alive – I suppose because my perception was that it might end at any second. It has only happened again once, in Cuba, when I almost wrecked my yacht and would certainly have been torn to pieces on the coral. But that only lasted an hour, not more than a month.

Yet within a week of leaving the *Al Ahood* off Dubai, I was back in the war zone in command of *Salvanguard*, fighting the fire on the burning *Tiburon*, 260,150 tons deadweight, loaded with crude oil. I subsequently towed her out of the war zone with my supertug – but that is another story, and on that occasion I was not in command of the salvage, for the roles of Selco and Smit had been reversed.

When leaving for Dubai I looked back on the green hull of the *Al Ahood*, now high out of the water, safely anchored. The ship we had worked so hard to save, so much sweat, fear and tension, so much courage and high drama, now a wreck to be towed to Taiwan for scrap. As the crew boat turned into the Dubai Creek I thought of another wreck, only a few miles away off the coast – so many dead, the fire, the smoke, and oh the screaming. But now the wreck had been under water for over twenty years, the bones of the dead long scattered, the memories of the wreck of the *Dara* fading.

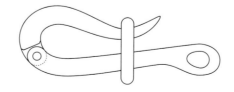

Ian Tew

Ian Tew was born into a seafaring family in 1943. He had learnt to sail by the age of seven, and later served his time with the British India Steam Navigation Company before becoming junior officer with Ellerman Lines and chief officer with the Indo-China Steam Navigation Company and Bank Line. He then worked for a year with a firm of admiralty solicitors in London before joining Selco Salvage in Singapore in 1974. After many years in salvage he went ashore in 1991 to run a small business on the south coast of England, and then in 1997–2001 he sailed around the world in the yacht *Independent Freedom*, retracing the route taken by his grandfather sixty years earlier. Ian's grandfather was the renowned transatlantic sailor Commander R D Graham, whose classic *Rough Passage* was republished by Seafarer Books and Sheridan House in 2005. Ian's mother was Helen Tew, who undertook a transatlantic voyage at the age of 88 and wrote about it in *Transatlantic At Last*, also published by Seafarer. Ian's own account of his round-the-world voyage was published as *Sailing in Grandfather's Wake* (Thomas Reed Publications, 2001).